The Last Days of Big Grassy Fork

The Last Days of
Big Grassy Fork

Hunter James

THE UNIVERSITY PRESS OF KENTUCKY

Publication of this volume was made possible in part by a grant
from the National Endowment for the Humanities.

Scholarly publisher for the Commonwealth,
serving Bellarmine University, Berea College, Centre
College of Kentucky, Eastern Kentucky University,
The Filson Historical Society, Georgetown College,
Kentucky Historical Society, Kentucky State University,
Morehead State University, Murray State University,
Northern Kentucky University, Transylvania University,
University of Kentucky, University of Louisville,
and Western Kentucky University.
All rights reserved.

Editorial and Sales Offices: The University Press of Kentucky
663 South Limestone Street, Lexington, Kentucky 40508-4008

06 05 04 03 02   5 4 3 2 1

Library of Congress Cataloging-in-Publication Data

James, Hunter.
   The last days of the Big Grassy Fork / Hunter James.
      p. cm.
   ISBN 0-8131-2215-5
   1. Hunter, James. 2. Hunter family. 3. Winston-Salem Region
(N.C.)—Biography. 4. Winston-Salem Region (N.C.)—Rural conditions.
5. Farms—Conservation and restoration—North Carolina—Winston-Salem
Region. 6. Landscape protection—North Carolina—Winston-Salem Region.
7. Agriculture and state—North Carolina—Winston-Salem Region.
8. Urbanization—North Carolina—Winston Salem Region. 9. Winston-Salem
Region (N.C.)—Economic conditions. 10. Journalists—North Carolina—
Winston-Salem Region—Biography.
   I. Title.
   F264.W8 J36 2002
   975.6'67—dc21   2001003410

Contents

1

Coffin Nails, Lynch Mobs, and the Rebirth of a City

I had come back to the town almost as a stranger. Maybe I wouldn't have come back at all, except that I heard the town was dying and didn't have much time left. Everyone had told me how it would be: the streets all empty; grass growing through cracks in the sidewalks; factories dark and idle; once-busy retail shops vacant and padlocked, with countless "for sale" signs in the windows; lynch mobs meeting in back rooms, hoping for a chance to snare and crucify the man responsible for the town's collapse.

In the thirty years that I had been away, off and on, prosperous "tobacco-stinking Winston," a one-time North Carolina boomtown, was now what the authors of *Barbarians at the Gate*, Bryan Burrough and John Helyar, later described as little more than just another "scruffy" factory town full of "tired old stores and tired old people."

Maybe it wasn't quite that bad, or maybe it was. I don't know. I do know that when I walked up Trade Street again and saw that a federal self-help agency had taken over space once occupied by one of my father's barbershops—well for me, the town might as well have been dead, buried and long forgotten.

I had spent more than five years roaming the South as a correspondent for the *Atlanta Constitution* and now in the summer of 1987 I found myself, ironically, right back in my hometown, caught up in one of the biggest stories of the decade. I had been obliged to take time out from covering an even bigger story, the collapse of evangelist Jim Bakker's

PTL empire, to see what I could add to dispatches being prepared for the next edition of the *Constitution*:

"RJR Nabisco Plans Move to Atlanta"

"Get back to Winston," my editor said. "They're getting ready to move your whole goddamn town to Atlanta."

Not exactly the whole town. Yet, to a lot of people, it might as well have been the whole town. The way I got it, the Winston I had known as a much younger man was now all but certifiably dead: the victim of an entrepreneur named F. Ross Johnson, who had come South as second-in-command of the newly formed tobacco-and-cookie combine RJR Nabisco.

Could Nabisco Brands find happiness in our "scruffy" backwater town, once known as the cigarette manufacturing capital of the world? Apparently not. Yet I liked the old place, which had great beauty as well as a grimy factory district, and wondered how good I would be at holding on to my objectivity, something I prized almost as much as my chaste conduct.

RJR had got its start in the late nineteenth century as a manufacturer of plug tobacco. In the twenties, with the introduction of Camel cigarettes, came its great breakthrough, and then toward the middle of the century the first hint of its imminent demise: the growing lung cancer scare. Ever since then the company had been rapidly diversifying, swallowing a whole platoon of smaller companies as a hedge against the potentially disastrous decline in cigarette production.

By 1965 the anti-smoking campaign was in full throttle, fueled mostly by a new breed of abolitionists, taking their cue from the same people who brought us The War between the States, Prohibition, and many other doomed, self-righteous ventures into social and political uplift. Twenty years later, its corporate books swollen with dozens of often-unprofitable acquisitions, RJR sought to absorb Nabisco Brands only to find itself gobbled up instead by the cookie giant and its chief executive, Ross Johnson. A real operator, Johnson was. Within a year he was in charge of the whole operation.

Came the day of his big announcement—"We're moving, folks."—and most of Winston's civic worthies, having been without real leadership since the death of R.J. Reynolds more than half a century earlier, suddenly got busy issuing all sorts of fraudulent statements as a way of assuring townspeople that the transfer of the corporate headquarters to Atlanta actually meant nothing—that the local manufacturing facility would go on making cigarettes as before. They even made it out that the move would guarantee the town certain "intangible" benefits Johnson supposedly was to clarify at some unnamed later date.

That's what they were saying in public. In private they were angry, befuddled, scared. Call out the National Guard! Bring on the lynch mobs!

As the days passed they at least pretended to fall for Johnson's spurious argument that the corporate headquarters needed to be separate from the various manufacturing divisions for the company to be truly effective in an ever more competitive market. Everyone from the mayor on down knew what he was really saying: since nobody else wanted anything to do with it, Johnson would indeed allow Winston to go right on making cigarettes. Yet it was all one: the real heart of the business was going elsewhere.

Johnson had learned to hate the town as a provincial backwater that had snubbed him as an insolent New York carpetbagger. Winston, he said, after he was safely in his Atlanta office, was simply too "bucolic" to serve as headquarters for a major corporation. When that got on the wires it began to look as if the lynching party would again find itself awash with recruits.

Johnson knew that no matter how high he might rise, he could never be a true insider in the town. The society matrons would see to that. He felt rightly enough that he stood a much better chance of ingratiating himself with the "beautiful people" of Atlanta, the South's foremost newcomer's town. In the end, walking off with old Winston's largest corporate enterprise—indeed, the largest in the entire state—was the one sure way to "drive a dagger through its proud provincial heart" (*Barbarians at the Gate*).

On my first day back in town I knew nothing of Johnson's motives and very little else about this sudden burst of disconcerting news. I kept thinking instead of all the old stories and legends that had made the town what it was before Nabisco's "Cookie Chief" had come along. I thought of all the ridicule Winston had taken down through the years, most of it undeserved, and how different and more complex was its history than that depicted by writers and journalists who thought of it as just another dirty, foul-smelling tobacco warehousing and manufacturing town, nearly as full of millionaires as factory workers.

Author-journalist W.J. Cash, writing of the town as it was shortly after the turn of the twentieth century, was the first to libel the place as a "tobacco-stinking" industrial quagmire, forgetting that fortunes were being made and a palatial lifestyle created not simply for cigarette manufacturers but for many of its other inhabitants—bankers, merchants, warehousemen, wholesalers, and even white collar professionals. Maybe Cash had never had a chance to experience the good, fresh smell of new tobacco being brought into markets on a cool fall morning. In his *Mind of the South*, he had dismissed the town as a monstrous and pathetic entity, "reaching out to swallow up the quiet old center of Moravian piety, Salem. . . ."

I had often heard scholars complain about the lack of documentation in Cash's great book, yet never did they fail to admit that it was certainly the single most influential work ever written about the region. Did it deserve quite so much praise? Cash had been . . . well, not wrong about my town, but certainly ignorant, and abysmally so, of its history and influence in banking and industrial circles. If he didn't even know that much, how could we put such a vast amount of faith in his other observations? Were we to treat the book as genuine social history or merely as inspired romance?

If nothing else, few other towns, certainly none in the Carolinas, if you don't count Charleston, had anything like so storied a past. Why there were still some who believed that if you hung around the factory district too long and were in the habit of breathing with your mouth open, your teeth would turn brown!

My thoughts kept drifting to a time when Winston was still a grubby factory town, desolate and spectral by moonlight, crowded and boisterous by day, a real coming place in those early days, before Prohibition and the Great Depression hit, with plenty of bars and whores and good times for everybody, especially during the tobacco marketing season.

For all of that I never knew of anyone who tried to fool himself into thinking that smoking cigarettes was actually good for you or even an innocuous habit that, at worst, could do you no harm. Not even the fiercest of tobacco partisans, among them the working-stiffs who labored away in those factories and counted themselves among the luckiest people on earth, believed all those Sunday comic strip ads implying that Camels could make you even better at whatever you were good at, whether race car driver, champion jockey, or Olympic high diver.

My father would always look at me as he was lighting up a fresh Camel and say: "Son, you don't ever wanta get hooked on these things. Stunt your growth. Take away your wind. Fix you so you'll never be at your best if you go into training for sports. Just remember that now. A real nasty habit. Just hope you'll never have anything to do with it."

That was a long time before anybody had even thought of smoking as a possible link to lung cancer.

Back when Cash was just beginning work on his incisive treatise, Thomas Wolfe, the greatest and most erratic of North Carolina novelists—more poet than novelist actually—had already begun to demean the town. In *Look Homeward, Angel*, he wrote, "There was forever in that town a smell of raw tobacco, biting the nostrils with its acrid pungency; it smote the stranger coming from the train, but all the people in the town denied it, saying: 'No, there is no smell at all.'"

At the time it was almost precisely the sort of town H.L. Mencken might have been thinking of when he described the post-World War I South as a "Sahara of the Bozart."

Soon all of that would change, first with the big money being poured into the Old Salem restoration, with even bigger amounts being spent to seduce venerable Wake Forest College to abandon its ancestral home near Raleigh for a new campus carved out of the lovely, sprawling R.J. Reynolds estate north of Winston-Salem

Maybe the best sign of all that Winston was becoming more than just another stinking industrial town was its ability to outbid Charlotte and Raleigh and Greensboro for the new North Carolina School of the Arts, founded amid the caterwaulings of legislators fond of describing it as "that toe-dancing outfit." The school's success was phenomenal almost from the beginning, contributing mightily to the metamorphosis of Winston into a major arts center. In one of his less felicitous phrases, futurist-author Alvin Toffler would later describe it as the South's foremost "culturopolis."

I had spent many a summer in the tobacco fields on my grandfather's farm, only six miles north of the city, and was always ready to defend Winston against blasphemers like Cash and Wolfe and other high-brow critics who liked to think of it as just another crummy nicotine wallow.

I could never read Wolfe's morbid dismissal of one of the most honored traditions in all of Moravian church history, its Easter sunrise service, without feeling a little stunned. Or maybe "puzzled" is a better word. His exposure to this extraordinary event, which annually attracts people from halfway around the world, left him feeling that he either had walked into a "ghoul fantasy of death returned" or had been an unwilling victim to some sort of "obscene feast."

Originally, all of my people were Moravians, long before they were Baptists, descendants of the German immigrants who had first settled our land way back in the middle of the eighteenth century, and even those of us who had gone over to the Baptists had always accorded those tough old settlers a special place in our history.

Well, at least the grass has not started growing in the streets, and we still have the smell that isn't there to remind us that we were once a big part of the New South story, even if we had never been much of a part of the Old South—and to haunt civic boosters with the terrible lurking suspicion that we might never ride nearly so high again.

Nobody would ever have guessed, in 1987, that with the approach of the year 2000 the old town would again be in the midst of a boomtown fever, seemingly unhurt by Johnson's action. We could have been left with nothing but a lot of "scruffy" old stores and a special, utterly delightful non-existent aroma that had caused such a stir among first-time visitors.

Now that I was back, preparing to cover the biggest story to hit the town since the still-unresolved killing of tobacco heir Smith Reynolds in 1932, I had a new sense of what local boosters meant when they referred to the smell of the "weed" as "the smell of prosperity." For it was certainly that. R.J. Reynolds and the cigarette industry had been responsible for transforming the town, during the early part of the twentieth century, into the largest and most prosperous in the state. The town was so rich in those days that many critics felt it had been irretrievably spoiled, that it had grown smug and presumptuous while remaining utterly provincial. Once known, not altogether correctly, as "the city of one hundred millionaires and no middle class," Winston-Salem would continue to flourish as an important commercial and financial center for more than three quarters of a century, despite its relatively modest size.

Those were big days in Old Winston, back before the lung cancer scare, back before the second big war, and even back before the turn of the century. Big days when farmers from all over northwest North Carolina and southwest Virginia came crowding into town for the market openings, with the melodious cries of auctioneers rising out of all the big warehouses. A time of carnivalism, drinking, whoring, gambling, revivals.

There were still plenty of natives who could remember the boom times of the twenties, when Winston, having joined itself to neighboring Salem, was still the largest town in the state. Some few could remember all the way back to the early days of that century, when Camels suddenly emerged as the first widely accepted cigarette on the U.S. market. Before that it was all cigars and snuff and plug tobacco. The first cigarettes had been overly sweet, overly laden with sickening Oriental blends. None ever caught on in America. But Camel, as the ads used to say, was a *real* cigarette.

Old Buck Duke down in Durham was soon in the fight with his dashingly successful Lucky Strikes. The American Tobacco product— "Taste a Lucky instead of a Sweet"—pushed Camels hard throughout most of the first half of the twentieth century, with first one brand and then another dominating the market. When filters came in, the company's Winston and Salem brands kept it on top throughout much of the fifties and on up into the sixties—until the coming of Philip Morris's "Marlboro Man."

By this time the town was no longer what it had been during the twenties. We could blame some of it on the Depression. Nothing was ever the same after the hard times hit. Truth is, though, the town had never really been on top of things since the death of the company's founder, back in 1918. For years after he left "No Business" Mountain in the nearby Virginia Hills and first rode into Winston on a tired mule, as legend has it, or maybe on a balky horse or even in a coach and six (he was no pauper even then), old Winston was one of the most turbulent places in the South.

Reynolds was a true marketing genius who swore to give old Buck Duke hell while his own operation was still part of Duke's American Tobacco Company empire. And he sure did that. By the mid-twenties, however, with its founding genius no longer around, the town had begun to drift. But it was the Depression that really altered the equation. The Depression was actually good for smoking, for helping maintain a certain amount of prosperity in the town, because people sure had to have those coffin nails even when they couldn't afford groceries. But the Depression brought something else besides hard times: it brought unions—or the threat of unions.

Roosevelt and his New Deal had scared the cigarette industry into taking a whole new look at itself. Now, for the first time, workers had the right to organize and picket and bargain as equals with their employers and even to go out on strike without getting pistol-whipped by Pinkerton detectives and their paid hooligans.

Would Winston be next? Boomtown mania suddenly was no more. Bring other industries in and you'll bring the labor organizers right along with them. They were right, of course. Unions, some led by communists, were already making headlines among the textile workers of the South. Before long, with this new prevailing mentality, Winston was just another company town, larger than most, but no longer the largest town in the state, and soon to be overtaken by Charlotte, a little later by Greensboro, then by Raleigh, and, finally, even as this is written, by Buck Duke's dinky little old town of Durham.

Nobody ever put it in the papers or made a public pronouncement, but the truth was that the tobacco company was full of shrewd operators who saw that the New Deal and the free hand it had given labor could be a real menace to the company. So it was that the town slowly began to draw in upon itself. But the people running Reynolds Tobacco in those days were plenty smart enough to know that they couldn't keep the organizers out by just refusing to issue them an invitation. The new managers at Reynolds kept wages high, right up there with what was being paid by American and other tobacco companies; created a superior health and pension plan (some say it led the way for the rest of the industry); offered pastoral counseling; and, after it became available, even delivered to each worker a free monthly copy of *Guideposts*, the inspirational magazine founded by positive thinker Norman Vincent Peale.

They had, in fact, produced the kind of atmosphere in which unionism would never thrive. The workers themselves would see to that: Get a job at Reynolds and you're set for life. A truism seldom questioned by even the most disgruntled of employees, if ever there were any who could have been said to fit that description. And who was I to pretend they were wrong? Its twenty-thousand-member workforce was loyal down to the last cigarette inspector or floor boss. Let the labor organizers appear, as they sometimes did, and there would always be trouble, sometimes big trouble, as in the late forties, when investigators for the newspapers found that communists had infiltrated the union local.

Still, there was no doubt about it: the town was already dropping fast as a major urban center long before Johnson came along.

The whole world had turned against tobacco now. We had hung on as best we could during all the big fights of the sixties: the package-labeling furor, the surgeon general's report that verified the tie between smoking and lung cancer, the presumptions of anti-smoking zealots bent on robbing us of our vast markets. It was a mighty long time, decades, in fact, before these supposedly "scientific" findings began to have any impact. On up into the late seventies, the RJR conglomerate was still getting more than half its profits from tobacco products.

"Get Ross Johnson!" That was all the cry when I got there. He was quite a fellow all right—more hated, I'm sure, than the character, whoever he was, who first thought up the link between smoking and lung cancer. People gathered on street corners and in cafes and in the backs of stores to talk about the despair and uncertainty he had brought to the town. And him nothing but an outsider at that. There was even talk that a lynch mob had gathered one night in front of his palatial mansion, the same as in one of those old Erskine Caldwell novels: *By god, if there were any real men in this town . . .*

It was sure the first time I had ever heard of anybody getting up the nerve actually to plan the lynching of a famous CEO hotshot. But maybe it was just a lot of fooling. Anyway, nobody had a rope. Or even a dummy to burn in effigy. The vigilantes eventually departed, to resume their angry talk on street corners, at Sunday go-to-meeting, on Little League ballfields. Wherever you found a crowd, small or large, you knew what the talk would be. The angry faces, the rage, the fists flying in the air.

Who was this character anyway? All people knew was that they didn't much care for a Canadian coming in and taking over the town. Not only that, he and his young wife were accused of ignoring all the proper social customs. Society matrons had soured on the man apparently long before anything was said about moving corporate headquarters to Atlanta. (Actually nobody would even have thought about that because nobody could imagine it ever happening.)

So how did he get where he was? How was one to explain his amazing success? How was one to reconcile his dubious beginnings as a lightbulb salesman and his long career in the middle ranks of Canadian industry with his new position as director of one of America's leading corporate giants?

Well, there was one way to explain it: social climbing and glad-handing, a familiar story to those of us who had grown cynical after years in the newspaper business. It had first paid off when he won the top job at Standard Brands, a company notorious for austere managing policies and sluggish profits. Johnson did little to change the latter. It was now that he initiated a whole series of marketing catastrophes, beginning with his introduction of such poorly conceived products as "Reggie!," a candy bar named for baseball star Reggie Jackson; "French Kiss," an insipid table wine; and "Smooth 'N Easy," a margarine-like bar that could be melted into a variety of gravies.

Johnson had a way of talking himself into positions of ever-greater responsibility. After Standard Brands had merged with Nabisco, he at once parlayed his position as No. 2 man into the top job. Now he was doing the same thing in Winston-Salem. Maybe he was only second-in-command in the new RJR Nabisco corporate structure, but anybody who had observed his career thus far would not have been surprised to learn that he was already working to squeeze out J. Tylee Wilson as CEO and get himself named top dog.

He was quick to see that nobody much cared for the Wilson; many of the other RJR officials soured on Wilson totally after he failed to inform them of long-standing research into what was eventually to become not his but Johnson's most notable market failure: a smokeless cigarette named "Premier."

Nobody could have guessed how badly Premier would turn out. But just about all the directors knew that they sure didn't care for Wilson, who never had more than tentative support from RJR's board of directors. At the right moment, Johnson pounced, announcing that his job at RJR Nabisco was finished now that he and other officials had completed the hard work of the merger and that the time had come for him to move on to fresh challenges. He had correctly foreseen, of course, that the directors would never stand for it. The directors, many of them new men, Yankee profiteers, brought in to provide muscle for a company that needed none when its founder was alive, were as quick to embrace Johnson as were the town's social arbiters to regulate him to the outer darkness.

Trouble surfaced in Winston's "closed" society when it became apparent that the restless Canadian and his wife, Cupcake, as she was disparagingly known to society matrons, could never placate the locals—even if somehow they could have passed themselves off as real insiders. In time he managed to alienate others, including former CEO J. Paul Sticht, an early partisan whose own big-spending ways seemed modest by comparison to those of "the Pope," as Johnson had been known back in New York, when he and his band of "Merry Men" were running Nabisco.

Eventually, Johnson knew much of the town was against him. First time anything like that had ever happened to him. He just had a knack for making himself popular with all the right people, and it had worked for him everywhere he had been. Now all these provincial rubes were closing the doors of their exclusive homes to him!

Well, he wasn't the first to experience this humiliation. No town ever had a "high society" more closed to outsiders than Winston-Salem. Not Charleston. Not Richmond. Not the most exclusive of New England retreats.

Those who had got their start selling lightbulbs would certainly never manage to fit in. They might occasionally make headlines on the society pages, but they would never be a part of the town's *real* society. That was only for people descended from the original builders of the town, the elder R.J. Reynolds himself, the Hanes family, which came from old Moravian German stock and had created a textile empire, and the Grays, who had been largely responsible for the growth of both the tobacco company and the financial giant, Wachovia Bank & Trust Company.

The latter at one time was the largest bank in the Southeast and, despite merger negotiations that ultimately would snatch it right out from under our noses, is still a dominant power in the financial world. All of these people, at least once a year, hold a closed gala of which there is never a whisper in the newspapers, and at which no outsiders are welcome. There has been so much intermarriage within the truly well-to-do that people unwelcome at these affairs liked to think future generations of Winston's power-mongers would turn out to be disfigured, chinless, and somewhat dopey characters like the latter day Habsburgs.

During Johnson's not-so-secret war with the social elitists (many of whom also had never got invited to that big secret party) perhaps he realized that one thing would be certain to destroy their devilish notions of superiority—depriving them of RJR Nabisco itself. It took him almost a year of dumping old enemies and wooing men who, till then, had held the real power of the town.

To prepare for the move, he began to drop hints about the need to separate RJR Nabisco's corporate headquarters from its operating divisions, which meant, of course, that he wanted to separate himself not only from the town and its snobbish social climate, but also from the stigma associated with cigarette production. Never mind that tobacco was still the real backbone of the business. When the talk became public, the town sneered again. Let him talk about economics, but everyone assumed that the real motive was pure spite.

I had seen him only once. That was on the day of a celebrated Rotary Club speech, which had been scheduled before the announcement of RJR's departure. By the time the big day arrived the news was out, and the affair was now being billed as a meeting at which we were supposed to learn about all the "intangibles" Winston was to get as compensation for losing its prized position as home to the state's largest corporation.

Would Johnson have the guts to keep his appointment?

Did he have what it took to face the very people he had summarily "ruined?"

Alone, maybe not. But with all those bodyguards he had brought along?

I guess that's what made the difference. Or maybe he had more guts than we thought. In any case, his appearance at Rotary drove the dagger in just a little more deeply.

I was there with all the other reporters, sitting almost next to the great man, at the end of the long banquet table, watching him closely: a big, square jawed fellow with an easy smile and full head of silvery gray hair. He gingerly and somewhat awkwardly puffed at a lean cigar without inhaling it. How many outrages would one day be remembered against him?

Yet there he was, standing up just as proud as you please and making his farewell speech to the Rotary Club within a week after he had announced that he was moving RJR's corporate headquarters to Atlanta. Every member was there, anxiously waiting to hear what he had to say. He sure didn't say much. I guess I somehow missed his allusions to all those intangibles that were supposed to make us prosperous again.

Prior to the meeting there had been a lot of grumbling among the Rotarians, as there was among everyone else. *Just plain stole the town you might as well say and not a damned soul willing to call him on it ... by god ...*

Not only the biggest industry in the town, but the biggest in all of North Carolina, as they never failed to remind themselves. Even the governor had finally thrown himself into the fight, thinking about all that tax revenue the state was about to lose. Anyway, there old Johnson was, sitting over his meal without eating it and pretending as best he could to enjoy his fine cigar.

Down at the other end of the table, all the TV cameras were in position, waiting for him to complete his talk so that the reporters could hound him with questions. But they didn't know Ross Johnson. While the Rotarians sat in stunned disbelief, Johnson abruptly ended his speech, which was nothing but platitudes anyway, flung down the cigar that was little worse for wear and hotfooted it out past the cameras and reporters without so much as a sidelong look, under the protective custody of a black man at least nine feet tall (so he appeared anyway) and known to associates, not inappropriately, as Mighty Joe Young.

The press was everywhere, TV cameras, reporters with notebooks at the ready. A lot of good it would do. No more speeches, said Mighty Joe Young. No more interviews.

We lit out after him anyway, in the best tradition of pack journalists, shouting questions. He strode straight on down the hall where a second aide was holding the elevator open. Johnson held his head high and stared back at us with another haughty sneer while the reporters kept trying to crowd onto the elevator with him. Mighty Joe Young flung them all back with what seemed like a flick of the wrist, leaving half of his attackers crumpled in a panicky heap while the other half went flying off downstairs to the parking garage.

Even small-town pack journalists don't give up that easily, but the elevator was too fast for most of us. Mainly I just stood and watched in bemusement, though I did get downstairs in time to see a lone female TV reporter shaking her hand in anger and disbelief. Johnson was already in his chauffeured limousine, laughing the laugh of man who was captain of all he surveyed, now making for the highroad to a new life among the beautiful people of Atlanta.

"What happened," I asked the girl.

"The crummy bastard slammed the door on my hand."

"You got a hand in the door?"

"That's all I got, except maybe a few broken bones."

"Did he say anything?"

"Laughed in my face and slammed the door. Looked like he was in a big hurry to get it slammed before I could get my hand out of the way."

"It's beginning to swell pretty bad. Sure hope nothing's broken."

"Don't know. Sure can't write with it the way it is."

"Something sure needs to be done about that guy."

By god, if there were any real *men in this town . . .*

That was the last anyone ever saw of Johnson around Winston-Salem, but we were far from hearing the last of him. He was already making headlines in Atlanta, which for some reason failed to fall for his suavely majestical presence. It wasn't long before we knew he would never really be one of the beautiful people of Atlanta either. Still, he managed to store up great treasures for himself in all the bank vaults of the town.

While raging against Old Winston's "bucolics" after making himself safe in his new glass-walled office tower, he went straight out and alienated the whole city of Atlanta with another of his impolitic after-dinner speeches. Again, the Rotarians were the recipients of his linguistic charms. At a dinner meeting Johnson loftily announced that the city needn't look to him or his company as the "salvation" of Atlanta charities, cultural organizations, social agencies, and educational institutions. As though anyone had ever asked him in the first place.

The newspapers began to write nasty columns about him:

"Don't Worry, Winston-Salem—
RJR Move Here Was No Great Loss"

A little later *Time* held him up as the ultimate symbol of American corporate greed, and he did everything he could to verify the assessment, lavishing untold millions on corporate jets, country club memberships, golf condos, and Manhattan penthouses; and on elaborate sports promotions that required the services of such high-rolling dignitaries as golfer Jack Nicklaus and Dandy Don Meredith, the wisecracking former Dallas Cowboys quarterback. He was always looking for new and more ostentatious ways to spend money.

Everybody thought he had finally outdone himself when he doled out twelve million dollars to build a hangar in Atlanta for his airplane fleet, which he liked to refer to as the "RJR Air Force." Common report had it that his main reason for building the lavish structure was to show up Coca-Cola, which had its own hangar right next door.

Well, it was about this time that the Pope concocted the wild scheme that would prove his undoing. He said he had been unable to pump up the company's undervalued stock prices, owing to the bleak future being prophesied for tobacco. Then he and seven other executives set out to buy the company at seventy-five dollars a share, taking advantage of the low stock prices and staking themselves to 8.5 percent of the equity.

Financial experts viewed the deal as outright theft. No objective student of the problem believed the stock to be worth less than 82 dollars a share, though it had never traded at that, and many believed its real value could be as high as 111 dollars. The cry went up from everywhere, "*What's the hell is it with this guy? He's trying to steal the whole goddamn company!*"

The way Johnson and his partners had worked it out, the deal would be worth two hundred million dollars as soon as the papers were signed and perhaps as much as 2.6 billion dollars within five years. Johnson alone looked to walk away with up to one hundred million dollars at a bare minimum, probably a great deal more than that in the years to come.

That's when Kohlberg, Kravis, Roberts & Co., the leverage buyout people, got into the game, shocking Johnson by immediately raising the ante to ninety dollars a share. Well, why not? After all, it was Johnson's own extravagance that helped convince KKR that the company was worth having at almost any price. The brains of the outfit was Henry Kravis, a Manhattan socialite.

Led by Kravis, the firm had created the leveraged buyout in the mid-1970s as a way of taking companies private, thereby insulating them from corporate raiders. But this was a bidding war that knew no bounds. Even Kravis was sweating before it was over. Shearson Lehman Hutton, the New York house that was putting together Johnson's deal, had another shocker waiting, raising the ante to one hundred dollars a share, not altogether with Johnson's blessing: every time the bidding went up his own projected share of the profits went down.

My god, was it possible that he would eventually have to make do with the fifty-three million dollar "golden parachute" he had negotiated for himself!

KKR would probably have dropped out at that point except for a surprising last-minute bid by New York's First Boston investment firm. First Boston came in with a complicated offer that would have been worth 118 dollars on paper, way higher than either the Shearson bid or KKR's second offering of 94 dollars. But only part of the offering was in money, the rest in securities, junk bonds, and something called stock warrants. Mostly just a lot of paper that might or might not have been worth its face value. The new bidders had based their proposal more on expectations than existing reality and were seeking to take advantage of a soon-to-expire federal tax loophole. All a bit vague. Apparently it never did get beyond being vague. At any rate the RJR directors were never exactly sure what they would be getting, and First Boston soon dropped out of the contest.

After weeks and even months of possibly the most bitter, frantic, and Byzantine-like round of maneuvering in corporate history the real bidding closed out at 109 dollars a share, with Henry Kravis a very nervous winner, already beginning to wonder how he would finance the immense amount of debt he had undertaken in order to outbid his rivals. A total of 25 billion dollars for a down-home company that Ross Johnson had transformed into a symbol of national corporate greed.

Meantime, the brokers had taken over the management of Johnson's bid, after he himself had lost interest—the more so as he watched his own carefully crafted benefits package shrink with each new offer. He had actually placed a final bid three dollars higher than the Kravis offer; but the board of directors simply did not care for Johnson anymore, and KKR's Kravis had earned their support if not their goodwill.

2

House of
Passage

On the day after I had written everything I could write about Ross Johnson and about the old town of Winston and its bucolics I went back to walk again the streets I had known so well as a child. Down Trade Street, up Liberty, down Trade again. All the places I had known when my father was looking toward a good, full life for himself and his family.

By the time he was in his late twenties, my father had already become owner or part-owner of a string of barbershops and rental houses, but he allowed drink and cards to get the better of him as the prosperous twenties faded into the Great Depression. All life seemed to go out of him after that. Toward his middle years, he began to prosper again and eventually recovered much of what he had lost, though he never could bring himself to give up drink and cards.

He had left the old homestead as soon as he was out of teens—in other words, as soon as he could escape the harsh demands of farm life, with its long hours in the corn and tobacco fields—and taken up the barbering trade, only with the hope that he could eventually earn enough to put himself through law school. But then came that old devil Depression, and, though it struck less forcibly in our town than in many another, simply because of the constantly rising demand for nicotine weeds, still it struck forcibly enough to end his plans for a career in law. Marriage, the war, his own advancing age . . . it was just too late for anything better once I had come into the world.

I walked the back streets, at an hour when there was no traffic, when the sun yet hovered just beneath the horizon, when a mist still hung heavily over the town. I walked south of the main business district through the old Moravian cemetery, studying the flat gravestones that signified the all-leveling democracy of death, a concept that had struck novelist Wolfe as somehow "obscene."

Bit of a crank anyway, Wolfe was.

I walked all through the old town, the cobbled back streets, the dirt paths, the side lanes, stopping to look at Salem's restored eighteenth-century buildings and the narrow, fenced yards so reminiscent of many a middle-European village. I got back uptown just as the sun was getting above the roofs of the factories and sat for a moment on a low stone wall that ran in front of the public library, no sound at all now except the clicking on and off of the traffic light above me as I stared up at it through the mist.

Even if Winston were still a foul-smelling industrial town, or only partly that, Salem was something else entirely—not the first of the Moravian towns, however, and for a long time not the most important. Six miles to the northwest stood the original Moravian settlement, Bethabara, Hebrew for "House of Passage," and less than a mile and a half north of there was the farmstead that had been in my family for more than a hundred years, overlooking those same rich bottoms where the Brethren had first grazed their cattle and where you could still see part of the old roadbed they had followed as they came to the end of their long, perilous journey from Pennsylvania.

The settlers chose the name Bethabara because their first settlement was never meant to be anything more than what its name suggested, a temporary way station that awaited the building of Salem, the central congregation town and administrative center. All of that would come much later. Meantime, Bethabara itself grew rapidly to become a commercial center of more than passing importance, rivaling Salisbury, another German settlement of note, as one of the two largest towns west of the fall line.

The story of how they got here begins in England, where Parliament had granted them preferred church status and where John Berkeley, the earl of Granville, son of one of the original lords proprietors of Carolina, had long been searching for reliable settlers who could bring stability and maybe even prosperity to his harassed land, which encompassed the upper third of what is now North Carolina. The Granville

District, as it was known, had proved almost totally ungovernable, acting as little more than a magnet for fugitives from northern settlements—penniless squatters, crooked sheriffs, drunken wastrels, long hunters, fur traders—while creating mass confusion among surveyors, tax collectors, and other despised officers of the Crown. Alone among the eight proprietors, the earl, a brilliant diplomat and consummate linguist, had refused to deed his share of the land back to the royal government when he learned that there was more to settling a country than emptying its mines of gold and silver.

By that time the Moravian Brethren had become known all over Europe for their piety and industriousness. In 1749, largely for those reasons, they won from Parliament recognition as an "ancient Protestant Episcopal Church," which carried with it privileges previously enjoyed only by Great Britain's Anglican establishment. Though Germanic in language and culture, they traced their faith and religious heritage to Bohemian martyr John Hus, who may be the true father of the Protestant Reformation. His death at the stake in 1415, brought about by his fiery and unrelenting opposition to the corruptions of the Roman clergy, set in motion a series of religious wars that disrupted Middle Europe for decades.

The Unity of Brethren, or Unitas Fratrum, as the Moravians then called themselves, also suffered long periods of persecution. The church flourished openly where it could, in secret where it could not, spreading through all the Slavic lands of middle Europe, building churches, schools, and printing houses. Came the counter-Reformation and the Thirty Years' War (1618–1648) and the power of the Unity was broken at last; its leaders were forced into hiding and eventually induced to make a new home for themselves on the Saxon estate of a friendly German count, Nikolaus Ludwig von Zinzendorf.

These people were exactly the sort of settlers the Earl of Granville had been seeking. By that time they had already established their first permanent American settlement in Bethlehem, Pennsylvania; and they, too, had been looking for a new land, to enrich their system of commerce and to preach to unlettered natives the joys of knowing Christ. Their prayers seemed answered when they learned of the earl's generous offer: one hundred thousand acres of their choosing if they would erect a town and bring order and stability to the land, together with honest, hard-working tradesmen to build up the country.

Granville got the settlers he wanted and a lot of others he did not care for at all, mostly Scots-Irishmen who later routed the British at Cowpens and gave Cornwallis a victory barely worth the having at Guilford Courthouse, crippling him so badly that he had barely enough horse and manpower to make his way to Yorktown and ultimate defeat. Whereas the Moravians had come by the hundreds, the other back settlers had come by the thousands and tens of thousands. They were the same men, many of them, who had first felled the forests and who, long before the Revolution, built a wilderness society that formed the basis for the great Regulator Rebellion that almost toppled Royal government in the Carolinas in the middle of the eighteenth century, years before the statesmen of the day dared speak of actual revolution.

They were a rough crowd, those old Scots-Irishmen, quite the opposite of the austere peace-seeking Moravians. Bare-knuckled brawlers, eye-gougers, knife-fighters, who nevertheless brought to these parts, along with a thousand other crafts and skills still being collected into books by antiquarians, one of the great cultural gifts of all time: the art of making good moonshine whisky. The Moravians, beholden as they were to the British, would always take the side of the Crown government against the Regulators, and it very nearly brought them to grief a thousand times during the Revolutionary era.

The Regulators were complaining about the evils of taxation without representation long before Patrick Henry got around to making speeches about it in Virginia's Colonial Assembly. Taxes were high and money short in the backcountry, but North Carolina's Colonial government was in the hands of an Eastern gentry class almost wholly indifferent to the hardships of the new settlers. Every time the legislature formed a new county in the back parts, it formed another down east so as not to undermine the dominant Tidewater political interests. It's well nigh impossible to say who were the most hated, the surveyors who constantly threatened squatters with the loss of their land or the sheriffs, bailiffs, and other Crown officials who tried without a whole lot of success to make them pay taxes on it.

Everybody knew where most of those taxes were going: not into the Colonial treasury but into the pockets of the collectors or maybe, in the form of bribes, into the pockets of Colonial judges. Well, along about 1765—maybe a little earlier in some places—the backcountry folk decided the time had come to "regulate" these sordid affairs. They took to dragging judges off the bench and throwing them into the street, horse-whipping sheriffs, bailiffs, justices of the peace, surveyors, and anybody else whose high-handed ways provided an excuse for a healthy dose of vigilantism.

When Royal governor William Tryon decided to levy a poll tax for construction of a New Bern palace, the Regulators rose up in a frenzy, gathering by the thousands at a river crossing near Salisbury, some forty miles to the south of Bethabara, and marching toward a last showdown with the Crown government at Alamance Courthouse, fancying that they were about to chase Tryon and his aristocratic dandies into the sea. It came to nothing. Tryon's regulars made short work of the undisciplined throng, driving them out of Carolina or back into distant mountain hollows where they would await a better day to take up their fight against the hated British and their surrogates.

Long before anyone had permanently conquered this land, long before there were vigilantes calling themselves Regulators and determined to bring those early Royal governors down a notch, before there were any angry Presbyterians fighting and drinking and fornicating in harsh river settlements, before there were any other white men in these back parts except an occasional hunter or trapper, the Moravians were already at work.

With the coming of the first permanent settlers, only ten in all, the town was up and going in a matter of weeks. They reached their new home on a cold December evening in 1753; within six months they were grazing cattle along our own Grassy Fork bottomland. We know all this because from the day of their arrival the settlers kept detailed records of each day's activities. Those records are unlike anything else in America, perhaps in the world—except, of course, for those other Moravian records stored in Bethlehem, Pennsylvania—and represent a uniquely valuable resource that historians are only now beginning to exploit.

A year to put Bethabara on the map. Odd that it should take another fourteen years before they got around to founding their central congregational town, ultimately to be a thriving commercial and theological center built of brick, not wood, built to endure, as indeed it has. Why so long for the Brethren to make up their minds? Mainly because for a right smart while it looked as though the Lord couldn't make up his mind, and no one ever doubted for a moment that He would have the final say.

How were the Brethren to sort it all out?

Well, not by prayers alone. Like a bunch of gamesters in the back of a saloon, they cast lots until they got the right answer. Crazy way to go about it, some might think, but the Lord had repeatedly sanctioned it as a proper way of ascertaining His will. It was not the work of a day. They would stake out a spot that looked like an ideal site for the new town, then they would gather to throw their lots, but the answer kept coming back: *"Nein. Wiederaufnehman."*

They spent more than a dozen years scouring the land and throwing their dice before at last they got the answer they had been waiting for. *"Jawohl,"* said the lot one day, and the Brethren went straightway to work, even though Satan himself had set his face against the task, coming into the town in the middle of the night, so they reported in their diaries, and breaking the handles of all their axes and hammers.

By then the country was really beginning to open up and Bethabara had become a considerable town in its own right. The old place is still there, remnants of it anyway: the distillery where the Brethren produced their excellent alcoholic decoctions (no double distilling it in old radiators as did some of those Regulators); the Potter's House, newly restored; the Gemien Haus where they worshiped; a reconstructed palisades similar to the place of refuge that protected both the pacifist-minded Moravians and many of their frightened neighbors during the hard days of the French and Indian War.

In Salem, the *Aufseher Collegium* or town supervisors dictated the location of every house, every garden, every commercial establishment, every sidewalk and meandering woodland path—certain paths for Brethren, others for Sisters, lest chance meetings occur with potentially devastating consequences. In the Moravian congregation town nobody did anything—from the ringing of bells to the taking of a partner in marriage—without the approval of the governing authorities. Not only did they locate your house for you, they also told you how many rooms it was to have, how many stories, how many gables and what color of paint to use. If confusion arose on some point, they could always retire prayerfully to a back room somewhere and cast their lots, and get the answer directly from on high.

With such guidance, the excellence of the Moravian handiwork spread far; the excellence of their good beer and brandy spread even farther. It reached the ear of Lord Cornwallis down in South Carolina and in good time at that. The tales drifting down from the Moravian towns prompted Cornwallis to bring his troops through on a rampage, to drink all they could and then haul away another ninety barrels or so toward Guilford Courthouse.

No one has ever determined whether it was the long rifles of Quaker "pacifists," who had recently settled at Guilford, or the potent schnapps of the pious Moravian Brethren that contributed to the poor showing of Cornwallis and his men at that last great, decisive battle in the South.

The Moravians kept their distance from both the great Regulator Rebellion and the American Revolution. Unlike the Quakers, they really were not pacifists in the truest sense (nor perhaps were the Quakers who fought at Guilford Courthouse), but it was a convenient and even necessary political pose owing to their special relationship with the British. Despite war and heavier taxes the Brethren prospered greatly during those years, boasting of it in their diaries, nor did they neglect their work as missionaries, the other great mandate that had brought them to Carolina.

This is not to say that all went well between them and their neighbors. During Regulator times and during the far more turbulent times of the Revolution these swarms of hard-bitten backwoodsmen—dark-browed Calvinists almost to a man—caused the Moravians much grief. Rowdy "Liberty Men" came noisily into their towns and stole everything they could carry away after drinking up all the liquor in the taverns and engaging in wild, bloody fights that frightened and amazed the pious Brethren, who were getting their first real look at backcountry "society."

Long before the war, when other pioneers were only beginning to find their way into the southern Appalachian foothills, the German settlers had brought civility and a thirst for learning into one of the most vast unexplored tracts of wilderness left in eastern America—cultural refinements hardly less sophisticated than those of Boston parlors or Viennese salons. The rigidly organized social order of *der Wachau* (or, in Latin, Wachovia), as they pleased to call Granville's hundred-thousand-acre gift, was truly one of the wonders of backcountry America.

They also brought in craftsmen of the highest order, brewers, distillers, master builders, deft artisans, strict dress codes, a Medieval-style guild system under which boys of about fourteen began studying with skilled tradesmen until they were competent to establish themselves in businesses of their own. Preachers, poets, musicians, composers—they all came, as well as politically shrewd business leaders who argued tactfully if not altogether correctly that their church was "pacifist" to the bone and that they would consent to pay a three-fold tax if the rowdy Liberty Men of that era would allow them to maintain their neutrality during the great rebellion against British authority.

All the music and sophisticated knowledge of eighteenth-century Europe eventually found its way into this isolated spot, just as did the Revolution itself at a much later date. The Brethren found themselves constantly caught up in some of the most beautiful music ever written, concertos and symphonies by Bach, Haydn, Mozart, while outside their houses, in the streets at nights, and in the neighboring woods, they could still hear the unsettling howl of the wolf and the cry of the cougar.

The more or less parallel settlement of this region by the Moravians and Scots-Irish Presbyterians, who made up the bulk of the Revolutionary armies, added a creative and, for all the havoc it caused, productive tension to frontier society. Before the war, the Moravians, ethnic opposites to the Scots-Irish in almost every way, provided men who could bring the Word to many a backwoods settlement that as yet had no preachers of their own. They counted on these same people to patronize the Moravian craft and pottery shops and make them hum with new business, and so they did; and it wasn't long before Bethabara was the chief trading center for all of northwest North Carolina.

The Moravians had also established a thriving trade with such places as Cross Creek (now Fayetteville), Pine Tree (now Camden), and especially the prosperous port town of Charlestown, way off to the south. They loaded their wagons with bear hides, deer and beaver skins, Seneca snakeroot, butter, tallow, beehives, grains of all sorts, candles, guns, and other raw products of the backcountry and made their way south toward a precarious crossing of the Yadkin River, just north of Salisbury, and so on into the low country of the Carolina Tidewater. Weeks later they would return with those same wagons crammed full of items to be sold mostly, though not altogether, at retail in the congregational store: salt, newspapers, sugar, spices, gunpowder, indigo, coffee, tea, needles and thread, tobacco pipes, hops essential to the production of "wholesome" Moravian beer, and an occasional Negro slave.

By the time the Industrial Revolution arrived in America, the enterprising Moravians, whose communal society had seen them through the first hard years in Carolina, now proved the most ambitious of capitalists. While most of the South was fighting to preserve its plantation society, the new young men of Salem had already begun to explore the possibilities of creating a much greater wealth in manufacturing.

As early as the mid-thirties they had voted to build one of the first of Southern textile mills, certainly the first to appear in what was still among the more remote sections of the North Carolina backcountry. (Was that one reason that The War between the States was inevitable, set in motion partly by Yankeedom's fears that their textile mills would not long be able to compete effectively with a Southern industrial economy that had ready access to raw cotton?)

Known as the Salem Cotton Company, and located west of the town on what the Moravians called Factory Hill, the building in which the mill was housed still stands and tells much of its own history, with eccentric stylistic details dating all the way from the late Victorian era back to early Jacobean times. Factory Hill was almost as much of a monument to the Lord as to their church. It had always been like that with the Moravians: Man manifested the work of the Lord in his life by the dedicated and consummate artistry of his trade or craft. In the church, a man could honor the Almighty with hymns and prayers. In the mill or in his craft shop he could do the same with the work of his hands.

Not that prayers were neglected even in the mill. Almost the first business of the church fathers after they launched their enterprise was to establish a Sunday school for the workers. Their next was to clear ground for a graveyard—two graveyards, one for the white mill hands, the other for slaves. As one walks through the old place he senses instantly that life of the antebellum mill was not unlike that of its late-nineteenth-century counterpart: a dreary and tedious business, often relieved by nothing except early death. Typical was the fate of twenty-three-year-old Caroline Lumly, who scrawled her own obituary on a fourth floor "graffiti wall" in the mill's female dormitory: "When I am (gone) from this place and numbered with the dead Remember Caroline Lumly that you seen my face when thease [sic] fine lines are read."

Though the mill was not a great success, not at first anyway, it represented a crucial transitional phase in the life of the town. Church elders were counting on their long commercial experience to see them through their first tentative excursions into textile manufacturing. Alas, the kind of experience they had gained through traditional methods did not count for much when it came to the manufacturing and marketing of finished textile goods.

Whether New England's dominant position in the Southern textile market of that day is the whole explanation for their failure is far from clear. Yet fail they did—miserably. They had originally envisioned profits of up to 20 percent a year. They never even came close to that. The story of the Salem Cotton Company therefore does not tell us as much as we would like about a great region rapidly turning to industry, but we do learn quite a lot about its first tentative gropings—in Salem as well as in the larger South.

The coming of The War between the States and a brisk demand for Confederate Gray finally put the mill on sound financial footing. In 1863 it passed into the hands of the F&H Fries Manufacturing Company, which had built a considerable reputation locally with its popular Salem Jeans: *They will finally wear smooth, but will never wear out.*

Frances Levin Fries, the family patriarch and guiding spirit of the textile enterprise, was an aggressive manager and unrelenting master of detail. He had spies everywhere. He and fellow entrepreneurs in nearby counties took turns at industrial espionage, sneaking into the North to inform themselves of the latest in machine technology and marketing techniques, and then returning to apply their newly acquired knowledge in their own mills.

Fries also had one other great asset that the Salem Cotton Company had denied itself: slave labor. His use of slaves in the mill at all levels brought much grief to the *Collegium*, not because they were bedeviled by questions of morality—the Moravians had owned slaves since before the Revolution—but because the practice seemingly ran contrary to the "orders of the community." By allowing his slaves to become proficient in the mechanical arts, Fries appeared to be creating a class of tradesmen who would begin to compete with the Moravian young for needed jobs.

The *Collegium*, which maintained a tight supervision over the Salem economy until the eve of the war—another reason perhaps that its early foray into the world of venture capital got nowhere—was forever at odds with Fries over this question. An artful persuader, this Fries was, attempting to convince his dubious overseers that he was by no means turning his slaves into skilled tradesmen; rather, as the keeper of the *Collegium* minutes states, they were to be thought of as mere "laborers at the machines."

A genial piece of sophistry that fooled no one. Yet the *Collegium* kept its peace, for who indeed would they find to take Fries' place? As one of his sons, Francis Henry Fries, was later to say, long after emancipation, "Many of these slaves were highly trained and key men, and all their places had to be filled when they left."

The elder Fries had borrowed many of the slaves from his father, who frequently complained that they were being worked too hard, whereupon they were finally sent home to labor under a more lenient hand.

"Or rather," as Francis Henry commented, "to work as they wished."

For all of his demanding ways, Fries, who introduced steam-driven equipment into his factory long before the war years, seems to have gained much respect in the community and within his family as well. His survivors spoke of him with unfailing admiration, possibly because he was willing to work himself a great deal harder than he worked either his family or his slaves. He even found time to keep a voluminous diary, which itself provides abundant evidence of the man's boundless drive. A typical entry: "Boys are rather worsted from loss of sleep so put Edmund Holland to carding and let them each take a nap. Run all night again. Holland up all night and boys half a night each. Brother tends boiler and engine till twelve—myself till morning."

The spirit of old Fries, who served briefly as mayor of the town, occasionally also as a member of the *Collegium*, and later as a state legislator, simply would not die. In spite of war and a desolation the Yankees called peace, his survivors carried on in grand style, managing to generate their own capital in a region so financially prostrate that it would one day find itself deeply in hock to Wall Street money changers. From this last and most enduring of Yankee conquests, which manifested itself in a colonial-like exploitation of Southern resources, the Fries heirs were singularly independent. Though money was short during those first hard days of Reconstruction, Salem was perhaps the only town in the South that was still passably solvent.

By the turn of the twentieth century the Fries heirs had built mills in Virginia and had entered the mercantile business in a big way. Their hydroelectric generators, created to furnish power for their spindles, soon lit the streets of boomtown Winston. Meantime, they invested heavily in streetcar and railroad stocks while energetically laying the groundwork for the Wachovia banking empire.

By late 1989 I was no longer busy chasing down stories for the Atlanta newspapers. That part of my life was over, and I now set out to reclaim a heritage in a slowly deteriorating farm that had been in my family for more than a century. I had spent so much time on the road there was precious little left to devote to the farm that was now to be home to me and my family.

I guess in a way I was already too late. The city that we once mistakenly thought had suffered a premature death was now threatening to overrun the old homeplace from almost every side. Try as he might, Ross Johnson failed to kill the town that had snubbed him as the savior of its largest corporation. His bidding war with KKR and subsequent stock buyout had made Winston more prosperous than ever and, little by little, it had resumed the grasping ways and boomtown mania that had dominated its earlier years.

By the time the bidding war was over, he had created a town with far more than the mythical one hundred millionaires who supposedly had run the place during the first quarter of the twentieth century, dumping an estimated $3.1 billion into the pockets of men and women who had spent most of their lives like almost everybody else: worrying about mortgages and how to stretch their paycheck from week to week.

Maybe you couldn't trace all the new growth to the vast amounts of money Johnson had loosed on the old place. But there was everywhere a new feeling of prosperity, and everywhere I turned nowadays I could see the big ugly nose of the city poking itself into our lives. Even before Johnson appeared on the scene, the expansion I most dreaded had begun slowly and inexorably out newly constructed University Parkway toward the woodlands and fields where I had hunted and fished as a youth. I had long ago realized that not even Ross Johnson was able to kill the town. I guess it was just too tough to die. A dirty, stinking, old town like that. Or, maybe, in a different way, it was already dead and just didn't know it yet.

Johnson himself was only a memory now, but he had left an enduring legacy of the sort he certainly had not anticipated. It must gall him even to this day, as he sits alone in one of those glass towers down in

Atlanta, resting beneath his golden parachute and wiping his desk smooth of imaginary dust.

When I thought about all that new money, none of which had found its way into my pockets, and saw the new Winston closing in on us, I began to look with growing dismay on the land that had once been a lovely part of the South's agrarian heritage, no longer as crazy about boomtown mania as I had been in earlier years. The land, the old post-Victorian farmhouse that was now our home, and the outbuildings, at least two of which had been built by Moravians way back before The War between the States, were still much as I remembered them from my earliest years, though I could see at once that they would not long so remain without a great deal of backbreaking work.

As for the rest, I could see very little to remind me of the good country of my youth. Gone from the low-lying hills just above the homestead were the white stables and silos of the old county farm, where some of us boys had once gone to watch the agricultural agents breed their cows. The Hanes textile manufacturing center stood there now, humming night and day with the manufacture of its successful L'Eggs product and soon to be bought out by the Sara Lee Corporation, which would cover half the valley with office buildings, splashing fountains, jogging trails, gardens. A whole new town in the making in a country that not long before knew little more than the cry of the mourning dove and the wail of the four o'clock freight train as it roared across our bottom.

Behind the textile mill was an old cemetery with gravestones piled high in broken heaps. Nobody ever again would be able to match the tombstones with their proper grave plots, certainly not in every case, though in recent years they have begun to try. I often think of how it was in those earlier days, how you could walk up in the hills above the county farm and look back south along a winding dirt road toward old Bethabara. On the near slopes herds of cattle grazed. Farther on was the train depot, gone now, and beyond that the lush lowlands bordered by hedge thicket, pine barren, and broomsedge field. Another road led west straight up past the Baptist church for which my grandfather had donated land, a gesture that presumably led him to believe he could rise up and deliver a drunken sermon or tearful confession at any moment of his choosing. Those moments were often indeed.

In the valley behind the church was the stream where, on summer afternoons, we boys sometimes went seining for catfish and perch. You could follow that stream past a stand of hardwood, a cornfield, an orchard, a hog lot. Then the land dipped and the stream widened to join the Grassy Fork, which stretched far away into the summer afternoon. On it flowed through willow and canebrake to join other creeks, which, in turn, joined the principal waterway in old Wachovia, the Big Muddy, an often-boisterous stream that grew to the size of a small river before emptying into the Yadkin basin.

In those days there was good seining in all of those streams. You worked your way out of the Big Grassy across the shallow rock bed beneath the railroad trestle and on out across the sunny meadow toward the train depot—then into the deeper timber, through waste places wild with great banks of honeysuckle and aster, with willows and black gum, the air heavy with a smell of moss, rotting logs, bloated marsh flowers. The water, checkered with shifting patterns of sunlight, ran swiftly and cleanly over the rocks, and only after a long drought could you find atop the water the thin stagnant film that now seems a perpetual attribute of all of our streams.

Then the city came. Nobody invited it. It just came—and stayed. I guess you could blame a lot of it on World War II, as well as on the new prosperity. With the postwar years had come the big diesels and the new roads and the whole country began to open up and we knew nothing would ever be quite the same again. Actually the city had been closing in on us long before we ever saw any real evidence of its presence. Because of the great forests that shut off the valley from the south and east, I suppose we had the feeling that we were somehow immune. The illusion lasted until about 1950, maybe a little longer.

Though much had happened during those first years after the war and during all the years I had been away, I could scarcely have foreseen that in time our farm and pastureland would be under assault from the developers and tax-mongers of tobacco-stinking Winston. I could again walk into the hills and look south toward . . . what? Very little that I recognized now. How different from the days when my grandfather had thought of the creek bottom and the tracks and the train depot as much a part of his personal possession as the land itself.

The whole valley was now one great clutter of houses and apartments, tractor sheds, warehouses, barbershops, filling stations, car washes, long stretches of land strewn with steel tubing, tractors, iron pipes—a horrendous agglutination of urban sprawl. While the countryside all around it underwent a methodical destruction, the old village of Bethabara was being just as methodically restored to something like its original state.

After every rain, the creek bottoms around Bethabara lay deep in water, as they had from the time of my earliest memories—only now, there were basements instead of cornfields to get flooded. Planners have a new name for this kind of place. They call it a floodplain, and, no, there was still no way to prevent builders from putting houses on it and selling them to an unsuspecting public. Later the developers would fill up those lowlands, forcing the water to seek other outlets, some of it gushing out into our own fields, some of it into the Mill Creek bottoms that lay much farther to the south.

Our new home needed work, the outbuildings needed work. Everything around the place needed work and a lot of it. You could hardly even call it a farm anymore, so surrounded was it by warehouses and crisscrossed by easements and rights-of-way and sewer outfalls, and so restricted by zoning covenants that I could scarcely add a doorknob to the house or repair a corncrib without bringing the city tax man down on me. Maybe we could blame Ross Johnson for that too.

My grandfather had built the place for his wife and ten children. Now there were only my wife and I and, for a brief while, much too briefly, our three children. Perhaps the wisest procedure would have been to abandon the place at once, call in the land-grabbers and tax-mongers, and tell them just to go ahead and take the hell whatever they wanted.

Well, I knew I could never bring myself to do that. Sometimes I walked back along the pastures and out where the old orchard had been and on up the white sand-clay road through the barn lot past all the farm buildings. My grandfather had moved at least two of them there himself, a log stable and a smokehouse, both built by early Moravian settlers.

I knew that somehow I would have to try to restore the old place to something like it was in my younger days, when the old farmhouse was still freshly painted, when the whole family would gather there for big holiday dinners and summer fish fries and family reunions. I thought about all the good times there before the war, all the childhood romps, the long afternoon searches for Indian arrowheads and Revolutionary artifacts. And always of my grandfather, a gracious and selfless man when he could stay off liquor, which actually wasn't very often. More than half a century after his death, he is still something of a community legend.

For some of us, the Big Grassy Fork still brims with fish, the white buildings of the county farm still gleam against the metallic blue of a summer sky, and the scream of the four o'clock freight still pierces the afternoon calm—and somewhere along a road in back of the Baptist church a boy is picking blackberries with his father and thinking of the good days when he at last will be a man.

3

A Glass
of the Finest

In the days of my innocence, I had no idea how far beyond our family's plantation, much shrunken from its original one thousand acres, my grandfather's fame had spread. But spread it had, especially after the great flood that washed away much of north Winston in the fall of 1916.

Even after I knew a great deal more, I never did know nearly enough. Nobody, for example, was able to say exactly how the old man had managed to escape the flood—which is to say, how he got out of the whorehouse where he had spent the night. Was he wearing his BVDs or nothing at all? And if nothing, who gave him whatever he covered himself with while making the long wagon trek back to the farm? It was November and cold. So he would surely have needed a great deal more than the bedsheets or towels or whatever he was hanging onto when he leapt out the window. Yes, and definitely something more than the leafless maple branches or fig leaves or pine foliage he yanked from the tree as he fell out of it and into the flood.

Ah, but that is only the beginning of what we didn't know. Apparently nobody ever learned the fate of his mistress either, or whatever he called the woman with whom he had spent the night. And nobody ever told me what he had said by way of explanation when he finally drove his horse and buggy into the big farmyard, or whether he even said anything at all or so much as hinted at the latest ignominy to befall him in the city. My best guess is that he didn't bother to explain himself in any way whatsoever. The family undoubtedly had to wait for the newspaper headlines: *City Reservoir Collapses, Killing Nine: Floodwaters Rampage through North Winston.*

Even then his wife and children would have had to guess at the whole truth. Or, maybe it wouldn't have been much of a guess. They had all known for a long time that when he stayed overnight in that part of town, he wasn't just sitting around cursing the drop in tobacco prices and hoping that the next day's sales would bring him a higher bid.

The Baptists of Bethania Station knew something else as well: that the old reservoir hadn't just given way for no reason. They knew it had been brought down by the hand of God Himself and wondered why He had waited so long to retaliate against booming, tobacco-stinking Winston's most notorious red-light district. He did a good job when He finally got around to it: Not a house left standing in the entire area.

Strange as it might seem, though, an awful lot about that flood simply did not add up. Why had He allowed so many good people to die, while my grandfather and all those dirty little whores escaped His mighty hand? Was the Lord saving my grandfather for a greater punishment? The Baptists of Bethania Station weren't sure. But why question the Lord's will? A thousand times they had been told that the Lord works in mysterious ways His wonders to perform. Just leave the old man to his own hard destiny.

I suppose, in time, my grandfather began to be proud of the deed and to supply some of the details himself. The way it later came down to me, the old man and his paramour had been caught in the act by the crash of the reservoir and had leapt to safety from an upstairs window just as the house was going under. Lucky that a good sturdy maple and a clump of fig trees were just within reach of the roof as they crept out onto it in the cold of the November dawn.

For years people would tell stories of those who had miraculously escaped death in the Great Trade Street Flood: the roof that collapsed and formed a protective canopy over a sleeping child, the black man and his wife who rode their bed to safety on the crest of the raging tide. But no one wanted to hear, or even think about, my grandfather's story. At least, nobody from the newspaper ever came out to interview him.

Could such a deed be left to fester in silence?

In the end, that was the question the Baptists of Bethania Station would have to ask themselves. Ultimately they did as conscience demanded: they began to murmur darkly against the old man and appointed a committee of deacons to investigate. The sorry and regrettable end of the story is that the deacons found themselves with no choice but to turn him out of their fellowship. They had turned him out before and would turn him out again. It was never easy, seeing as he had given the congregation land on which to build its church and then more land to create additional parking space for horse-drawn buggies and Model-T's and then still more land for picnic tables and softball fields and outdoor toilets.

Not only that, the man had given land and money for the one-room schoolhouse where my father and other children of the community got most of their education. "Grasshopper College," as it was known, was another unfortunate casualty of the bout of development fever that has swept our community in recent years. During his sober moments, which were mighty few as he approached his middle years, my grandfather had done many another fine work for the community. There was a time, in fact, when he enjoyed the respect of all who knew him and would upbraid his card-playing companions for using even the mildest sort of oath in front of his sons.

When he was drinking? Lord, what a difference! Once, while my aunts were in their teens and were planning a party to celebrate sister Grace's twelfth birthday, they realized their father was out in the granary so drunk he couldn't find his way to the house. That was just fine as long as he stayed where he was, but they could only imagine what an embarrassment it would be if, by chance, he did find his way inside before the party was over—and which of the young women would become the object of his inevitably lecherous attentions. My father and two of his brothers hit upon a solution: they found an old logging chain, tied him to the granary wall, and kicked the bottle out of his reach. They counted on his being sober and in a forgiving mood by the time they set him free.

"Why he never said a single word to us in anger," my father told me. "He took us boys aside, gave us each a quarter and thanked us—that's right, thanked us—for protecting him against his own worst instincts. One of the very best men in the world as long as we could keep him away from that bottle."

The people had heard all those stories—though certainly never one quite to match the story of his escape from the whorehouse just as the floodwaters were about to wash it out from under him—and laughed about them for years. Maybe the church deacons even wished they had never heard the tale of the notorious flight from the flood and had never been called to act upon it. Yet the dark truth was out, and the churchly mandate was clear: *Turn the sinner out from among you, lest ye perish by the way.*

The trouble with turning my grandfather out of the church was that inevitably the day would come when it would be absolutely essential to invite him back. That would be the day when the board of deacons realized it needed still more land.

In this case, it took less than six months. The church especially needed land for parking, now that the motor car had become a way of life for many people. The cemetery was fast running out of room, and eventually the authorities would need to think about putting in seesaws and high slides for the grade-school children. They knew that if there was land to be had, it would have to come from Mr. Sam, whose farm bordered every corner of the church property.

So the day came at last, with the deacons knocking timidly at the front door. Not to talk of land, not yet, anyway: only, hats in hand, to invite him to deliver a short public statement of faith and contrition. There would be plenty of time to talk of the land after he had resumed his old place in the Amen Corner, where his presence had been sorely missed.

The old boy must have surely laughed at that. He was drunk by the time he got to the church, and naturally went into every detail of his unfortunate "accident," adding hardly a word of faith and contrition. Sakes alive, and that was only the beginning. Once he had the pulpit, he sure god would make the most of it, and before long the deacons undoubtedly began to wonder how badly they needed all that extra land after all.

Well, what did they expect? Everybody who knew him at all knew he would never fall down weeping and moaning before the congregation, which, I guess, is mainly what was wanted—certainly no more talk of his unseemly presence in a bawdy house. Did the deacons really believe they could reason him into compliance? How many times had they seen it happen before: Mr. Sam leaping to his feet in the middle of a revival, casting the visiting evangelist aside to take over the pulpit for his own use, and roaring at the astounded congregation like a demented prophet from the wastes of ancient Samara?

His testimony of contrition was bound to be more of the same . . . except that there was something a little different about my grandfather on this night: for the first time in his life, he flourished a walking cane. It was some slick article, too. Chrome-tipped and polished to a fine high luster and fitted with an ornately carved handle, it had the look of a cane that had been ordered special for the occasion—and did that old sinner make good use of it!

No one had ever seen the church so packed, people standing all around the walls and even gathering outside in the dark. They figured it was bound to be just about the best show they'd had around there in many a year. They sure guessed right.

The Baptists of Bethania Station had heard him many a time, drunk and sober. But they had never before heard him at his glorious best, just drunk enough to be lucid, just sober enough to have remembered everything in the way of wrongdoing ever committed by any parishioner living or dead. Adultery. Sodomy. Blasphemy. A famous murder that had been covered up as a suicide. A thousand drunken binges by men now perpetually sober. A *ménage à trois* no one knew about until the culprits were found in an act of garish seduction in the very baptismal font of the church, which back then was nothing more than a walled-up portion of a nearby creek.

My grandfather swung the cane menacingly around at the congregation, waving it like the rod of Aaron, as he roared off into his main theme, his mustache twitching as though it had taken on a life of its own.

"Oh, it was a glory to hear, I tell you," my Uncle Frank used to say. He had seen it all and was always anxious to supply the details: "He would look all around with a kind of steady, measured, studied look that would have done credit to the more demonic revivalist in the land. Yessir. Then his voice would start out real low, and he'd say, 'There's a mighty scarlet woman in this church tonight!'

"Then he'd just stop for a minute and look around at all those women, as if every last one of them was guilty of something or other that they weren't prepared to put in the church bulletin. And that cane, he just kept swinging it till he had pointed at every female in the congregation. One fine show, I tell you. He swung it towards Mrs. Fannie May Beeson and then towards Mrs. Gloria Cranfield or maybe towards Mrs. Jane Washburn, and every head would follow. Old Lady Washburn!

Can you imagine that, for goodness sakes? Ha ha ha. Then he would rare up and just let it all fly, 'Is it you, dear sister! Or you, my pretty sweet!' Then I saw him pointing it right straight at Mrs. Ruby Overcash and Mrs. Kathleen Littlejohn. And I'm telling you, everybody was growing more than a mite restless, and there were enough red faces in that place to have started a conflagration. Why, the fidgeting in those back pews was like the sound of a thunderclap just beginning to make itself heard way back in the west."

Uncle Frank would cry down his sisters, who kept telling him to "hush" and to tell no more of that "devilish story." Uncle Frank would go right on, walking about the room and crying out like the old man himself.

"Well that old cane just kept swinging. Like some kind of divining rod scenting out the next deep well of evil. Yessir. It stayed for a right smart while on Mrs. Peggy Sue Cavendish, who kept trying to do something with her hands and who seemed mighty relieved, I'm telling you, when she saw that it had swung on over toward Mrs. Ola May Pritchett— and everybody knew what *she* was."

The cane kept right on swinging until hardly a one of his "suspects" had been left without at least a hint of something dark and evil in her past. Then he suddenly bounded out of the pulpit and down into the aisle and dropped his voice an octave or two while the deacons glanced worriedly at one another with dripping brows. He looked all around the congregation, pointing to one and then another of the parishioners, catching some of them two or three times apiece and grinning a little as he did so, until finally he was pointing directly at Mrs. Della Andrews, whose good work for the church had not made everybody entirely forget her dubious past.

Right there was where the cane came to a flat, dead stop. "Oh, *yes*, brothers and sisters, I tell you there's a mighty scarlet woman in this church tonight!"

"Well," said Uncle Frank. "That woman got her switchy little tail out of that church in one more big hurry and never came back. Yessir. That's the flat truth of it, if it was ever told. And let me tell you, that old buzzard followed her all the way to the door and kept yelling at her as she vanished amid the snickering crowd of onlookers that had gathered outside to have a couple of drinks while enjoying the show."

"Oh! It was terribly wrong of him to do that," Aunt Cleo always said. "If she erred in the past, she had confessed her sin, and it was all behind her. And for him to bring it up that way, well, it was such an embarrassment and such a terrible, terrible shame."

"What did she do?" I asked her once.

"Well, she left the church."

"I don't mean that. I mean what did she *do*?"

All I got for my trouble was a slightly contemptuous stare.

No matter. I already knew the story. Mrs. Andrews had lost her first husband while quite young, hardly out of her twenties, and soon gained the reputation for being a loose woman. Her name wasn't Andrews then. It was Summers. Hettie Summers. She began to use her other name, Della, after she had come again into her dignity. Different men had had a go at her, and my grandfather, I'm sure, not the least among them.

Mrs. Andrews, or Mrs. Summers rather, had been a good-looking woman and was greatly sought after once she had become the favorite topic of community gossip. A stranger named Andrews who moved into our community after retiring from Reynolds Tobacco Company — "with a real bundle," everybody said—either knew not or cared not about the rumors that had befallen Mrs. Summers.

They were soon married and spent almost five years as an exemplary Christian couple before she was again a widow and still a fine-looking woman not yet out of her thirties. But no one ever said of her that she had reverted to her earlier un–Christian ways or that she was in any way responsible for the arsenic found in her dead husband's liver. Well, I don't know. The old fellow's mind was just about gone; who was to say that she had not been peppering his tomatoes and French fries with rat poison?

After Della's departure, the cane kept waving, and the old man kept shouting. The deacons looked on in a fit of absolutely feverish agitation as the stories unfolded, loathe to tolerate such outrageous behavior yet unable to say anything because they really did need that land to expand their parking lot and provide more space for the cemetery.

"Woe! I say. Woe to a people that sells itself into lust and venery! Ye who seek the most prominent seats in the sanctuary, that your prayers may be heard, that your tithes may be given with much ceremony, ye who are the very rock of our salvation and yet walk forth in secret with stretched-forth neck and wanton eye, mincing and making sweet music as you go, do you not know—you scarlet women!—have you not heard, does not your own Bible tell you that in that Great Day of Judgment, the Lord, yes, even He, the most high God, will know the lusts of your heart and in that day will discover your most secret parts!"

Some show it was, and collections were up considerably for quite awhile. Well, I never did hear it said that my grandfather couldn't hold an audience or that anybody ever walked out on one of his sermons. Except, of course, for Mrs. Della Andrews. The way I figured it, Mrs. Andrews, during her life as Hettie Summers, had had the audacity to reject my grandfather as a lover. Otherwise he wouldn't have ruined it for himself like that. She was still, as I say, quite a looker, again unattached, and it wasn't like him to overlook the possibility of a wildly lecherous act to transpire on some later and infinitely scandalous day.

Such, anyway, was Mr. Sam's "confession," and it was way too much for the deacons. Land or no land, he simply would have to go. My grandfather unintentionally spared them the onerous task of ejecting him from the pulpit by ejecting himself. With one last swing of the cane, he flung himself clean out across the communion table and landed flat of his back, with the altar flowers turned upside down on him. He had to be fetched home in a litter, with the sin rampant in his heart and his name still stricken from the church rolls. Banned again, and maybe for good this time, almost as if some evil papist had cast him under an everlasting interdict.

Not so everlasting as all that. Unfortunately, the interdict did not endure nearly long enough to suit anyone who wished to see Christian harmony reign in our Baptist community. In six months the deacons were back offering my grandfather another chance to redeem his errant ways. He threw them out of the house. They had to wait at least a year before they could get anywhere near it, and it must have been another two or three before he went anywhere near the church.

Let the deacons come calling, and he would have guessed, long before their appearance at his door, what they wanted. There had been talk of more land, more expansion programs. There even had been talk of a brick church to replace the crowded frame building where I spent many a dreadful hour as a child.

By this time he was drinking more than ever, trying to forget what Herbert Hoover and the Depression had done to his life. Try to tell him that FDR's New Deal was only more of what Hoover had wrought, and you would likely run the risk of disinheritance—or worse. Once he had been a wealthy landowner with a fine future as a gentleman farmer. Now, thanks to Hoover—and just leave Roosevelt the hell out of it—and some bad luck with the crops, he was little more than a dissolute man of means, still looked up to when he was sober or when the church needed expansion room and roundly shunned when he was drinking. Which meant that he spent his last years almost alone, because in his last years, just before the Second World War, he was seldom, if ever, completely sober.

The truth is, my grandfather was no longer a wealthy man. He had thrown away too much money on drink and women. Then came the Depression and imperiled the fortunes of everybody trying to make a living out of the land. But the needs of the church were great, and in another six months, the deacons again came knocking at the door. An uneasy lot they were, talking of little except the weather and the crops and the political disasters of Herbert Hoover before finally getting to the point.

The brick church. The picnic tables. The seesaws. The outdoor toilets. More room to park all those A-model Fords beginning to appear in the community. More room to bury the dead.

Chairman Faust, clearing his throat, explained that the feeling within the congregation was that my grandfather was now a changed man and that the church could count on him to conduct himself with the dignity appropriate to his years and that it would be a mighty fine thing to see him back in his old pew, leading the prayers and the singing.

"Why," said the old man, rising all at once and chasing the lot of them out across the yard, "you sanctimonious sonuvabitches! I'll see you in hell first! Learn to eat your dinners on the Lord's good earth like the damnable swine you are!"

He grew older and, yes, he now began to walk with the cane that had once been only for show. But he no longer stopped at the houses of all the widows in the neighborhood or vanished for long drinking weekends in town. He was often just out walking the land.

It was along about this time that he got it into his head to buy a train. Not just any train: the steam-driven passenger train that stopped twice a day at the Bethania Station depot on its Winston-to-Wilkesboro run. But first he had to see if he could operate the thing. We learned of all this by merest chance when he caught up with the steam engine one

Sunday afternoon at the depot and tried to bribe the engineer into letting him take a turn at the throttle.

The depot was a busy place in those days. A lot of activity around there on weekends, before the automobile brought an end to weekend excursions by railcar. The railroad had first come through in 1893, about the same time it was poking its way down half the coves and hollows of the South. Nobody minded it in those early days, when my grandfather was alive. The trains were big and slow and friendly, not like the loud bullying diesels that came along after the war. During the first half of the century the tracks seemed like just another natural-born part of the landscape, a companion to the deer and gray fox and raccoon, as much a part of our lives as the waters of the Big Grassy Fork or the cry of the mourning doves or the encircling slopes where herds of Angus cattle grazed.

Those railroad tracks sometimes led us on long treks into the backcountry, where we would pick blackberries or hunt for Cherokee arrowheads or shoot quail or simply lose ourselves in the wild mottled splendor of an autumn afternoon. The train that went up each morning to Wilkesboro came back late each afternoon to discharge its passengers and sit there for a moment at the depot panting and shaking like a great fettered beast gathering itself for the last slow run into town.

Except for our soul-saving summer revivals, our family reunions, and our seining expeditions along the Big Grassy Fork, the passing of the afternoon passenger train was about as much excitement as we ever had in our lives. We could hear it coming from a long way off. Then we would look up and see it as it rounded the curve out of the forest and stretched itself out for the long, leisurely run through our bottom, its great iron wheels pounding out a merry rhythm as the engineer tossed up his hand at us and sounded the whistle for the crossing.

So it was that my grandfather got it into his head that he wanted to buy that train and make it a permanent part of the farm, maybe a kind of museum piece for which he could charge admission. At least that's what he told everybody. I think the first time the notion struck him was way back in the early days of the Depression. Trouble was, about the time he got the idea, the railroad decided to change engineers. He and Royce Bumgardner, who had been on the run for years, had been close friends who often drank whisky together and sat up for many an all-night poker game.

Now that Royce was gone, the railroad every year or so would put a new man on the run. Naturally my grandfather took it as his bounden duty to break each of the new fellows in good and proper. Why, he'd hear that train coming, and off he would go, hopping along on his cane almost as fast as a young man could run and just plain daring that train not to stop! My grandfather would catch up with it about the time it was slowing for the depot. He would start out not even looking at the engineer. He'd walk all around the locomotive and tap at the big wheels with the cane. Then he'd get down on his knees and squint at it from underneath. Then he'd back off a ways and stand looking at it with the practiced gaze of a man who sure knew his trains. All of this carrying-on would eventually catch the engineer's attention. About the time he came down to see what it was all about, my grandfather would take out a fat roll of bills and stand looking at the new man on the run: "Well?"

At first the new man wouldn't get the joke. My grandfather would look at him with a show of exasperation. "Well, son, speak up! You've got a train to sell. How much you want for the goddamn thing?"

Finally the new man on the run would laugh and say something like, "Gimmie fifty and its yours."

Then they would have a big laugh together, and my grandfather would insist on a drink or two to seal the "deal."

There came a time, however, at least once, when the new man on the run turned out to be a sour fellow who didn't much care for the joke, nothing like old Royce, who had once let him take a turn as "engineer." He even went so far as to report my grandfather to the authorities. Well, that didn't get him very far. The authorities reported it to the sheriff, a fellow named Ernie Shore, who turned out to be an old friend. Actually, he was more than an old friend; he was a former big leaguer who had played with Babe Ruth and had been the first man ever to pitch a perfect game in the majors. The old baseballer, then in his first term as sheriff, came out to talk to my grandfather about all the trouble he'd stirred up. I think they mostly wound up talking about baseball and having a drink together. Anyway, it wasn't long before the old man was out trying to buy the train again.

I never got to know my grandfather as well as I would have liked— mostly just as a sad old man, drunk all the time, well into his bottle before the first church bell rang on Sunday and drunk enough by the

time everybody arrived for the big noon meal to attack his wife of fifty
years as a sluttish hypocrite who deserved nothing less than a good thrashing. That was mainly because she was always trying to hide his liquor.
After ten children, she had long ago stopped caring about his women.

One Sunday, just as we were arriving for the big dinner, we heard a
loud crash inside the house. Then here comes my grandfather, nimble
on both legs and my grandmother right behind him, holding him by his
collar with her good right hand. Then the door opens and the old man
sails right past us into the dust. He lands on his back, blinks a couple of
times and looks up at my father with a sour grin.

"Well, Cletus," says he, "what'd we gonna do? That old mama of
yours has done gone and got herself drunk again!"

Whenever he really got into the bottle, he would always start talking politics. By this time, he was no longer able to bed all the widows in
the community. All he had now were the good memories of his days as
a political comer. He never ran for anything and never rose particularly
high as a "boss." But never mind all that. A lot of important people in
town had thought of Mr. Sam as a "man of sense" and had sometimes
sought his advice on real estate deals and eventually chose him as a
precinct registrar.

He did a real good job with those registration books. He kept them
right in the house with copies of the few other books he had—the Bible,
some verse anthologies, an early history of the state, and a bound copy
of the speeches of Henry W. Grady, the Atlanta editor who preached,
for official consumption, a wonderful doctrine of reconciliation between
North and South and, more privately, to his Southern audiences, a different sort of doctrine crucial to the rise of the Jim Crow movement.

At one time, a lot of people thought my grandfather's own gift for
public speech could have carried him far. I doubt that they would have
got much disagreement from the Baptists of Bethania Station. Some
spoke of him as a likely candidate for Congress, perhaps even as a future
senator. Drink got to him a long time before that day came, but he did
what he set out to do and did it well: As far as I know, no black man or
scalawag or populist "co-conspirator" ever got his name on one of those
registration books.

People had just about forgotten about Reconstruction when Herbert
Hoover and the Depression came along to remind them of the bad old
days. My grandfather just wasn't prepared for anything like a Depres-

sion. Maybe as a younger man he would have worked a lot harder and spat right in the teeth of adversity; but he was getting on in years now, and drunk all the time, and living on his memories of the old politics, threatening Effie Belle with death and damnation if he ever again found her hanging around Mr. Will Goslen (that "dagblasted Republican scalawag" she had chosen as a clandestine lover) and brooding over all those old speeches and editorials that orator Grady had made famous and that almost nobody else remembered anymore.

He had nothing but his bottle and the thoughts of a wasted life— and yet a glorious life, too, in its own way—and that big full box of news clippings to remind him of the good days when a black man still knew how to tip his hat properly and to keep him otherwise amused while contentedly taking care of the evening chores.

The good days were vanishing even before his death. Neither he nor any of his children ever voted for anybody but a Democrat, even though my mother had constantly warned my father that Roosevelt was creating "a sick world out there." The world of Norman Rockwell was vanishing fast. The old world of Walt Whitman had vanished a long time ago. What would the new world order be like, and how long before Roosevelt would get us into this "rotten war?"

Maybe my grandfather never truly understood how much change had already come into his world until the afternoon a black man boldly knocked at the front door and introduced himself, politely enough to be sure, and asked to see the registration book.

"You must be a stranger in these parts."

"New York," the stranger told him, almost as though he expected a vigorous handshake and warm congratulations.

My grandfather, I'm told, was only momentarily stunned. Just long enough for him to take it all in. For the first time in his twenty or more years as a registrar, here was a black man asking to see the books. Not only asking for the right to vote, but so little informed of our ways that he didn't even have the gumption to go around and knock at the back door. That wouldn't have gained him the right to vote, but it might at least have gained him a civil refusal.

The old man said no more. He was on top of the newcomer in an instant, yelling for someone to call Sheriff Shore and moving like nobody had seen him move in years. You would never have guessed that he was half crippled. He was moving as fast with the cane as he had once moved without it, the black man ahead of him by only a step or two as they lit out across the yard and down the dusty road toward the depot, my grandfather lashing at him every time he came anywhere within striking distance.

The old man got as far as the depot before losing him for good. He flung himself onto the platform and tried to catch his breath, maybe beginning to feel a little sick from all that running on top of an afternoon of hard drinking. A great disappointment it must have been that he was unable to knock the black man half senseless. But at least the family had been spared one more embarrassment. The old man didn't see it that way; all he saw was that he had missed a chance to get a large congratulatory headline in the morning *Journal*: *"Old Town Registrar Whales Daylights out of Negro Who Forgot His Place."*

Nobody ever knew exactly what happened after the chase. Sometime after dark, my grandmother became mildly curious as to his whereabouts, and my father came over with two of my uncles and they got lanterns and flashlights, and went down the road toward where the old man had been seen to disappear. They found him lying in the middle of the road, his hip broken and at first thought he was dead. He must have taken a real tumble as he tried to feel his way down the steps from the platform. We later found out that he had also suffered a mild stroke.

The ambulance men brought him in on a white cot. We were all there by that time, in the darkly lit house, wondering if the old man had died before he'd had a chance to seek penitence for a lifetime of sin.

"Oh, there's still plenty of life left in him," old Dr. Martin assured everybody. "But I can't see that hip ever mending properly, not at his age. Seriously doubt that he'll ever walk again. As for his mind—well, we'll just have to wait and see."

"So he will live then?"

"Yes. He will live. There will be a lot of pain. I can get him something to help him ease it. But perhaps a nice toddy once or twice a day would also be beneficial."

"Ha!" muttered my aunts. Now that they had him as a prisoner in his own house, he would be lucky ever again so much as to get his hand on a bottle of good drinking liquor.

Poor old guy. I never liked the room where they put him. I remember how he lay there all that winter with a somber hearth fire going, his whole manner wild and anguished now that he was being denied the daily ration of whisky that had become his life, his mustache drooping like a soul in torment.

I couldn't understand what the fuss was all about at the time, but I knew from watching him that he was having to endure one more horrible torment for the sake of his spiritual well-being. Later I would wonder if there had ever been so devilish a torture in decent Christian civilized society since Torquemada invented the Spanish Inquisition. Three months of total sobriety, with the headaches and blackouts coming ever more frequently, his eyes bright and mournful, he himself little more than a shrunken wax figure, his wrinkled old face like a sallow sponge tossed up on the high bulging pillows. It was as if somebody had stretched an invisible noose around his head and was drawing it a little tighter each day.

The bawling would go on day and night. "Whisky, Effie! Goddammit, bring me some whisky!"

He latched on to every visitor and begged for a little something to help him ease the pain. My father and some of my other uncles did what they could, but all of their sisters were watching mighty close and it was precious little anybody could get away with, even when the old man was in his greatest need. He never got a drop of liquor from anybody in the house, not even from Aunt Grace, who had loved the old man more, or at least had been more tolerant of his ways than any of the others, despite the way he treated my grandmother, and was a lot more adept at handling him than her sisters.

Grace had been sitting in the dark bedroom crying when the three men brought him in from the depot. They placed him in the bed on which he had not slept in years, his wife's own bed, so that now she would have to find another, and left him there with condolences—and with the sure taint of sin on him from head to foot.

From what I knew of my grandfather, I could not imagine him ever making peace with God in his sickbed if he had never found time to do it back when he was going to church every Sunday. All I can say is that those were terrible days. I was only ten, and I spent many an afternoon with him in the big room, the gray winter chill hanging over us even with my constant stoking of the fire.

A lot of afternoons my cousin Jesse Frank and I were about the only company he had. I sometimes doubt that he ever knew we were there. He would fall asleep for two and three hours at a time. Now and again his eyes would pop open, and he would wildly fling himself to a sitting position and try to climb out of bed, only to fall back with new pain in his hip and the tears gushing out. He would cry out for his wife, who was remorseless and unbending despite her reputation for Christian charity and mostly just ignored him entirely. Then he would call for Grace or Ethel, who always came in and tried to calm him down, but who never brought liquor.

He kept his cane with him, hiding it under the sheets and, at the right moment, grabbing it to lash out at anyone who came to look in on him, hooking it around his visitor's neck, drawing him close to the bed, and offering good money if the fellow could get him a little something to see him through the evening. I'm sure he had plenty of whisky in the house, ingeniously hidden from his wife and daughters. Just a question of getting at it.

"These damnable and hellish women! They've turned my life into a perpetual torment, and may they rot in hell for it!"

He was a growing scandal to the Baptists of Bethania Station. Wasn't this the time, now, for him to start thinking about penitence and humility and the waters of life rather than to go on thirsting after the one drink he would never enjoy again?

The refrain went on hourly. "Damnable hellions! Murderous and bloody women! Did I bring you all up as Jezebels to plot my destruction? Let the dogs eat me in the street! Do you hear me now? Let the dogs have my carcass and nibble at it until there's nothing left but bones for you to pick your damnable teeth with! And let my soul rot in Hell to your heart's content! Go ahead and have your way with me, you bloody eyed creatures of the night—but at least let my last hours be passed in some semblance of peace!"

They never brought the bottle and wouldn't have brought it even if they had known where it was—except perhaps to smash it before his eyes on the hearth—no matter how thirsty or blasphemous or tearful or angry he got. Almost six months he lived that way. The Lord's punishment, everybody said. It must have been awful. I wondered if I dared try to find one of those bottles and sneak it to him. Would it be worth one of those shiny, new fifty-cent pieces he always gave me for my birthday?

One evening along about dark, a chap known only as "the Bastard" appeared at the old man's bedside. His real name was Reggie Dawson, but the old man had never called him that. Born out of wedlock to Mr.

Sam's oldest daughter, the Bastard was no more welcome in that house than a populist or an "uppity" black or one of those Republican scalawags. His sister, also illegitimate, had moved to Detroit city as soon as she was out of high school and become a streetwalker. For a long time neither of them had dared come near the house without waving a white flag. Little good it did. My grandfather had never shot at his granddaughter, but Reggie? Many was the time he had taken dead aim on him and cut loose with both barrels. Whether the old man was only trying to drive him off the property or was simply too unsteady to get off an accurate shot and drop him where he stood, no one could say. Probably aiming over his head: his aim was too good for him to have missed so inviting a target.

Now, however, on this raw January evening, all that had changed, for the Bastard had brought the one thing he hoped might win him the old man's favor—and what else could it have been except his favorite brand of hooch? Who knows what Reggie was thinking? Maybe he figured eventually he could get himself written into the old man's will.

The old man was asleep when he got there, and Reggie assured his aunts that he would simply pull up a chair and wait until his grandpap woke up. Then they could have a nice little chat. When the old man first saw the Bastard, he reached for the cane. But the Bastard reached for something else—a pint of Old Glenmore, which he whisked from his topcoat and thrust into the old man's hand. That liquor was gone in ten minutes flat. My grandfather was content again, and the Bastard, illegitimate sneak-thief that he was, had suddenly replaced me, or maybe Jesse Frank, as the old man's favorite.

Reggie drove a transfer truck and usually could come only on weekends. The old man grew increasingly impatient awaiting those visits and got awfully nervous if the Bastard—I don't remember if he ever got around to calling him by his real name—had not appeared by early Saturday evening. This worked fine for about a month. The old man would go peacefully off to sleep after a rousing good time talking about the days of his whoremongering and drinking binges, and the Bastard kept himself just sober enough to get out of the house without arousing suspicion.

One evening the old man did not fall asleep as usual, and his visitor did not depart on schedule—the same evening that my Aunt Beth, a hard case if ever there was one, had come in from town to prepare the old man's supper and read scripture to him.

"Why, Miz Bessie," old Reggie said, "ain't you de champ, though! Why me and the old gentlemuns here done had us a nice little talk and done cleared up all our previous mizunnerstandin.'"

He swatted the old man with the now-empty bottle. "Ain't that right, champ? Why, Miz Bessie, we done come to such a fine unnerstandin' that we just natu'rilly felt it called for a little toast. Tell um 'bout it, champ!"

The old man fell into a sort of drunken trance, while my aunt dropped the supper tray all over the Bastard and went after him with both hands.

"Why you sot? You drunken sot! And who in the name of all that is holy had little enough sense to allow you in this house? You lowdown scoundrel! Have you ever once made the slightest effort to read your Bible?" By this time she was striking him with both hands and both feet, driving him out of the room, down the hall, and right on out through the front screen without his even taking the time to open it.

"Do you hear me sot? If you ever step foot on this property again, I'll have the law on you. And if I ever, ever hear you call me 'Bessie' again I'll see you in Hell! Do you hear me? Do you think there is a single soul in this house that doesn't know perfectly well who stole your grandmother's finest set of china? And all that fine silverware?"

Well, I was sorry to see it end that way—sorry that the Bastard wouldn't be bringing us any more of his Saturday night entertainment. When the old man came to himself, he relapsed into the pure torment of those endless winter days, and good old Reggie went off to whatever destiny awaited him without ever getting himself written into the will.

As March came on and as the old man sank lower, the big question was whether he had ever been truly saved. Once saved, always saved. That was the Baptist salvation—and never mind about all his drinking and whoring around. And all those favors he had done the church? To say nothing of all the times he had exposed the hypocrites who ran the place. Still, the old question rankled: Was he truly in a state of grace? Was he, in other words, actually planning to die without knowing where he stood with the Lord? Was he hoping to embarrass his relatives in death as he had so often in life? No one could say. The most distinguished theologians in the community came to wrestle with the question, every member of the board of deacons as well as the Rev. Parker himself.

Now the truth was that Parker never did have much on the ball as a deathbed preacher. He had been pastor of the church from my earliest days, and I guess if he'd been the man he thought he was, another more fashionable church would have snatched him away by this time. Anyway, nobody was ever right sure whether he was able to get across to my grandfather that if he had never truly professed Christ, he was a doomed man.

Mr. Sam had professed Christ, of course, a thousand times, and when he was really drunk, he was sometimes so persuasive in the pulpit that he could talk others into coming up and giving themselves to the Lord. But when people thought of all that and his whole sordid history, it was hard for them to remember a single time that he himself had professed his Savior in anything like the proper spirit.

Preacher Parker did his best to be reassuring, but his captive, confound him, just didn't seem to get the point. Had the old man ever been truly saved, with all the shouting and crying and screaming that was the only sure sign among the Baptists of Bethania Station that a man's heart had been touched and touched forever by the Holy Spirit? Had he gone up to the altar, if indeed he did go up, with an understanding of the important step he was about to take in his life, or did he go up there, God forbid, only because it was expected of him?

Nobody could remember. Even my grandmother was not quite sure. So long ago, so much forgotten. Nothing left but to rely on my grandfather's word for it—and a lot of help that was! He refused to talk about it at all. He would merely scowl and take a swipe at anybody who came near the bed looking as if he wanted to pray and then, mollified, would offer him good money if he would smuggle some whisky into the house.

Parker came each afternoon to give him a proper lecture. But all he could get out of him was, "Preacher, all I'm asking—and I'm only asking it, not demanding it—only asking you to slip me just one little drink." Parker sneeringly ignored these idiotic requests and talked to the suffering man as though time was short and the hour near when he would no longer take pleasure in the things of the world.

One afternoon the preacher repeated himself once too often.

"The pleasures of the world be damned, you good-for-nothing scoundrel!"

The old man half rose out of bed in spite of the pain. "You dirty, lowdown, good-for-nothing scoundrel! Come to this community in a broken down Tin Lizzie that wouldn't make it up the last hill. Now driving a big shiny Buick, the likes of which nobody else in the church can even afford! And you talk to me about the pleasures of this world!"

He got his hands around the preacher's neck and surely would have choked him for a fare thee well if someone passing in the hall hadn't heard all the gagging and the muted cries for help. After that, Preacher Parker didn't sit so close to the bed anymore, and you got the idea that the only reason he came around at all was for the sake of appearances.

Would my grandfather burn in Hell? Had he committed the unpardonable sin? We all knew what that was: blaspheming against the Holy Ghost by refusing once too often to let Him into your heart that He might there abide and be with you always and you with Him, even until the end of the world. Amen.

Sometimes the old man lay there listening silently to the preacher; other times he struggled feebly to his elbows, cursing and screaming and trying with all his might to get his hands on his tormentor's throat.

"Just one more time, Parker, and you're a dead man. Who made you rich, Parker? You steal all that money we gave you for the Foreign Mission Board? Come here with one suit of clothes to your name and now sporting a wardrobe that couldn't be matched by Solomon in all his glory! How much did you spend for that Buick, Parker? Tell me, Parker. Where're you gonna spend eternity? Tell me that, Parker, and I'll go to my grave content!"

Toward the end he grew more somber and began to talk, as he had in years gone by, of the woman known to the family as Sweet Adeline Furchess. The house was suddenly in a fit of consternation. Were all those old rumors about Mr. Sam and Sweet Adeline once more to plague their lives? Now, even in the last days of Mr. Sam's life, the Furchess woman was still a striking, exciting woman. She must have been well into her seventies; yet she looked barely fifty—a very seductive fifty, at that.

Sweet Adeline had little in common with the boozer she had brought with her into the community and passed off as her husband. Sweet Adeline was not at all what you thought of when you thought of a country woman. There was even talk that she was something of a "hoodooer." She had not aged as other women in the community and still had the same devilishly captivating figure of her younger years and the high, almost haughty cheekbones of a born aristocrat.

I'm not sure when she and my grandfather met, only that their affair had been the talk of the community for quite some years and had ended only because Mr. Sam grew tired of sharing her with all those "haints" that seemed to have taken up permanent residence in her pine-boarded house and once, so it was said, shoved her husband out of his own bed. He had known from the start, of course, that she was seeing other men.

Now all was forgiven. Mr. Sam needed her and was willing to abide her countless infidelities, having convinced himself, perhaps with reason, that he was her favorite.

"Phone her," he kept shouting. "Tell her to come on down here and that she'd damn well better be prepared to spend the night!"

His daughters—all except Aunt Grace—just stared him down with withering looks of scorn.

"Perhaps," she said one afternoon. "Perhaps for this once we should do as he asks. Why shouldn't he see whoever he wants to see at this critical time in his life? And why should we pay so much attention to Mr. Parker and all those other church people? Why shouldn't he have at least one drink a day, if that's what he wants? What possible harm could that do at his age and in his condition, when everybody knows he'll never be able to get out of that bed again?"

"Grace, girl, sometimes you cause us to worry about you," Aunt Cleo replied. "I certainly hope it is without reason."

He often called Grace to his side. Not only his youngest, she was also his favorite, the only one who had never had to go to the fields or do a speck of housework. And she was certainly her father's own child, that girl was, closer to him in her adventuresome disposition than any of the others, even if none of them wanted to admit it.

"Time," he would say. "Time, my sweet. The time that waiteth on no man."

"Please don't say so, papa. It's so disturbing to all of us to hear you speak like that."

"The pain, daughter—why it's something fierce, girl. Mighty, mighty fierce. Just one little taste, daughter, one more little taste of that delicate concoction that maketh glad the heart of man! Put here for the nourishment and redemption of mankind by the good Lord himself! Help me, Grace. Help me, my sweet."

"I'll see, papa. I'll just have to see what I can do."

Precious little it was, with the eyes of those "murderous birds" on her every moment of the day. Before she could ever get him a drink, they would all be there to drag her off to vespers or some such. Evensong as the church chimes began to sound. They never gave up trying to save him, even at that late hour, and never stopped asking the Lord to forgive him for his godless obsession with Sweet Adeline Furchess.

He never did get the drink. And it began to look as though he would never again get to see his old lover. As I say, Aunt Grace was as helpless as the old man himself, what with my other aunts ever on the alert for some falling off of righteousness in their youngest sister.

It was about this time that he went into his last decline, no longer crying out for liquor or shouting curses at his jittery daughters, threatening them with death itself if ever he could escape the confines of his sickbed. He was different somehow. His daughters' prayers only brought the Furchess woman more frequently to his mind. He now talked of her almost incessantly.

Aunt Alma and Aunt Effie B. and especially Aunt Cleo were absolutely undone to think that that woman's name would even come up at such a time as this, when they were doing all in their power to get the old man to understand that his soul itself was in jeopardy. Were they actually afraid that Sweet Adeline would again work her magic and raise up the old man so that he could carry out his threats of vengeance? No one doubted that they would have been in a hard way if ever he found himself able to walk again.

"The one true love of his life," Aunt Grace would murmur.

"What a thing to say," Aunt Cleo said, without conviction. "Poor mama. I suppose it doesn't matter now, but she has not always been past caring, you know. Why she cried and cried and cried that day she lost her wedding ring in the yard."

People had always thought there was something a little strange about Sweet Adeline Furchess, even before she began openly exercising her powers in behalf of her fellow man. There was a definite taint of witchery about her. If the stories about her were true, she was certainly the loveliest witch ever to live in our community and surely one of the most gifted in the ways of the Unknown.

There was also talk that she had been known to raise people from the near-dead, if not from death itself. She was said to have held mysterious rites at her farm home, and sometimes we boys of the community would sneak up there and throw rocks at it. By that time the old place had definitely begun to show the effects of Furchess's sorry ways. Needing paint, the shutters half falling off, no grass in the yard.

Well being a healer was just about the worst thing you could possibly be in a church community like ours. The story was that she had restored sight to the blind and made the lame to walk and committed all sorts of other blasphemous acts. Naturally she was no longer welcome in the church. The word of her miracle work had got around the community in a hurry, though not nearly as fast as the news that she had taken a fancy to my grandfather.

It was after that that the murmuring against her suddenly took on a more ominous tone. One summer night there was another delegation of churchmen at the old man's door, the preacher with them, quoting a familiar refrain, "Surely all witches and sorcerers among you shall die and not live!"

"Which of you men brought the rope?" my grandfather scowled.

Nobody had thought to bring a rope. I suppose the deacons doubted that hanging would do the whole job—that the only sure way to get rid of a witch was to burn her to death. My grandfather explained that she was "a fine woman" and warned members of the delegation to get on back to their homes and their wives and their own affairs.

Back then, Parker hardly ever came to the house or left it without working the conversation around to Sweet Adeline and her mysterious exploits, explaining that the Good Book was most explicit on how the church was to deal with such people and that nothing less than a swift retribution would serve to placate an all-seeing and ever-merciful God. Were her good works not in themselves the most powerful evidence against her? What of their own peril? Would not they themselves, the deacons, who had their mandate straight from Bible, surely answer for it if they were to ignore the word from on high and refuse to revoke her church membership—or, better yet, shoot her down in her tracks?

They contented themselves at last with striking her name from the church rolls, not because they felt that they were necessarily acting in strict accordance with the scriptures, but only because it was plain to everybody that even if they were to take her to court, the judges were so corrupt they would never believe she had actually cured the blind and the lame or, if she had, why such "devilment" should be punished as a crime.

Still, for all her blasphemy and good works, the church missed Adeline. Her good singing voice in the choir, her unquestioned powers as a healer, her uncanny ability (so it was said) to throw dread into the heart of the Devil himself!

Not a bad person to have around in an emergency.

It was during one of those emergencies, after my grandmother had kicked Mr. Sam out of her bed for good, that my aunts unhappily found themselves in Sweet Adeline's debt. On this occasion, Mr. Sam had just got back from town after a big round of drinking and decided to make his presence felt at what must have been one of the dullest Wednesday night prayer services in memory. I say this because it was one of those times when he decided to take over the pulpit for his own purposes. So he did, after a brief and mostly uncontested struggle with young Parker, who, as Uncle Frank later said, immediately tried to make it appear that it was his idea.

"Bless God! Amen! Mr. Sam has a word for us tonight! God bless you, Mr. Sam! Perhaps there are others who wish to come forward to-night and offer personal witness to the work of the Lord Jesus in their lives!"

A bad moment for my grandfather and more embarrassment for the family. He had barely got to the pulpit when he fell right out of it in a drunken seizure. Dead for sure this time! Suddenly his old lover was there, bending over the old man—he was barely into his forties—and uttering some sort of wild incantation that didn't sound like anything from the scriptures.

Why was she there anyway? The deacons warned her that she would be endangering her mortal soul if she were ever again to step inside that church without being invited to do so. Yet there she was, in the hour of my grandfather's greatest need, talking to him in what people later said was the "unknown tongue"—definitely against the rules of the Bethania Station Baptist Church. There was such a stir among all the right-think-ing parishioners that no one noticed Mr. Sam was not only back on his feet but sober as well. Adeline had never boasted of her gifts—and strang-est of all, she had never been able to work her miracles on that worthless husband of hers.

We were now well into March, but there were no warm days, and the hearth fire blazed constantly. The old man occasionally fell into a slumber from which it sometimes appeared he would not waken. He had suffered another small stroke and would fall asleep for long hours that were a blessing to us all. One day he woke and sat straight up, suddenly as alert as I had ever seen him.

"Where's Adeline? Who was that a-speaking to me just now?"

The old man could never get it out of his head that she had been in the room with him all that time. As he himself slid perceptibly toward the unknown, he began to speak not *of* her, but directly *to* her, as though she were hovering over his bed. Maybe she was at that. Even now, after so many years, the room bothers me somehow, haunting me with a strange, almost unearthly quality. I sometimes feel as though I have seen for myself the vision that must have obsessed my aunts almost nightly: the old man suddenly out of bed, his mustache bristling, with the ghost of Sweet Adeline on one arm and his cane on the other, moving toward them like a stalking vampire come hot and vengeful from the forests of Transylvania.

Which of them would be able to withstand his wrath? Which of them would have the temerity to ask him if he'd found it in himself at last to cast all of his burdens on the Lord?

Adeline! Adeline!

The unspoken word forever hung in the air like the faint, vibrating chord of an unseen harp.

Adeline!

The sudden appearance of bosomy, dark-haired Aunt Beth at the door, last seen on the night she had banished the Bastard from the premises, put a quick end to all that wild talk about inviting a witch to preside over Mr. Sam's last hours. It squelched almost all kind of talk, among the men and women both, my aunts casting a wary eye at their husbands and their husbands beginning to wet their lips as they again felt the seductive power of their sister-in-law.

Aunt Beth had grown up in an old mill town south of Winston and had suffered great impoverishment and neglect in her youth. I don't know exactly what it did to her, growing up in a place like that, but it must have put a lot of iron in her bones. It would have been difficult to live a truly decent life in a place like that, but somehow or other she had found God long before marrying into the family and had become one of the most formidable Christians of our time, with a brusque take-charge manner that did not always set well with the old fellow's daughters.

On this evening she had heard somehow that Mr. Sam needed her in the worst possible way. I don't know how. No one was ever quite certain how she found out half of what she knew; she seemed almost to have certain witchly powers of her own. All I know is that nobody seemed really surprised to see her in this last desperate moment of the old man's life.

She marched straight to the bedroom and slammed the door. "Get out of that bed, Sam James!"

Sort of a funny way to get started, I thought.

"Have you read your Bible today? Now you get up from there, and put your faith in the Almighty God! Do you hear me now?"

Having heard that she was on her way out there to pray for the old man's soul, I sat crouched in the corner behind a pair of heavy green dusty drapes and watched her go to work on him, quoting passages of scripture like some frantic jungle shaman and again ordering him to "get out of that bed and act like a man."

"Sam!" she barked. "Why are you worrying your family half to death? Don't you know they have nothing but your welfare at heart?"

Then came more scriptural quotations. "'In that day men shall beg for death and shall not find it! And all drunkards shall be cast into the lake that burneth forever with fire and brimstone!' Do you hear me, Sam? Now why don't you just get out of that bed and get down on your knees and beg forgiveness of the Lord Jesus and stop putting your family through all this strife?"

I'd made a horrible mistake by coming in there at all. She could turn on me in an instant, just like Sweet Adeline, and shoot rays of thunder into my body and stop me flat dead still and just leave me there for the clean-up woman to sweep out in the trash. No escape now. Her voice had become more frantic and her incantations more incoherent as she again ordered Mr. Sam to get out of that bed and get down on his knees before the Lord.

The old man just lay there and listened. He did not move at all. He had not spoken from the moment she entered the room, at least nothing that reached my ear, which was strange since Aunt Beth had always been his favorite daughter-in-law. Though she had made quite a reputation as a leader in churchly affairs, the old man had always believed for some reason that they shared a common cynical view about the world and the general worthlessness of mankind. But now all he did was just lie there, staring at the ceiling. He didn't even have strength left to comment lecherously, as he almost always had before, on her "really nice set of titties" and how just looking at them made him feel like a young man again. No one else had ever had the nerve to say anything like that to Aunt Beth. You always expected him to go after them like a hungry man after an exotic melon.

My aunt again soared off into another staccato of scriptural quotations. "What profits it a man if he gain the whole world yet loses his own soul! Tell me, Sam. What else do you hope to gain in this world? What hope do you hold for the hereafter?"

Even amid all her shouting, a strange stillness had fallen over the room, unlike any I had ever felt. The old man said nothing. I realized after another minute or so that my aunt had stopped speaking as well. I looked out and saw her peering closely into his eyes and taking his pulse.

"Sam? Can you hear me? Sam?"

She and I must have realized at just about the same instant that she had been talking to a dead man all this time—that he might very well have been dead before she entered the room to save him for the Lord. Not a word had he heard of the sermon that might have put him on the road to eternal life and given my aunt another miraculous deathbed conversion.

An awkward situation, but Aunt Beth was always at her best on such occasions. She immediately flung open the bedroom door and announced that the old man was indeed saved, and that even now he was climbing the golden staircase to heaven.

"Dead?" said one of the daughters. "Hardly seems likely. Do you mean papa is dead?"

"He passed from us even as I was repeating to him the verses of scripture which brought him to a new life in the Lord."

I was never sure whether she actually believed any of that. I had a lot of doubts about it, to tell you the truth. Maybe he had managed to speak a word or two as she came into the room, but I really think he had been long dead before she hauled out even the first of her redemptive messages.

Mainly what I was thinking was that I sure didn't want anybody, especially Aunt Beth, to know I'd been in there observing her last rites. I sneaked out through the back bedroom and then went out and stood at the lower end of the hall, all innocence, listening to the grownups as they mourned the passing of the old man and celebrated the deathbed conversion—so Aunt Beth described it—that had taken him straight up to Paradise.

"With every expiring breath—exactly nine, and I counted every one—he said to me that he was ready to accept the Lord Jesus as his Savior and that he was truly sorry for the sinful life he had lived on this earth and that he felt the first real peace and comfort he had known in years—perhaps had ever known 'Saved for Jesus,' he told me. 'Saved for the Lord!' My goodness, and none of you heard him? 'I'm coming home, Lord!' he shouted. 'I'm coming home.' And with his very last breath he turned to me and said, 'Good old Beth, I bless you, girl. God bless you all.'"

She seemed to have convinced herself that it was really true. Maybe it was best that way. Nobody else would have to know. At least not until I got around to telling them. I knew very well that the old man had never said anything of the kind, or anything at all for that matter, but it was one more big relief for the family to believe otherwise and another great triumph for a woman whose good works in behalf of the Lord had won her quite a following among the truly influential people in our town. That was the galling part: to have to give her all the credit for doing what none of them, his own blood kin, could do for themselves.

Some years later I went back to the little church—the brick church, not the old frame building that had been the scene of my grandfather's most glorious sermons and also the scene of many a frightening hour for me in my youth—and looked at the new stained-glass windows recently installed to honor its many God-fearing patrons. It was lovely and quiet and I was alone.

As I was leaving out through the back of the sanctuary, a memorial plaque in one of the windows abruptly caught my eye. The church had consecrated it to the blessed memory of my grandmother, Martha Hunter James, who had also had a Sunday school room named after her. Nothing surprising about that. Then came the shocking part. Right beside the name of my grandmother was the name of the old sinner himself. Another fine old gentleman of blessed memory, Samuel Augustus James. My own grandfather. Well, after all, he had done quite a lot for the church, first and last, and time, I suppose, had wiped the slate clean of his many transgressions.

I stood contemplating not so much the bronze memorial as my own feeling. Was it pride? Did I wonder anew at the hypocrisy my grandfather had always hated? I just wasn't sure. As I went up the stairs and started on out through the back of the church, I suddenly heard, somewhere off in the gloom, from the general direction of the baptismal font, a scalding burst of laughter so mocking and so sneering that I almost had to believe that the old man had seized one last chance to condemn the Baptists of Bethania Station to eternal torment.

Only my imagination, of course.

"It was very thoughtful of the church to do that for him," Aunt Grace told me later. "As I've often said—and truly I have always meant it—he could be as fine and decent as any man who ever lived in this community as long as he stayed away from liquor. And you know, I actually do think he found the Lord at the last."

"Thanks to you-know-who."

Aunt Grace looked away for a moment and then in a much smaller voice said, "Yes, I suppose we do owe her a very deep debt of gratitude."

She put her arm around me as we walked on. "We've been told so often—and I suppose it really must be true—that the Lord most certainly does work in mysterious ways His wonders to perform."

4

Mister Will's
Revenge

I was very nearly grown before I knew the whole story of why my grandfather and Aunt Effie's husband-to-be, Mr. Will Goslen, never could
sit down and talk out their differences like men of quality, and come to
a satisfactory meeting of the minds. At the time he was squiring Aunt
Effie B., I was much too young to grasp all the ramifications of their
falling out. I knew Mr. Will was an important man in our town, but he
was also a Republican at a time when the South was still trying to get
over Mr. Lincoln's war and was just becoming acquainted with Mr.
Hoover's Depression.

Not only that: Mr. Will, a starchy sort, didn't seem at all ashamed
of his politics, which might have been all right as long as he didn't try
and take over city hall. At times, in fact, he seemed absolutely proud of
himself. As editor and publisher of the *Union Republican*, a periodical
dating back to carpetbagger times, he kept drawing attention to himself
in the most outlandish fashion during an era when other members of
his party had mostly gone into hiding.

On the Sunday afternoon in 1929, when he appeared at the back
screen of the old homeplace, the big question was: How on earth did he
ever find his way out to so unlikely a spot, and what, in God's name,
could be his business? It was one more big joke when we got the answer:
he had taken a fancy to my Aunt Effie B.

The second oldest of ten children, Aunt Effie was already in her
thirties and, therefore, long past the age for a seemly marriage. But she
had taken a part-time job in that same summer at Mr. Will's printing

establishment, and, wonder of wonders, the publisher, though at least twenty-five years her senior, found himself suddenly caught up in a wild infatuation. For Miss Effie to have made such a match, and that at an age when she had long ago been consigned to a life of spinsterhood, her sisters would have been willing to forget all about Mr. Will's politics even if they'd been able to say exactly what they were.

"For the life of me," Aunt Cleo kept saying. "I can't understand why it should matter how a man votes."

Except she never talked like that in front of my grandfather, for whom politics was reason enough for the likes of Mr. Will to be thrown out of the house. Even though my grandfather would have been far gone in drink by the time his visitor got there—as he always was with the last tolling of the Sunday church bell—he nevertheless was a man to hold fast to his principles. Which meant that Mr. Will, grimly determined even then to take over the house, hardly got inside the back screen before he was picking himself up out of the dust of the backyard and shouting, "More will come of this!"

"Who invited him out here?" Grandpap wanted to know. "Just tell me that, goddammit, and they can take their goddamn bags and follow him right on out to perdition!"

Well, that put everybody to thinking. Was it really possible that Mr. Will was the first Republican ever to get inside the house? It was possible, all right. Truth was, no one had ever heard of such a thing. And it sure wasn't as though Mr. Will could hide who he was; as I say, he seemed positively proud of it.

"My Lord, Effie," Grandpap shouted. "Have you lost even the little sense that God gave you? You know what's gonna happen to you if I ever hear tell of you throwing in with a good-for-nothing nigger-loving scalawag?"

"Papa, I'm sure it was only meant as a friendly visit."

"God spare me another, and the rest of us as well."

If we hadn't known it before, we certainly knew by then that nobody ever felt more strongly about his politics than my grandfather. The old man had come of age during Reconstruction and had spent his best years defending the Southern way of life. And then to have a low-down good-for-nothing scalawag enter his house just as high and mighty as you please?

Despite his drinking and card playing and fondness for loose women, my grandfather still carried himself as a man of some standing. He even read books on occasion. But mostly what he read, when he wasn't stomping on Mr. Will's *Union Republican*, was Henry Grady's Sunday *Constitution* (a magazine-style version of the Atlanta daily), which carried its message of Southern "redemption" and white supremacy into almost every household from Texas to northern Virginia.

Grady had indeed made a grand music in the South of his day. He was not yet forty when he died, but his message of enterprise and progress, always based on the Yankee ideal, lit lamps of hope all over the benighted South, and few public men have been more widely mourned at their death. Grady spoke, and perhaps not hypocritically, of the "good, loyal, hard-working darkies" he had known—faithful servants who had stood by their white "masters" all during the war. Yet there was no place in his New South for such men. Their way had been clouded by the bitter memories of too many "bad niggers"—tools of Republican radicals and carpetbaggers and scalawags, whose only thought in those first years after the war had been to dominate the South by means of the black vote.

Out of this nefarious crowd of intriguers, Mr. Will had come. What no one talked about anymore, at least not in front of my grandfather, was that our family and Mr. Will's family were distantly related. Both Mr. Will and my grandfather were direct descendants of those German-speaking Moravians who had settled our Piedmont country way back in the middle of the eighteenth century. My great grandfather was the first to renounce his heritage, and he had survived many an eye-gouging fight with men who insisted on calling him by his old German surname of Jacobus. So, by the time Mr. Will arrived on the back stoop—nearly two hundred years since the Moravians' arrival in the wilderness—my own family was no longer Moravian. The best of my family, like my grandfather, were hard-drinking English-speaking Baptists who did not care to remember that many Moravians had refused to take up arms against the British during the Revolution. Mr. Will and many others, however, had held on to the old ways. Maybe that is why they also managed to hold on to their money during those first hard years after the War—old money that did a lot to build up the banks and industry in our town, tainted though it surely must have been by its association with pacifism, cowardice, and betrayal.

Still you have to hand it to a man like that Mr. Will. In spite of his austerity and his dignified ways and his immaculately tailored white suits and his straw boaters and his pearl-handled walking canes, he must have been a fellow of considerable courage. Otherwise he scarcely would have risked coming to the farm at all. He could hardly have been foolish enough to think he could talk sense to my grandfather. He would have known of the old man's reputation, just as the old man would have known of his. From what I knew of Mr. Will in later years I am quite sure he managed to hold on to all of his dignity even as he was getting knocked out of the house.

"All this fuss over politics," my aunts would say. "Doesn't Effie B. have a right to her own life?"

Well, maybe. Not quite yet, though, not for a long time to come. Mr. Will, he sure was a persistent cuss, and who ever would have thought he would demean himself by agreeing to clandestine meetings with my aunt at the local railroad depot? It went on like that for almost ten years. Not once in all that time did Mr. Will ever get close enough to the house to be spotted by my grandfather or any of his spies. Mostly Mr. Will and Aunt Effie would meet on Sunday afternoons, mingling furtively with the crowd that had come to welcome the four o'clock train from Wilkesboro. Or, if there was no train, Mr. Will would just sit there in his fine suit with his legs hanging off the platform and the pearl-handled cane across his lap, waiting until my grandfather was drunk enough for Miz Effie to slip safely out of the house. Sometimes, when they were in an especially daring mood, they would ride about the country roads in Mr. Will's shiny black Packard convertible. Top up, of course.

That old depot stood almost long enough to accommodate my aunt and her affianced in their need for a secret relationship. After 1938 or thereabouts, the trains no longer stopped in Bethania Station. My grandfather died on a cold evening in early 1940, leaving the way open for his daughter's marriage and for my newest uncle to pay his first uncontested visit to the farm, after which some of us began to long for the days when he hadn't been allowed near the place.

The wedding took place in April of 1940, scarcely a month after the old man's death. Miss Effie left the Baptist church to become a Moravian, and, now, for the first time in a long while, certain members of the family remembered that they, too, had once been Moravians—though none would pretend that they had ever been Republicans.

"I really think we have treated Mr. Will most unfairly," Aunt Cleo said on the day of the wedding.

"He doesn't seem like such a bad sort," another said. "Maybe it's just taken awhile for us to get to know him."

"Frankly," said yet another, "I have never understood why we should have made such a fuss over a body's politics."

"Effie is really most fortunate," Aunt Cleo said. "She shan't want for anything again. I wish the same could be said for the rest of us."

"Indeed! I think that we all owe Mr. Will a very great apology."

The day for Mr. Will's triumphant entry into my grandfather's house had come—a day in early April, soon after his marriage. It was cold for April, and we had started a fire in the parlor. I had never seen such a crowd in all the years I had been coming there for my grandmother's big Sunday dinners. Promptly at noon Mr. Will's fancy new Packard, all black and shiny and bespangled with chrome, came zooming up the drive. My cousin Jesse Frank and I greeted him from a discreet position behind the smokehouse:

"Scalawag!"

"Big dirty Republican scalawag!"

Mr. Will kept straight to the mark, striding stiffly and disdainfully up the back steps with his bride, who had grown more than a little plump in her ten years of waiting.

"Scalawag!"

Moments later Jesse Frank's mother appeared at the screen. "Come, children. Come in, and meet your Uncle Will."

"We've already met him," Jesse Frank said.

"Well, come on in, and speak to him anyway."

By that time the newcomer was all the way inside. He moved with a mighty purposeful stride, still bristling no doubt at the memory of that ignominious afternoon in 1929 when my grandfather had sent him crashing to earth next to the backyard well house.

"Christ almighty!" Jesse Frank said. "He's in the house. Mr. Will is in the house!"

Not only was he in the house, he had begun to look it over with a certain proprietary air. He also had taken a gander at his gold watch, as though calculating to the second the amount of time he could afford to squander on our big country family. One of my aunts led him into the parlor. Mr. Will, after all, was a city man at a time when our town was still the largest in North Carolina and, therefore, cared not a jot for our old ways and backcountry traditions.

"Please have a nice seat here by the piano, Mr. Will."

He stood instead at the hearth, a little restless, not smiling, tapping the bricks with his cane, looking quite out of our class with his precisely trimmed mustache, ivory jacket and checkered vest, and gold watch fob dangling to his waist. After dinner, he rose with a haughty sniff and went striding back to the parlor, where he surely meant to start hogging all the fire. The others wiped their mouths, left their desserts half eaten, and tore after him in a powerful big hurry.

"We've certainly not seen enough of *you!*" Aunt Cleo said.

"Indeed, we have not!" said Aunt Alma.

"We hope you won't judge us *too* harshly!"

Mr. Will said little or nothing. He just stood there, leaning on his cane, maybe wondering how he could work all this into an editorial condemning the Democrats as the party of rum, Romanism, and rebellion. When he spoke at all, it was only to say something critical of Roosevelt, which made everybody, except Mother, a little nervous. My aunts all looked at each other as if waiting for someone else to answer. Except for my mother, who had a little smirk on her face; she had been brought up with Republican sentiments and had always looked on FDR, especially after he brought back beer, as the "man of sin" spoken of in the Bible, believed by many to be the Antichrist himself.

Nobody could think of anything to say. Instead, just about everybody in the room went up one after another and fawned after the great man. Even my father treated him with decency and respect. He felt as strongly about his politics as my grandfather—as strongly as Mother felt about her own—but he had a whole lot less of the angry German inside him. In other words, he was "natured" so differently, as everyone said, that he just couldn't work up any fuss about a Republican, even a Republican as wealthy and unbending and ornery and dignified as Mr. Will. All the same, I could look at Father and tell what he was thinking: *Why that fella ain't nothing but a confounded scalawag, and it looks like there ain't nothing ever gonna change him.*

Mr. Will kept taking out his watch and giving it the once over, as though not quite certain he was getting the correct time. Once or twice he put it up to his ear and shook it. Then, along about two o'clock— much too early for anyone who wanted to show his "good" side to be leaving—he looked over at Aunt Effie and called out harshly, "Time, Effie! Get your things."

Miss Effie was off gossiping in another part of the room. "I don't care," she was saying. "I don't care, I tell you. I don't ever care about being one of the Elect. If I can get to heaven by the barest skin of my teeth—well, that's quite good enough for me! What does it matter if I can't sit by the right hand of the Lord, as long as I can manage to squeeze in through the gate!"

Mr. Will repeated himself once or twice, shook his watch again, and then struck the bricks more sharply with the tip of his cane.

"Come, Effie, I say! Let's go!"

He hooked his cane around her, which took a bit of doing, and guided her through the draperies into the dining room, not looking back or saying "thanks for the big dinner" or anything of the sort.

Then they were gone, with members of the family left to stand gawking at one another uncomprehendingly. One by one my aunts drifted over to the windows or front door and stared after the big Packard as it moved back down the drive.

"I'm sorry to have to say this," Cleo told Aunt Grace, "but it's beginning to look as if Papa was right."

"Well, he had certainly read his share of books—I can testify to that—and for all his faults I think you have to admit that he knew human nature through and through."

Jesse Frank had followed our aunt and new uncle out to the backyard. I found him standing by the well house with a rock in his hand.

"Gonna bust out his window lights?"

"Dunno."

"How about his headlights? Gonna bust them out?"

"Dunno."

"Shoulda let all the air outa his tires like we planned."

"Well, I'll sure get him next time. You'll see!"

I wasn't so sure. "Looks like he's too much a part of the family now. First thing you know, everybody's gonna start expecting us to treat him like a regular human being."

That was asking an awful lot, and I knew Jesse Frank would never come around to my way of thinking unless there was something in it for him. That was the thing about my cousin—always thinking of himself. His father had plenty of money, mostly from selling bootleg whisky in the back of his store in East Winston—what we called "colored town" in those days. So, Jesse Frank had learned to expect an awful lot from everybody. He had always tried to finagle the best pieces of candy from my grandfather when we went out for the big Sunday dinner, and if Mr. Will had given him the spanking new silver dollar he had halfway expected, everything would have been just fine. As it was, I knew my cousin would never give up until he had put a big old dent in that nice, shiny Packard.

Even my mother, for all of her Republican sentiments, was not quite sure what to make of Mr. Will. "I've certainly tried my best to know the man," she said, somewhat wearily, as we drove home that evening.

"It's his politics," Father said.

Mother looked at him with the look that said she knew very well he had been drinking again and that if she had to pack up and leave home just one more time, it would sure-to-God be the last time he would ever lay eyes on her.

"How much have you had to drink, sot? And will you please tell me what on earth his politics have to do with it? Many's the time my father told me that Roosevelt was destroying this great country of ours, and the Lord knows we have lived to see his words come to pass."

"Lord, honey, you know he saved the country. And Mr. Will, why he's still praising that Hoover to the skies in that little paper of his."

"When did you ever take time to read his newspaper?"

"In the shop. It comes with the mail."

My father had operated a string of barbershops on Trade Street in the middle of the downtown warehouse district in earlier years. I had seen Mr. Will's paper in almost all of them at one time or another, together with back copies of *Time, Colliers*, the *Saturday Evening Post,* and *Blum's Almanac*, another of Mr. Will's family of publications. So he had at least two counts against him: first, he was a Republican, and second, a Moravian.

"Your own people were Moravians," Mother would say. "So were mine."

She would go on to explain that she was still a Moravian at heart, even though he had been dragging her to the Baptist church all these years and that, furthermore, her own father, who was a very smart man and could play six musical instruments, certainly deserved a great deal of credit for being able to foresee the great evil Roosevelt was bringing on the country.

"Just because of the beer," Father said.

"Not just the beer."

Mostly it *was* just the beer, because everything changed for her in the early thirties, after the Prohibition laws took flight. That was when my father, so she always said, began to betray a fatal genetic flaw— "weak blood," she called it—by staying late at the barbershop or pool- room on Saturday nights and drinking a round or two with the boys.

"If you want to know what I think," she said, "I think everything that has happened since that man has been in the White House is the act of a criminal mind, and I can tell you right now we will not get off easy: we will all have to pay for it."

"My lord, honey, don't go bringing Roosevelt into it. He saved the country."

"Saved the country? That filthy gangster? Is that what you think? *Ruined* the country, you mean. He'll have it coming right down around our ears before you know it."

"Lord, honey, you know the Republicans ruined it."

"The Republicans? Was it the Republicans who fed all those pota- toes to pigs when people were going hungry in this country and then took the pigs out and shot them before anybody could get so much as a spare rib? Was it the Republicans who plowed under all that tobacco and cotton? Was it the Republicans who taught the Negras to get on their high horses and, yes, brought that filthy liquor back into our lives? I can tell you this, papa was a very, very smart man, and he knew exactly what he was talking about when he said this country would never be the same again. You watch: first thing you know, Roosevelt and that devil of a wife of his will have all those Negras sitting right next to us on the street- cars, just as biggety as you please. And now with this war coming on . . ."

"Why do you think Roosevelt would want to bring down the trol- ley line?"

"Why? You ask me why? Well, let me ask you: why would he want to bring the country down?"

I sat listening to them from the backseat, their heads pointed down the long narrow highway toward home and the moon beginning to rise. It would go on like that for months and even years, all the talk about who brought on the Depression and who got us into the war, with Mother always insisting on the last word and Father grinning at her indulgently and maybe a bit foolishly around the butt of his dying Camel.

"I suppose you actually think that that devil is going to keep us out of war," she said. "Well, I can tell you right now, he won't. Not on your life. You watch, there will be a big war, all right, and we'll be right in the middle of it."

I had first heard about the war in 1937 or thereabouts. I was only five, and Jesse Frank and I were playing in the dirt under his house on Patterson Avenue; that was just five years or so before his father got rich off the black market and bought a big, pillared neoclassical home on Robin Hood Road. I felt a great gloom settling over me as we sat there in the dirt talking about how we would all probably die in the war and how there would be Nazi spies lurking in the woods and bombs dropping all over the town and how, when it was over, the Nazis would own the very houses in which we breathed and ate and slept.

Later, I would think about all that again as I listened to my parents talking at the supper table. Mother would explain that none of the fighting would have been necessary if Roosevelt hadn't secretly sicced the Japs on Pearl Harbor and how the big hypocrite was almost certainly the Great Beast of the Apocalypse, if not something much worse, and how we all might as well be in perdition anyway, what with the country now thoroughly awash in liquor and all the Negroes getting above themselves. Father would sit there with the long ash curving off his cigarette and his single gold tooth glinting, grinning the grin he always saved for her worst moods. "Lord, honey, haven't I told you how Roosevelt saved the country? I just don't know where we'd be right now if it hadn't been for Franklin D. Roosevelt. I just don't know."

Then he would turn back to his old Philco radio, working the dial through all the static until he could find the Gabriel Heatter newscast. Most of the time I was right there with him because Gabriel Heatter came on right after the Lone Ranger, probably the only man in the world who could have rescued the United States from Roosevelt and the Japs at the same time.

"There is bad news in the world tonight," Gabriel Heatter would say. "Lucky Strike Green has gone to war!"

Mr. Will never did get over being unfriendly. I'm not entirely sure whether it was his politics or whether he was just that way. As my grandfather always said, I don't guess he could help being what he was, but he might at least have tried to show some sense of shame.

"A mighty hard man to know," my father used to say. "Holds himself mighty high."

For a long time after his ceremonial visit to the farm, we did not see Mr. Will at all. After the war, with gas rationing at an end, he generally showed up for the big family gatherings, but we sure didn't get to know him any better. He would get out of his Packard, exchange pleasantries with everybody he was unable to avoid, and then move off to establish a little hegemony in a far corner of the yard and wait for Effie to bring him his food, leaving the rest of us to decide for ourselves whether we wanted to pay him court.

Mostly, we didn't.

The last time I remember seeing him there was the summer of 1946. We were halfway through the tobacco harvest and the August revival, and the family was holding its first big reunion since before the war. Jesse Frank and I had gone seining with our fathers and some of the other men and had brought back a fine catch of catfish and perch from the Big Grassy. As usual, Mr. Will and Aunt Effie didn't show up until all the hard work of preparing the meal was over—the fish cleaned behind the smokehouse and cooked over an outdoor grill, the sawbuck tables set up, the great bowls of potato salad and slaw and succulent cakes and pies brought out from the kitchen, the big urns filled with tea and coffee, and the Lord praised and thanked beyond all measure for bringing us all together to share in His wonderful bounty.

We watched Mr. Will as he got out of the car and set out across the yard like a halfback dodging tacklers in the open field.

"I'll take care of him this time," Jesse Frank said as we came back from sneaking a smoke. "Just you wait and see."

By the time Mr. Will got to his remote outpost at the corner of the yard and planted himself by his walking cane, Jesse Frank was waiting for him amid a great outcropping of hedge and hollyhock.

"Big dirty Republican scalawag!"

Mr. Will didn't turn, didn't move at all. He just sat there beneath the walnut tree with his hands motionless on top of his cane and waited for his plate of fish.

"Scalawag!" Jesse Frank shouted. "Scalawag!"

He still didn't turn, and Jesse Frank fell silent when Aunt Effie came hoofing it over there with a heaping plate of fish and dessert and a glass of iced tea. He would probably want coffee later, and she would see that he got that too.

Just as he settled in to eating, in that sort of genteel way he had,

Jesse Frank crept out of the bushes, stood up for a second and fished something out of his back pocket: a penny box of stick matches. He got out a couple, planted one between Mr. Will's sole and shoe leather, and had just ignited the other when the publisher rose and spun furiously about. He hooked that cane around Jesse Frank's neck and sent him sprawling back into the shrubbery. Jesse Frank set up a blubbering like none of us had heard since the night Aunt Polly threw herself at the foot of a visiting evangelist and confessed in front of the whole church a youthful indiscretion she had carefully kept hidden for more than forty years.

"That Jesse Frank," Mother said later, "such a crybaby. And him almost fourteen years old. Thelma has simply spoiled him to death. I have no brief for Mr. Will, but I really don't think he struck Jesse Frank at all."

Neither did I. Even if he did, I'm sure now that it was a blow aimed not so much at my cousin as at my long-dead grandfather, or perhaps at the entire family—the whole conglomeration of yellow dog Democrats that had brought him such grief for lo these many years.

"More will be heard of this!" he cried, as he flailed away at the bushes.

The whole yard had fallen still. My aunts and uncles all stood with their plates and faces caught in a kind of fantastical still-life portrait, glaring first at us and then at Mr. Will as he turned from the shrubbery and planted his straw boater on his head, flinging his plate of fish to the four winds, and stalking off purposefully toward his car.

"Come, Effie! Come, I say!"

Gone again and this time for good, out of the yard and out of our lives forever—or at least until the night in 1952 when the funeral home phoned to say he had died of a heart attack. He'd had a weak heart for many years, and his illness had greatly alarmed Aunt Effie. The story was that in recent years she had scarcely ever allowed him to climb her ample frame in the night anymore for fear that the exertion would finish him off. Now it had! It was a good six years since I had laid eyes on the old scalawag, but I have to say that nothing about him had changed. He lay there among the flowers, looking as stern and dignified in death as ever he had looked in life.

It wasn't long before we got the rest of the story: Mr. Will had not left Aunt Effie so terribly well fixed after all. The embarrassing truth was that he had all but denied her any share of his estate, and, of course, everyone knew why: it was his only way of getting back at my grandfather for all those years of ignominy—for never having been allowed near the house and for being forced to fulfill the one great passion of his life among the furtive, demeaning shadows of the local railway depot.

"Can you imagine such a thing," Mother said one Sunday as we were on our way home from the farm. "I'm told that she is to get only the barest stipend—that everything has been put in a trust fund to be overseen by members of Mr. Will's own family. I suppose she will have enough to get by on, but perhaps not as well as she would like. I think that is what Cleo called it: a mere stipend."

"Well," Father said, "what else can you expect of a Moravian—and a Republican, to boot?"

"Have you been drinking?"

"Not a drop."

Father may have been at least partly right. When it came to spending money, Mr. Will had been hard even on himself. In spite of his great wealth, he had lived in a relatively modest home on Poplar Street all these years. I say modest, yet it was quite a nice house indeed by ordinary standards, a two-story white frame dwelling with green shutters and ivy climbing up one of the chimneys. Miz Effie got to keep the house, or at least live in it; but its ultimate disposal, like everything else, was left in the hands of Mr. Will's family trust fund. Apparently the family itself got the bulk of the money and doled out Aunt Effie's share in meager monthly installments.

After Mr. Will's betrayal, the family once again suddenly stopped talking so fondly of its Moravian heritage. Whenever I reminded my aunts of it, they would simply look at me as they had on the day I came home from college to announce with Nietzsche that "God is dead." I suppose now they were right to hate Mr. Will. After we found out about the trust arrangement, we all hated him far more in the grave than we ever could have hated him in life.

"We certainly did everything in our power to be civil to the man," Aunt Cleo would say.

"How could anyone have done more?" Aunt Grace would say. "And now this."

For the first time, my aunts began to talk of my grandfather with something almost like respect. After all, he was the first to have seen through Mr. Will.

"Papa drank far too much, and he did not treat Mama at all well in his last years," Aunt Cleo said one Sunday afternoon. "But he was in many ways a very wise man, a very thoughtful man."

"I often saw him with a book in his hand," Aunt Grace said. "And I think all of us will now have to admit that when it came to knowing all about human nature, he was the shrewdest of us all."

"Certainly when it came to Mr. Will."

So it would go. They eventually came to talk with something almost like fondness for the man who had often embarrassed them by drinking far too much and by openly consorting with the whores in our town and, most of all, by exposing the adulteries and fornications of the women in our own church. Let the subject of Mr. Will come up and they would all of them nod with appreciation as they looked up at their father's portrait, which still hung above the parlor mantel.

"Well," my father would say, "those Moravians always did hold themselves mighty high." And Mother: "Hush, won't you? Won't you just hush?"

Even though Aunt Effie had gone over to the Moravians at the time of her marriage, I'm not sure she ever won wide acceptance. In fact, I am certain she did not. Years later a Moravian lady of great piety and reputation said as much when I spoke with her one afternoon about a book I was doing on Moravian "pacifism."

"Miss Effie," the lady said, not unpleasantly. "She was, after all, only a convert."

I don't suppose Effie B. ever had the presence of mind to explain that her people had all been Moravians once—or maybe the thought just never came fully home to her.

After all this I began to understand a little why old Jacobus, my great grandfather, had repudiated his German heritage, challenging anyone who presumed to remind him of it to a "fair fistfight" and refusing to speak a word of good Deutsche even though he had grown up with it as his first language.

Maybe that was also why Aunt Effie, toward the end of her life, chose to come home and to be buried among her own people. Or maybe she had done so only because the Moravians still had a rule prohibiting men and women, whether married or unmarried, from being buried in the same section of a graveyard. They were often a hard-living, hard-drinking lot, those old Moravians, but lust had always been a worrisome problem—an intolerable if necessary evil in life and not to be countenanced at all in death. So, in the end, Aunt Effie finally got to come back home, to the immense gratification of everyone in the family and to the great vindication of my grandfather.

"No, we certainly cannot deny that he often let liquor get the best of him," Aunt Cleo said. "But he was at heart a good man. And a perceptive man."

"Especially when it came to Mr. Will," said Aunt Grace.

"Well, we all know this much at least," somebody else said. "Effie B. certainly was a lot happier knowing that she was finally to be back among her own kind."

5

Mama's Little Boy Lost

I first knew my Uncle Luther as little more than a peddler of eggs and butter, forever fawning at the back gates of the rich and mighty in our town, often returning home with stories of how Mr. R.J. Reynolds II had invited him onto his patio for a nice companionable chat or how Mr. James A. Gray, the banker, had once allowed him to peek through the porch screen at his newly remodeled kitchen and entrance foyer. Strange that he could not have known those men on near-even terms, as had my grandfather. Stranger still that he ever took up the peddling trade at all. But say this for him: he was the only one of five brothers to stay on the land and hold it in great reverence for all of his long life.

My grandfather had drunk good liquor with all the town oligarchs and joined them for cards and borrowed their money and occasionally paid it back, but Uncle Luther saw nothing of this in himself. He saw himself, I suppose, as only a struggling dirt farmer who counted himself fortunate when one of his clients briefly invited him into their houses, always through the back way, to get a glimpse of the fine carpeted rooms and lush parlors where they held their decadent parties and orgiastic rites.

Back home, his sisters would shake their heads dolefully and talk among themselves: "What can we do for Luther?"

That was the great cry after their mother's death in 1950, and what could be done for Luther now seemed only too obvious: just hand over to him all our good land for a price way below its market value. There were murmurings against him from some of my other uncles, who did not feel they'd got a fair shake and, driven on by a set of angry wives, were just about ready to give him a good thrashing.

All for nothing.

"Poor old, half-blind Luther," his sisters would say. "Poor old Luther. Why he's never had a real break in life. Staying here on this old farm to take care of Mama, while all the others were fleeing into town. Just don't seem fair somehow."

Well, they went right on talking that way, even after they found out about all his jimmying of his mother's will.

Poor Luther. Poor peddler.

Nobody ever talked about how he was also the only one of ten children to have been in the army and how he had marched through many of the greatest cities of Western Europe and had learned all about the perfumed decadence of a world the rest of us had never seen. A lovely memory that stayed with him all of his life, yet changed nothing. Just another peddler of eggs and butter among the tobacco and textile millionaires. Why even his wife, the daughter of a well-to-do Winston merchant, had fallen victim to advanced senility when she was barely into her forties.

It was true that for many years after my grandfather's death, Luther came every day to look after the milking and the haying and the tobacco crop. His five sisters had all married and moved away; and his brothers, as soon as they reached the age of twenty-one, had hotfooted it into the city. My own father had gone to Cincinnati and Pittsburgh and Canada and Kansas City to work as an itinerant barber before coming back to Winston to settle down, marry, and seek the fortune that was forever slipping out of his hands. Another brother got his start as a grease monkey and eventually acquired his own auto distributorship. Uncle Frank, of course, had done best of all; he married well, developed a booming market for bootleg liquor out of the back of his grocery store, and when World War II came, drew down another easy fortune selling sugar and other scarce goods on the black market.

None of that for Luther. Unlike the others, his long years of hard work in the corn and tobacco and wheat fields, when a man had only his hands and the most primitive tools with which to work, had not turned him against the land. He was just a sad old guy in a lot of ways, and it was easy to feel sorry for him, especially with that eye problem he had. None of the others would ever miss the farm as he would have missed it, because none of the others had forgotten their hard lives as children, the call from the foot of the stairs at 4:30 each morning, "Time to get moving, boys. Time to get on outa here and take care of that milking!"

My father would spend his whole life talking about the hard, cold winter mornings when he had to make his way to the barn by lantern light; the long hours of plowing corn in the hot sun, of suckering tobacco and priming it as the August dog days came on, more long hours of hanging it in the barns for curing. But unlike the others, especially the women who married into the family, he had little to say when the time came to settle my grandmother's estate. He took his $7,500 for the forty-five acres that would soon be worth ten times that amount and never once protested his loss.

"Cut out the heart of the farm for himself," snorted Uncle Frank, who needed the land least of all, "and made such a tangle of things that none of the rest of us would have access to our share."

But his sisters all said, "Poor old Luther, Mama's little boy lost."

I was eventually to get the farm, simply because I was the only male heir—my cousin Jesse Frank having died at sixteen in an auto accident—and also, I suppose, as a sop to satisfy a promise Luther had made to my father as part of the settlement. In those days, of course, I never figured I would get it at all. I figured Uncle Luther would manage somehow to lose the little piece of paper on which the agreement was scrawled—if, in fact, there was a paper.

A peddler without ambition, without even the pride to keep the place from falling into a state of disrepair that would have outraged my grandfather had he lived to see it. When Luther acquired the estate, everybody thought he would make something truly extraordinary out of it. After all, he had never minded hard work, and he was still a tough old coot, always anxious to be out and going, even on the coldest days.

How was it, then, that when my wife and I went out to have a look, after age finally caught up with him, I could scarcely recognize the place I had known so well as a child? Little more than an embarrassment to those of us who had once counted ourselves proud heirs of Mr. Sam, who had bought the place in 1893 and turned it into a profitable and well-kept enterprise despite all the time he spent running after drink and fallen women.

"Some people are just plain damn common, and it doesn't make any difference how they're brought up," I kept muttering, sometimes to myself and sometimes to my wife, Mary Ellen, still very much the fetching, green-eyed girl I had first laid eyes on more than sixteen years earlier.

"Well, you have to remember that his eyesight is poor," she would always remind me. "Perhaps he just can't see what needs to be done."

"I've heard talk that his eyesight isn't as bad as some have said."

"Do you think the government would pay him if it wasn't as bad as he said?"

"Would you trust the government to know the difference?"

Anything gone wrong with the farm? My uncle would always make sure that his eyesight got the blame. "Well," he would say if you happened to mention that one of the barns needed work or that the hay was beginning to look a little moldy, "you know I can't see." Then, as though to make his point, even after you'd been in deep discussion with him for half an hour or more, he would fling himself right into your face, squinting horribly and saying, "Who'd you say this is that I'm talking to now?"

He was always careful to pull this stunt when some of the other relatives were around, knowing that I had suspected his eyesight was much better than he pretended and maybe thinking he could finally throw me off the scent. Still, if he were managing to put one over on the government, I guess you had to figure that that in itself was quite an accomplishment. Because everybody knew that his failing eyesight, however exaggerated it might have been, had nothing to do with his service in the army. I always felt a little better about him when I thought about it like that—at least until the day I learned of his plan to will almost half of what he had left from my grandfather's once princely holdings to the church.

I didn't remember anything like that being mentioned at the time of the settlement. The way I'd always heard it, we were to receive the farm intact—that it would come to us as it had come to him. But there was a kind of terror in him in those days, a kind of frightened laughter, and I was sure he had lost the paper by now and that if we got anything, it would be only because he needed us to look after him in his old age. You could see in him in those days what might have been seen in many a Medieval magnate or crowned head who, in penitence for sinful lives, had lain on their deathbeds and signed over their castles and landed estates to the pope and his church.

My uncle had grown up under another kind of belief—the Baptist belief in faith, not works, as the only sure guarantee of heaven. He had heard it from his earliest days. No one could remember the last time he had missed a preaching service. He was always there. Sunday morning. Sunday evening. Wednesday night prayer meeting. All the church suppers. Dinners on the ground. The first in the door of every revival, and the last to leave.

Even so, I'm not sure that old Baptist message of a lifetime ever fully took hold. I guess he had been scared all his life. Unlike my grandfather, a drunk and energetic whoremaster almost to his last days, my uncle never touched liquor, never swore, never carried on with loose women—or for that matter with any other kind.

We were not even sure he had ever done much carrying on with his wife. She had been sickly and emotionally distraught for the whole time he had known her, yet she was also a lovely girl who had been brought up to a life of privilege, and nobody could understand how a poor half-blind farmer who had spent his best years delivering eggs and butter to the back doors of the rich men in the city could fare so well in the game of matrimony.

In his last days, after we moved out to take over the old place, he went to work in predictable fashion. We had given up our own home, at his insistence, after promises he never meant to keep—or meant to keep only in part. For, indeed, he had already promised the church at least three-quarters of his land.

What he didn't know was that my wife had something in her lockbox almost as valuable as the land itself: a power of attorney drafted by a sympathetic aunt, actually one of those angry wives who had made such a fuss at the time of settlement. The paper gave her sweeping powers over all of his belongings, and many was the time I cursed the depth of her Christian commitment because I knew she would never use that paper to take the first dime or the first scrap of land from my uncle. He eventually learned of the paper, to be sure, with some show of alarm, since he trusted no one and was never sure he would not be left alone and helpless in his last days. He accepted with an uneasy laugh her suggestion that they call in the lawyer to revise certain key provisions of his will. She was a slick one all right. In the end, much of what had been destined for the church and charity would come back to us. I suppose he convinced himself that he was merely being generous—a trait long dormant, if, in fact, that is what it actually was.

My wife and I were both working and unable to settle into our new digs right away. Our belongings, accumulated over fifteen years of marriage, would have filled his house and maybe another half again as large. So it was that I came in unexpectedly one winter day to hear him telling my aunts how greatly we had failed him at a time when he needed us most. I didn't say anything, but when my wife came in one day and found those same aunts rummaging through our things with flashlights, like explorers studying an Aztec ruin, she lost her Christian composure for one of the few times in her life and had quite a lot to say to my uncle.

"And who'd you say this young lady is that I'm a-talkin' to now?"

That put an end to all those exploring expeditions. Not the talk, however. I would come in early from work sometimes and hear my uncle and his sisters sitting back in the kitchen laughing at our "uncivilized" ways. After one particularly galling episode, I grabbed him up by the shirt collar and was about to send him for a nice ride across the wide kitchen table when it came to me that he was, after all, an old man. He laughed his nervous, frightened laughter and came over to me and got up in my face and squinted at me like always: "Who'd you say this is that I'm a-talkin' to now?"

Nobody in the community knew any of that. The whole countryside came out to honor him at his funeral. There was much talk of building a statue to the man who had lived all his life for the church. Or, at the very least, of putting up some sort of memorial plaque. *Poor Luther. Mama's little boy lost.*

Despite certain last-minute revisions in his will, the Baptists still came off quite well, much better, I'm sure, than if my grandfather had still been in charge. The Baptists were quite decent about everything. They at least asked permission when they came to haul away the tobacco barn he had promised them so that they might transform it into a recreational building. It was one of only three on the place. I had not wanted the Baptists to have much of anything, especially the tobacco barn that I was planning to restore as a studio apartment.

"Gotta stop them," I said, grabbing my double-barreled 12–gauge shotgun from behind the kitchen door. Plenty of firepower in that old gun, the same my grandfather had used to shoot holes in the doors and ceilings and to knock toupees off unwelcome visitors and casual passers-by.

"Put that thing down! We can't stop them. It's in the will!"

"Confound him. Confound him and his goddamn will!"

I gloomily watched them raise the barn on wheels and roll it off across the pasture toward a turn in one of the small creeks that fed the Big Grassy Fork. There had once been a baptismal pool there, banked up with smoothly rounded creek rocks, with steps leading down the banks beneath the shade of the big oaks. The scene of many an adulterous midnight tryst.

Now, years later, I think of Uncle Luther lying there during those last weeks before his death. I began to feel really sorry for him and even tried to forget all those times he had come up to me, squinting in my face and saying, "Just who is this young feller I'm a-talkin' to now?" I watched him as he lay there, each day growing a little more distant, shrunken, dying, his grip still fiercely strong even in his last hours. When he was able to speak at all, he would always cry out for sympathy, for someone who would understand how much of his life he had devoted to others, how much he had given up so that everybody else would have more. I watched him, the only one of the brothers and sisters who had finally got it all, the big farm, the house, and the array of historic barns—two of which dated from before the War between the States—and allowed it all to fall down. Would they ever really build him a statue? Worse, would I be the guest of honor and asked to deliver a little homily?

All I can say is that the rest of us, the younger generation, could see him for what he was, when his own sisters and at least some of his own brothers and the U.S. Army could not. But that was before his death and before we found the diary that in some ways altered still further all our feelings about my uncle. It didn't tell us anything about the man we knew; instead, it told us an awful lot about the other self that had somehow got trapped inside him and had stayed there as a prisoner for the rest of his natural life.

An astonishing find, that small leather-bound booklet, not so much for what it had to say about the closing days of the First War, no not that at all. Only surprising in that a man so seemingly lacking in ambition, with so little curiosity about the great world, so beaten down by life, with almost no self-respect, with hardly a creative spark in his body except when it came to making up all those lies about his eyesight—that such a man would have had the interest or found the time or for that matter had the sense to understand that he was witnessing a pivotal moment in modern world history. I kept hoping he would prove to be a diarist with a superb eye for detail. Well, he was not exactly that even though his diary was indeed a bit more than the collection of inconsequential scribblings we surely would have been bound to expect. And for a man, whose only claim to an education was six years or so at my grandfather's little "Grasshopper College," his command of the language was far from contemptible.

As I pondered the words of a man who seemed ready to face any challenge I couldn't help but wonder what caused him to swell with pride every time someone brought up the incident that won him his childhood nickname of "Mama's little boy lost." He had gone through life thinking of himself that way and enjoyed telling the story on himself, laughing as he spoke of it—how he had once driven his sisters to a party and was waiting for them timidly in the buggy when a couple of girls just his age came out—he was sixteen then—and a fine time they had at his expense!

"Why," says one, "If it ain't Mama's little boy lost. Come all the way to the big party and won't even come in and say 'Hello.'"

The others laughed, and I suppose he must have tried to join in the laughter, as they mocked him in singsong fashion.

Here's Mama's little boy lost. What're we gonna do with Mama's little boy lost?

Anyway, the name stuck, maybe because he believed himself only as a poor hapless creature who never quite found out what to make of the world. So it was that in time he became the skinny, niggardly coot we always remembered from the big Sunday dinners at the farm, full of resentment for those he somehow thought had it better than he did and were always seeking to gain some sort of advantage over him.

If we had found the diary without ever knowing our uncle we would have concluded, I'm sure, that he was a man of parts, perhaps even of fortitude, not even afraid of the loose women in all those European towns half shot to pieces by opposing armies. I kept asking myself what could have changed him into a frightened, suspicious little toady, who would never feel entirely comfortable walking up to the front doors of the town patriarchs.

He was the only one of my grandfather's sons of the right age to go to war. He saw no action, but it was the one great adventure of his life. We knew that much because we knew he had never had any others.

The more we read from that little diary the more we came to realize that he had not always thought of himself as "Mama's little boy lost."

It was almost as though a vital part of his personality had escaped him somehow, driven underground perhaps by my grandfather's dominating, if drunken, personality. In those days he had not always thought of himself as a nobody, a man to be sneered at by the patriarchs in our town even as he was delivering them their weekly portion of eggs and butter.

I suddenly found myself wondering how he could have gone out into the great world and seen so much of Europe and the lovely decadent life of showgirls and whores and all the great cities and the antique elegance that the war had not entirely destroyed, yet have been content to come home and live the life of a man much resented by the rest of us for his back-biting ways. I wondered why he never spoke of those days with anything like the zest that had found its way into his written words. Most of all, I found myself longing anew for a land I had seen only once, and that briefly, and yet had seemed far more like home than this almost alien Piedmont country in which I had come to manhood. Ah, I thought, to have the chances he had had—to walk again along the great rivers of Europe, to stride the ancient cobbles of a thousand cities that had been great centers of trade and culture when our own land still echoed with the cry of aborigine and panther!

He did not enter the army until the fall of 1918, only six months before the Armistice. He could not have known it would be over so soon, and he seemed almost anxious to get to the front and to experience the dangers of actual battle—he who avoided confrontations even of the most innocuous sort in his everyday life back home. There was no terror in him then. It was as though Europe had called up in him a being whose existence had been unknown even to himself. He had heeded it briefly—then forgotten it entirely.

Why?

As an eighteen-year-old off to war, he appeared to feel real excitement at being back in the land of his ancestors. He landed at Brest in September of 1918 and in his subsequent march across France, he took every moment he could spare from drill to describe the splendors of the French countryside, of the towns and villages, of Orleans, Chartres and dozens more. It was almost as though he had lived his whole life in the five months he was abroad and that nothing else mattered. The country seemed more beautiful all the time. The fields of Champagne. The Argonne forest: "The most beautiful scenery I had ever seen or expect to see."

He was wrong about that, if only because he hadn't seen Germany yet. He could not have imagined the great beauty of that land when all he knew of it was what he had seen in the propagandistic headlines of his hometown newspaper. He found it hard to imagine that a nation of such scenic charm could have produced the barbaric hordes who had burned all the great libraries and cathedrals of France and Belgium and destroyed all those lovely little French towns.

He learned how to shoot and how to handle a gas mask. He was part of the Forty-second Infantry Division and had landed with every intention of facing those same barbarians in the trenches. The officers pushed his company hard. Twelve miles a day by foot. Thirty-five men traveling in a cattle car barely big enough for twenty. Yet there was no whining or complaining in Uncle Luther's little work of prose, nothing at all to remind us of the man he was to become.

I never have given up wondering what forced him to turn inward and take refuge in a life of shadows, in pathos and sorrow and, yes, even in blindness. There were no complaints about poor eyesight during his European adventure. In his spare time he would often go off hiking with some of the other men, determined "to see as much as I could of France."

Not till the very day of the Armistice did he and his troop start for the front. It was a bit of a disappointment, even though the drilling did not stop, the long nights of guard duty, none of the hardships of an army life. Later, he learned with great satisfaction that he would be going to Germany after all, as part of the U.S. occupational force.

They marched on into *Deutschland*, just as though the war were still there. Maybe it was. On one occasion he wrote that his company had been held up for hours by an exchange of artillery fire. What was he feeling at that moment, as he at last saw all the old German towns, the lovely mountains, the castles, the storied Rhine? Did he feel cheated out of his part of the war? Was there no terror in him at all, none of that unwillingness to face up to life, which is what most of us would later remember about him?

I suppose he had most of all wanted to see Germany. It was easy to forget that his own father was a full-blooded German and that our fore-bears were all German and to conclude from the war propaganda that they were indeed only barbarians.

Until we found the diary, we did not know that some part of the old Moravian tradition—the obsession to know and remember and chronicle everything that came within their realm of experience—was still strong in my uncle. Not a day went by without a diary entry of some sort. He would stop at the sills of burned-down houses or on rock walls during a break in the long marches to jot down whatever came to mind.

It was lovely as they marched into the Rhineland. The company camped at a place called Niederbresig. "There is another town just across the river," he wrote. "Just back of the towns there are high hills and it is very beautiful to look across the river from one town to the other and I see the deep green valleys and high hills in the rear."

By the second week of December, they were deep into Germany. One senses the excitement in him as he approaches the fabled land of ghosts and dreams and mighty castles. He is always looking ahead to the next day's march. He was in a country like none he had ever seen, great mountains rising before him, fields clean after the harvest, long narrow roads carrying him past gnarled old orchards and rambling stone walls overhung with the branches of apple trees.

Many whose ancestors came from those parts have experienced the same magical lure of the old country. Perhaps it is something of what my uncle felt—that somehow it had been his own home in some distant misty age long forgotten, somewhere deep beneath the darkest rivers of memory—remembered dimly somehow, or rather felt, not remembered, as he looked at the country that had been home to many generations of Jacobuses and other unnamed Germanic peoples, men and women who had adopted the pietistic Moravian faith and eventually found their way as a communal society into the hills and valleys of Piedmont North Carolina.

Christmas brought the first real relief from military duties, even though the Armistice was now more than a month old. On that most nostalgic of holidays, he must have thought of the big country dinners back home on the Grassy Fork. Yet, for some reason, he did not write of home, only of what lay ahead, the great beauty of the land, the good fresh pork and mashed potatoes and rice pudding that he and his company had enjoyed as their own Christmas feast.

They marched on into Mandenscheid, a place near Trier, believed to be the oldest town in northern Europe. One evening he found himself seated at a table with a lightbulb dangling over his head, allowing him to spend the whole night writing for the first time since he had been on his European adventure. He had never known the same luxury at home, in the very land where electric light first made its appearance, and would not know it for another fifteen years, until the coming Franklin D. Roosevelt and the Rural Electrification Administration. If he perceived the irony, he failed to record it in his diary.

Back home, he finally threw over everything of that old culture and, unlike his father and grandfather, was apparently proof against all temptation. Did it have to be that way? Everything in his diary cried, "No!"

To those of us familiar with the indoctrination techniques of the Baptists of Bethania Station and who knew my uncle in later life, it might have seemed odd even then, even when he was eighteen, for him to have fallen very far from the paths of eternal righteousness. Unless they had seen the diary. Maybe he just didn't write about that part, though he did once hint at it. That was the day he had stopped to make an entry on a low stone wall near a burned-down German house.

"A good woman tried to get me to come in the house to write, but I told her I could write here all right."

I hated that in him and wanted to imagine a different fate: he goes into the house, accepts a glass of wine—not the $3.50 stuff either—and is soon seduced by drink and by the woman herself, a widow and perhaps a former adulteress or woman of the streets, greedily sexual, who teaches him more than he would again have a chance to learn in all of his ninety-three years. One hates it for him even now. Perhaps by the second or third glass, he would have been committed to a different kind of life entirely and would never have grown into the hard-bitten, unrelenting Baptist he was later to become. So that we would never have come to think of him as just another sneaky little farmer who had inherited bad blood somewhere, and nobody wanting to say whether it was from the English or German side—whether, indeed, it had come all the way down from Charlemagne or Pépin the Short.

I hate it that we did not know about the diary before he was gone. At least, then, we would have known he had not always been destined to the life of a niggard. He must have known that himself, at least in some dim part of himself, yet he came back anyway to live out his life as a measly peddler, the diary itself forgotten or, at best, no more than a keepsake to remind him that he had once been young and full of the wild and sweet and sordid things of youth.

Even now the great mystery—the "why" of it all—remains.

He might have had the good days and drunken, wildly sinful nights in Trier to remember and, perhaps, would have come home to build a different kind of life, a more expansive and generous life, out of all the good memories of liquor and women in the wreckage of all those old German towns. Perhaps he would have become something more than a grasping old man, coaxing his mother to alter her will so that his brothers and sisters would be unable to claim a fair share of the old homestead—though precious little help his sisters were: *Poor Luther—no life of his own, how thoughtful and loving of him to stay with the farm and to spend his best years looking after Mama.*

He would have enjoyed a certain status that none of his more adventuresome brothers could have claimed. He could have escaped the snare of the Baptists, or at least have been able to live out his life without the feeling of doom and damnation that seemed always to be hanging over him in his last days. He would not have had to go as an old man and ask for a secret Baptism, fearing that his first as a child had not taken, never realizing that the second, kept hidden from other members of the church, would be a mere mockery of his own more fervent attempt to make peace with God. He would have forgotten or put to the side the one biblical passage that would have reminded him of how foolish and unproductive he would find the secret immersion of his old age: *"He who does not confess me before men neither will I confess him before my father which is in heaven."*

He lost sight of how differently everything might have been because he had forgotten Germany, his own past, his own chance for the good life of drunkenness and fornication. Even if it did not have to last forever—that life—as it had with his own father, it could perhaps have lasted long enough to have saved him much torment.

Back he came to the town that one day would know him only as a peddler, never again to leave, never again even to speak of returning to the Continent. So how could any of us know whether he regretted the thought of all the liquor he had not drunk or the memory of all those fast women to whom he had not made love?

He would not have understood the Lost Generation, the expatriates who did not want to come back, who could never feel comfortable again after experiencing the wonders of Europe, the marvelous world that emerged always fresh and new and incredibly old and unbelievably lovely, no matter how often armies had marched across it, no matter how often it had been burned and ravaged by senseless war, turning *hausfraus* into ravenous nymphomaniacs and good, right-living country boys into men of adventure and intoxication and connoisseurs of the good life of wine and endless fornication. He could have lived without all that frightened laughter in his voice and died without all the terror in his eyes.

It just plain didn't work out. By the time I knew him, he was fast becoming, if he had not already become, what he would always remain, what he always was from the first day I ever knew him: a peddler of eggs and butter, fawning at the back doors of the rich and mighty in our town. A good thing those old boys never got around to pestering him about his land. Fortunately or otherwise, the church got there first, and I got there barely in time to keep the preachers from getting it all! If the town "patriarchs" had stuck their noses into it before he decided to hand over to me a good portion of the old homestead, I would *really* have had a fight on my hands. And poor old Uncle Luther, what a quandary! The church, the patriarchs, or his own kin? Heaven, Hell, or Purgatory?

6

My Debut
as a Wine Snob

As an embattled freeholder struggling without much success to save a family farm from extinction—the farm that was now my home—I ultimately hit upon what seemed an ingenious plan, not so much to save the house as to save the land itself: I would become a famous winemaker, whose product would prevail over the lesser vintages of our area and assure me a permanent place of refuge amid the towers of a growing city.

All of our agricultural authorities had persuaded me and dozens of other would-be wine snobs that we could hardly fail. They assured us that nature had conspired in some mystical way to bless our land with precisely the right amounts of rainfall, sunlight, soil diversity, and dark nights of the moon to transform our Piedmont countryside from a land that had known only the cultivation of tobacco—pernicious weed!—into a region soon to be acknowledged as one of the premier wine-producing regions of the world.

This was heady news. Night after night we crammed into the auditorium at the agricultural office to hear fat men in T-shirts praise the coming greatness of our Piedmont vineyards. The *vitis vinifere*, source of the great wines of Burgundy and Bordeaux, would be brought in, nurtured with knowing hands, and, in time, convince itself that it was right back home amid the castles of Avignon.

It didn't quite work out that way. *Vitis vinifere* proved disconcertingly recalcitrant. No matter. For the truth was, as we all knew by now, one could become a wine snob without knowing anything about grapes or, for that matter, very much about wine.

I am not sure exactly where I went wrong. All of my early experiments with *vitis vinifere* were a disaster. Morning and evening, my vines drooped with a lassitude that betrayed an indefinable and sorrowful homesickness for the old country. I had often felt that way myself, convinced that it was my true home as well—the old country—and so it was not too surprising that when their hopes despaired, mine went into an even speedier decline.

Our other vintners had much the same kind of luck. Everything had been calculated by logarithms and mystical calibrations to prove that *vitis vinifere* would be right at home in the North Carolina Piedmont, that this was indeed a country created from the beginning as a land that could not fail to produce great wine. Somehow, though, it just wasn't working out. That was when we discovered French hybrids—good, stately grapes that combine the best of *vitis vinifere* with disease-resistant American varieties. Maybe the wines produced from those grapes would not put to shame a fine *Haut Brion* or elegant *Medoc*, but they have had their advocates among those whose opinion was not to be despised.

So I again set to work, churning lush meadows on which cows had grazed peacefully for more than two hundred years into an implacable morass. I labored without a break during one of the coldest winters in memory, getting the posts set, the vines established, and the land properly drained and fertilized. By mid-April the vineyard finally took shape—long rows of stubby vines, yet to produce their first green shoot, laid out in a military-like phalanx on the wide upland slopes between our farm home and the Baptist church.

Well, none of it worked out exactly as we had envisioned. But I was happy in my naiveté and, for a long time, haughtily counted myself as a charter member of the Upper Piedmont Wine-Tasting Society, a fraternal order that lobbied for favorable licensing laws and crowded around big fires on winter nights to talk the good talk of grapes and wine lore. There would be long and intense discussions of balance and flavor, of "audacity" and bouquet and acidity levels, of golden Rhenish in tall slender bottles, of princely Chardonnays and feisty German Moselles, at once unpredictable and ever rewarding.

Our principal retreat was a spacious vacation home on the Yadkin River—our host an Albanian restaurateur who had made a fortune in steaks and gravy and was now looking for something finer in life. One gazed in awe upon his chrome-plated vats and urns and cooling chambers, at his many shelves crowded with tumblers, casks, weird alembics, hydrometers and thermometers stuck in thin-necked bottles.

Those were heady days all right—good days full of the promise of imminent prosperity, fame, and the right to be drunk as often and as completely as you pleased. So it was that on a certain Sunday afternoon in early September came the big wine-tasting event of the season. Everybody who aspired to greatness in our society crowded into the Albanian's riverfront lodge, many carrying under their arms the proud homemade vintages they secretly hoped would overawe the French and California wines spread about for sake of comparison.

I knew there would be difficult moments. Naturally I had read everything I could find on the ceremonies of wine-tasting and had practiced all the right gestures in front of my bathroom mirror. I still wasn't sure I knew enough. A heavy burden that drove me out to buy a $35 wine-tasting manual of this complex ritual, guaranteed to teach you every nuance. I went to work once more, this time to master the fine and subtle art of "smelling," a complex procedure approximately as intimidating to the wine novice as one's first brush with advanced Germanic philosophy.

In this case they were almost the same. German was all the rage that year. I had spent most of it at Old Salem, as director of an editorial program looking toward a commemoration of the 1976 Bicentennial year, and like a lot of my fellow workers at the restored Moravian congregation town, I had taken up the study of Deutsche with an almost frantic zeal, preparing myself—as were the others—for an autumn decorative arts tour of the Fatherland.

The tour would take us through seven countries, and we would be obliged to poke around in a lot of musty old museums and Gothic cathedrals and at least pretend to take an interest in all sorts of arcane lectures and Medieval artifacts. But there were compensations: good German wurst and sauerkraut and Wiener schnitzel. Dutch banquets and fine Danish pastries. Long walks through elegant gardens and along storied rivers and through old walled cities that looked out on some of the most delightfully scenic country in the world.

It was there, in the Fatherland, under the guidance of a Lutheran minister named Fred Weiser, a great round man who acted as our tour guide and whose theology was essentially no different from that of the Moravians, that I made my first acquaintance with a true European-style *weinprobe*.

Though I learned little of the language, and have long ago forgotten that little, I still feel a tinge of the old excitement when I think of our nocturnal visit to the ancient Deutsche "*Weinstrasse*," or German Wine Road, and how I came away with a single burning admonition: "Alvays schmell!" Such was the advice of Herr George Erben on that long ago night in the little town of Deidesheim, as my companions and I crowded into his Medieval cellar and gathered around a long table to watch him uncork a 1938 bottle of *Trockenbeerenauslese* that would have sold for 1,000 marks, or 400 American dollars. "Alvays schmell!"

It was late by that time, and we had tasted many a fine wine that evening, from the least expensive to the plainly unaffordable. The *Trockenbeerenauslese*, a rare vintage made from grapes just barely nipped by the frost, so as to concentrate all the sweetness and richness in a special way, was the most unaffordable of all.

I was almost the only non-Moravian in the crowd, invited to come along because of my work at Old Salem and because I had recently written a book about the Brethren's role in the American Revolution, which, of course, had been to avoid it with every means at their command.

Anyway, I had never lost respect for the Moravians, for those old settlers who more than two centuries earlier had suffered great hardship as they struggled to open up our Piedmont country to the civilized world. I kept thinking about my own ancestors and how they, too, were among the first of the church's many pioneers to make their way into the Carolina wilderness and what a great shame it was that their descendants had strayed off and got themselves lost in a cloud of wild Baptist sermonizing.

So maybe it was then, on that long ago night in the Fatherland, among the descendants of my own German-speaking relatives, that I first decided—maybe without even realizing it yet—that somehow, someday, I must find a way to make wine my life and myself the preeminent wine snob of the Carolina backcountry, a truly imperious pipe-smoking character, soon to be written up in magazines and celebrated at literary soirees.

What a disappointment! For the Moravians behaved shamefully that evening. Although their forebears had been great imbibers of wine and schnapps and brandy and all kinds of whisky, later generations of these pious folk had developed a certain Baptist mentality and, to put it plainly, would not do Herr Erben the courtesy of so much as sampling his exquisite Rieslings. They simply poured it all out, from the two-dollar-and-fifty-cent stuff right on up to the four hundred-dollar *Trockenbeerenauslese*.

Herr Weiser, a sometimes irascible tour guide, had warned that such behavior would be the very worst form of bad taste. Strictly *verboten*. Better that they had stayed at the hotel in Kaiserslautern and watched televised reruns of *Casablanca* or *Gone with the Wind*.

Ah, the great irony of it all! The idea that Moravians had departed so far from the customs of their own people! They were a proud and selective and—some would have said—even a snobbish lot. In the eighteenth century their breweries and wineries and distilleries had been the pride of the Carolina back parts. Wasn't that why the British Redcoats paid us an unwelcome visit during the Revolutionary times—so that they could sample unlimited quantities of good Moravian schnapps?

It was partly to remind the tour group of its forgotten heritage that our bilingual Lutheran guide, known to some of us, not altogether correctly, as *der grosfader*, had scheduled this nocturnal *weinprobe*. Never mind all that. Almost to a man (and woman), they seemed bent on utter sobriety. Herr Erben had thoughtfully provided receptacles into which the excess wine might be poured. There were many bottles to open, and we could not have been expected to drink it all. But neither were we expected to pour it all out.

Maybe Herr Erben didn't notice at first. A small darkish man full of merriment and spirited cries of "Probst!" he had greeted us with each new bottle as though it were a treat specially distilled for our edification and enjoyment. "Alvays schmell!" he would cry, as his assistants filled our glasses. "You must alvays schmell!" Next would come the formality of the "schmell," another cheery cry of "Probst!" and then the good taste of the wine itself.

For everyone except the Moravians. Despite their scandalous behavior, Herr Erben was unperturbed. Out of the darkest recesses of his wine cellar came his four hundred-dollar bottle of *Trockenbeerenauslese* as though he had either failed to notice the insult or made up his mind to treat it as an idiotic American idiosyncrasy. He wiped off the dust and cobwebs and shouted "Probst!"

"Alvays schmell!"

"This is rare," said *der grosfader*. "It means that he likes us very much. Indeed, this is a moment we will all want to remember. In all my visits here I have never known this to happen. Not this. Not with his best thousand-mark vintage."

Maybe our host only meant it as a compliment to Herr Weiser and the other Lutheran minister traveling with him. Because even as the *trockenbeerenauslese* made the rounds, our Protestants were busily emptying this most hallowed of wines into their already-brimming receptacles. *Der grosfader* quivered with unbelief and then with the beginnings of rage. After all, it was only his long and friendly acquaintance with Herr Erben that had prompted so unusual a show of hospitality. Up and down the room he waddled, his Rabelaisian frame palpitant with barely suppressed emotion.

"Don't you people understand? Haven't you even been listening? How dare you embarrass me this way! Don't you realize what this wine costs?—that it was only because of his special liking for us that . . ."

Herr Erben was still smiling imperturbably as we rose to take leave of his wine cellar. It had not always been a wine cellar, just as Herr Erben had not always been a vintner. It had once been a cattle stall, and on the white plastered walls, above the half-timbering, hung many a trophied *auerhaun*, a type of tiny European woodcock. We flung ourselves back out into the night after the wonderful, if shameful, evening in Deidesheim, across the dark unsteady courtyard toward the moving gates and onto the not-yet-moving tour bus.

"Absolutely inconceivable!" said *der grosfader* as he slumped heavily into his seat. "I could have killed them all!" He shook his head wearily. "Without doubt I could have wrung their necks right off their shoulders . . . every last one of them and left them buried on the spot!"

A sudden lurch as we started off, making our way rapidly across the dark night of the German Rhineland and through many small unlit Palatinate towns—and then once more into Kaiserslautern, a city more American than otherwise, with an American-style hotel full of Coke machines, wall-to-wall carpeting, softly lit bars, and desk clerks who spoke English without an accent. A place, it seemed, where one might again feel at home even if some of the magic of the evening had been lost.

Well, I thought about all that during those last days before my "coming out." The good days in the Rhineland, the shame of the Moravians. Then came the afternoon that everything was to be put to proof.

Had I learned enough?

As it turned out, I found that when I most needed the benefits of my Rhineland experience, I could remember very little of what I thought I had absorbed—with help, of course, from my wine-tasting manuals. It had all been very romantic and very wonderful that night in Deidesheim. Yet I now realized I had brought away no deep or lasting impressions of the proprieties of wine-tasting itself—only that single admonition, "Alvays schmell!"

No one had seemed impressed on those occasions when I talked of my vast experience on the *Weinstrasse*. Everything would now depend on what the instruction manual had described as my "gustatory receptors." And, of course, on my delicate and sophisticated sense of "schmell." I only wished that I had learned more. "Schmelling" wasn't everything. There were too many other ceremonies, other proprieties. As I joined my fellow vintners and wine connoisseurs at our Yadkin retreat, I imagined again a thousand perils lying in wait for the unwary. A hesitation at the wrong moment, a gesture insufficiently mastered, even an expression that wasn't just so—and there goes your reputation as the backcountry's most famous wine snob.

The bottles had been arranged on a large table at the front of the lodge. I circled the table with a certain flair, schmelling this and schmelling that. As I completed my circuit, I decided to try a certain "audacious Cabernet" that had been recommended by a tall, silvery-haired gent whose name I failed to catch. He nodded deferentially, pouring a glass for me and another for himself.

"A most excellent nose," he said.

"A very fine nose indeed," I said, somberly matching my expression to his.

"And yet withal"—he paused and stared with momentary suspicion at the glass—"a certain—ah, shall we say, vegetal quality?"

Vegetal quality? As I said, I was not prepared for everything. But maybe I could bluff my way through. My wine-tasting manual had been quite specific: "Everything depends on the receptivity and sensitivity of one's olfactory and gustatory equipment." And there was always the lurking threat of fatigue—the possibility, in other words, that your taste buds or "gustatory equipment" would become worn out with tasting so many different kinds of wine. The whole aim was "to exhaust the possibility of bringing out unwanted odors without exhausting one's olfactory and gustatory receptors."

The gent looked at me questioningly—and I at my glass with an air at least as suspicious as his own. Were my receptors exhausted? Was there still time to cleanse my palate with a sliver of brie and get back in the game? Lucky for me I had memorized something else from the manual: "Swirl the glass violently without spattering your neighbor or yourself. If anything is there that shouldn't be, violent swirling will bring it out."

A certain vegetal quality, eh? Well, we would see about that! I gave my glass a violent slosh, as directed, and thrust my nose boldly over the rim.

Alas—too late. I found that I had indeed spattered my neighbor as well as myself. An imposing drop of the audacious Cabernet hung from my nose, another from my neighbor's seersucker, darkening slowly, like a fresh and possibly mortal wound. The fellow looked at me—with an air overly reproachful, I thought—and swiftly turned away, holding his hand over the wound in a manner stiffly reminiscent of all the old pictures of Napoleon at the height of his glory.

It was suddenly quite cold and lonely in the crowded room. Before making for the door, I paused just long enough to look back once more at the man in the seersucker. He did not meet my gaze. He stood a little off from the others, his brow wrinkled in an ecstasy of concentration and his hand still lifted—in that same accusing Napoleonic gesture— across the front of his jacket.

I realized as I raced for the car that it was all over, finished, the beginning of a distinguished and exotic career gone for naught. No more winter nights sitting around a big fire talking wine with the Albanian and his guests. No more Sunday afternoon wine-tasting binges, at which everyone was allowed to become gloriously and excusably drunk. Because it was wine. No more exquisite Rieslings, crisp Chardonnays, good claret that puts new life in the bone.

Nothing left now but to struggle on alone in my vineyards, fighting off the ravages of downy mildew (not to be confused with its cousin, powdery mildew) and a thousand other infestations that have indefinitely prolonged my "coming out," if, indeed, they have not ended all hope of it forever. The nematode has had its say. Black rot has taken its toll. Anthracnose made a belated appearance. Then came the dreaded Dead Arm, to say nothing of assorted other blights and galls that finished off everything the birds left behind. For all I know, even the boll weevil may have got into it.

I try to hold on to my pride, pretending that my shame is at least not so great as that of the Moravians. And the dream persists. Even now

I cling to the hope that my Grassy Fork Reds and Grassy Fork Whites will one day stand side by side with the great wines of the television commercials. The ghost of Orson Welles will be there. And the inestimable John Gielgud. Or perhaps some young fellow with an elongated countenance that immediately identifies him as one of Europe's "youngest and brightest wine-tasting authorities."

You know the type I mean: a sybaritic young man in silken sleeves and scarves, his shirt open casually at the collar and, around him, other wine authorities of note, all nodding and gesturing just so. The sybarite takes another long slow look at my Grassy Fork Red, tilting it slowly and lovingly toward the light, while, from the middle distance, comes the sedate yet stirring strains of a Baroque concerto. The young man is all one with the music and the wine. Again he lifts his glass with a practiced gesture and knowing nod—and then, as he thrusts his "olfactory receptors" boldly over the rim, he cries, "A most excellent nose!"

And the others all nodding and saying:

"To be sure, a most excellent nose indeed!"

7

Lord of
the Manor

Despite all of my pretensions, I eventually had to acknowledge that my venture into wine making was an inglorious failure. Not only were my vineyards a shambles, so were my ambitions to set myself up as a reputable wine taster. Worse, I knew I could not again step foot inside the Albanian's riverfront retreat, except as a kind of failed court jester whose appearance would only start the real wine tasters to whispering behind their hands. An ignominious and even disastrous end to what had once seemed a noble calling.

Still, after taking over the family farm—what was left of it after the profligate ways of my grandfather and the slovenly ways of my uncle—I never got over a powerful calling to restore our rustic domicile to something like its original glory. I found myself almost alone in believing I would ever be able to finish the job. No encouragement even from the people who had grown up there.

"Why, son, you'll never save that house. Nobody on earth could put that place back into its original shape without spending himself into bankruptcy."

Such was the advice of my rich uncle Frank, the one-time grocer who had made a fortune at bootlegging and on the wartime black market and who had decided—though I did not know it at the time—not to leave me any of the money that would have made the restoration make sense. He had no other heirs—his wife dead, his son killed at sixteen in an auto crash. I did not like to think of myself as counting on all the money I seemed destined to inherit. Neither would I have guessed that he planned to leave it all to charity!

Uncle Frank was not by himself in trying to talk me out of what would certainly would be a man-killing project. Everybody who knew anything (or perhaps nothing) about the restoration of old houses was saying much the same. Somehow, though, I just couldn't let it alone. I kept thinking about all the good times I'd had there as a child—back when I still lived in the city, about all the big Sunday dinners and October corn shuckings and family reunions. I thought about all the historic buildings my grandfather had brought there in 1893 from an early-eighteenth-century Moravian homestead on a hill less than a mile away, most of which had either fallen down or were long past saving. Was I to allow the family homeplace to fall into the same state of decay, its memories lost amid a pathetic stirring of dust and a crumbling foundation?

Uncle Frank just looked at me and shook his head with a certain deprecating air. "I tell you, son, I believe it's time just to let the bulldozers have it." No sentiment in him at all. But he had also had restored a lot of houses and built quite a few as well, or had them built, so naturally everyone thought I should look to him for advice.

Even my father, who had wanted the place for me, said much the same. "Too much expense, son. Too much heavy work. A lot of places out there on that farm to build a place more to your liking. Why—but I guess you must know this already—every time we get a little rain, that basement floods so bad you've got to get down there and bail out all that water before it gets to the furnace. And there's been at least one time when you didn't make it. Nope. Looks to me like you're just asking for more headaches."

The house had burned in 1915, and my grandfather, though wise in his rare moments of sobriety, made the ignominious mistake of building it all back on the original foundation, which dated from long before The War between the States. Nothing but lime and creek clay for mortar back then, which is why we now faced the prospect of replacing the entire underpinning. My father and his brothers had all pitched in to help rebuild the house, and they were mighty proud of their work. "Every piece of lumber came right off the place here," my father kept reminding me. But I guess they were also aware of the mistakes they had made. "Frank's right. Just go on and live in it like it is until you can build your own little place. Too big to maintain anyway. Built for a growing farm family. You don't need anything like that."

There wasn't much chance that I would take my father's good advice. Or anybody else's. After all, at that time, I was still in my glory years as a promising vintner and horse breeder, a monarch of all I surveyed and a rising entrepreneur who one day would take his place in a society dominated by cigarette producers and underwear makers and would go to all the best parties and write best-selling novels and become a kind of dictator of cultural norms—yes, and still young enough to have seen in the once-majestic homestead a potential everybody else had overlooked.

I have even developed a speaking relationship with at least some of its ghosts and remembered things about it I had never been told. How could I have gained such knowledge? A great mystery in the old place, as well as an awful lot of private history. I just didn't see how I could afford to let it go.

"Think about it," I kept telling the naysayers. "All the history there. We don't wanta save that? How you gonna get that back in a new house?"

No need for more talk. Surely a man out to make a name for himself as a preserver of the land, who sneered at the efforts of developers to pollute the Big Grassy and was soon to make his mark as the most astute winemaker (this was all before the failure of my "coming out") and rancher in the county could transform the old house into a manse that would bring in photographers and journalists by the dozens and dominate the pages of the big architectural and restoration magazines for years to come. I had even built a huge stable in between taking assignments for an Atlanta newspaper and had tried my luck with horses for awhile before being flimflammed by a man I had deemed an honest tradesman.

Once I had latched on to the idea I never for a moment strayed from it: my grand design to restore our family homestead into a masterwork of venerable and enduring beauty. Quite a job, to be sure, as we had known from the start. First I would have to rip off all the asbestos siding with which my uncle had covered the house shortly after World War II, in the great days of the asbestos siding fad—and pray that the authorities would not find out I had violated all their new rules for removing the stuff without getting it into the lungs of everybody who ventured within a mile of the place.

The asbestos was only the beginning. Lord, I would have to replace almost all of the old tin roof, all of that old foundation. I hated to see it go, but I don't suppose a foundation in itself, regardless of its age, is worth a whole lot as an artifact.

I would have to get rid of all the tasteless flowery wallpaper Uncle Luther had put up; I would have to rip out all of the worn, dusty carpets, if any of us expected to draw a decent breath again. I would have to rip the tacky bathroom tiles off the fireplaces and restore the brick. And, of course, the chimneys themselves had begun to fall down—one, two, or three bricks at a time, depending on how hard the wind was blowing. We had all of us learned never to walk near any of those unstable parts of the house when it looked as though a storm might be coming up.

One of Uncle Frank's last words to me, just before he died, was that I had undertaken the impossible and that the house would never be worth all the time and money being put into it. But I had convinced myself secretly that where the others had seen themselves as mere tenants of a falling-down farmhouse, I would shortly be perceived as an architectural genius of rare taste, a wine connoisseur comparable to all the best vintners of France, a winner of all the big horse races—in other words a true lord of the manor, something we had never had in our community. My family, although my grandfather had come close before he let liquor get the best of him.

I figured it this way: All the people of my father's generation had no real sentiment in their bones, no deep feeling for the place, even though they had grown up there. Perhaps it was my mission, coming along as I did, to see in it what they could not. As I say, I was still young enough in those days to feel capable of mastering almost any enterprise. Now that I am no longer so young, I bow to the wisdom of the older generation. Even so, it was a mission that, once undertaken, whatever my age, I would have felt absolutely compelled to bring to a successful end.

I realized almost at once that the real function of all my uncle's flowery wallpaper was simply to hold the plaster in place. When the wallpaper came down, most of the plaster came with it. That was when I made another astonishing discovery. All over the house, in all of the outer walls, my grandfather had inserted brick nogging as a kind of primitive insulation—something his Moravian forebears had themselves done when building their congregation town of Salem. So there was a lot of tradition in that old brick nogging, even if nobody could see it and even if it was next to worthless when it came to keeping out the wind and cold. Tear it all out. Was that what was now facing me? Suddenly the job had become a thousand times bigger than I would have guessed even in my most pessimistic moments.

There was still time to get away: to change my identity and to make a name for myself in another country. What comfort in that thought! What a shame I couldn't bring myself to go through with it! It would have been so hard: leaving the kids behind. My wife. But anybody could see that it was the only sensible way out. Still, there *was* a lot of sentiment in the old place. For more than a hundred years my family had lived in the house. And now to throw it all over? No, I just couldn't think about all that right now. I would think instead about all the days and weeks I had spent there as a child. Memories of wheat threshings and bean stringings and even all of those long hot days in the tobacco fields. And the October nights when we all gathered in the upper pasture for the yearly corn husking, coming in later to a massive kitchen table laden with great slabs of ham and fried chicken and all kinds of freshly cooked vegetables and pumpkin pie and big falling-down coconut cakes. All that and much more: the big Sunday dinners and summer fish fries when the men came home drunk from the river, after seining all morning and drinking half the afternoon away, their wives furiously shouting at them while they laughingly dragged the women inside and tried to get their clothes off, and occasionally succeeded, with angry shouts turning into maniacal giggles.

Ah yes, and who could ever erase the memory of one of my girl cousins coming out of her room half naked with a six-shooter in her hand—and right there in front of the Baptist preacher, himself a bit of a lecher—after her husband had torn off her best summer dress in a frantic effort to get himself "a little piece."

"I wish that young'un could learn to be a little more circumspect," Aunt Grace had said.

"Can't believe she would actually have shot him," someone else said. "But, after all, it was her best dress."

"Well, who knows what she might have done if there hadn't been so many of us around. She's always had an awful lot of Papa in her."

Long before I got very far into the restoration, I had learned—with what humiliation I even now find it hard to describe—that I was not destined to make a fortune in grapes and wine after all. It seemed to me, as the preacher said, that the days when "thou shalt have no pleasure in them" were already fast upon me. Maybe I would never write a best seller *or* win the Kentucky Derby. Was then my whole purpose in life to save the family homestead? If not I, who? Nobody else even *knew* about the ghosts, much less had found it possible to communicate with them.

By that time my reputation had begun to suffer. People slowed as they passed the house and then gave a big laugh as they sped off again. A lot of talk at church and around the community.

"Yup. Just like his grandfather. Drinks too much, wastes too much money. And when's the last time he ever gave a dime to the church? It's that sorry Jacobus blood. Yessir. Those old Germans, all of them a cut from the same old cloth."

Well, damn them all. At least I still had the house and the land. I knew that the city was creeping perceptibly closer almost by the hour: a clangor by midnight and noonday as the shopping centers moved closer, as new roads took shape, loud sirens wakening you from sleep, drunken shouts from a taproom that had set up shop almost directly across from the Baptist church. The city had indeed surrounded us on every side and had thrown out its grappling hooks, just waiting for the right moment to seize the whole farm.

For years, even before the warehouses and fast food joints appeared, the tax people had been looking over our place with an evil eye. I thought again about what Uncle Frank had said before cutting me out of his will (if indeed I was ever in it at all): "Maybe it just isn't worth it, son. Any improvements you make are only gonna raise your taxes. Maybe the best thing would be just to let it alone or hire a bulldozer to come and push it over." He shook his head grimly as he spoke. "Just can't imagine you wanting to spend so many years of your life trying to the old place back into shape."

I just flat out wouldn't listen. It was one big mess, no matter how you looked at it, and, maybe as Uncle Frank had said, I was about to embark on an undertaking much too ambitious and grandiose for a man of my limited resources. Call in the bulldozers? Wife Mary Ellen would never agree to it. She had developed a strange sort of fondness for the place, as though it had come down in her family instead of mine. Maybe it really would be best just to go on and get out of the country. Mexico. The Caribbean. The Côte d'Azur.

Just as I was ready to pack my bags, along came a fellow promising to make me a million dollars as a horse breeder. He almost took me for everything I had, which fortunately did not make him a whole lot richer or me a great deal poorer. Like a thousand other clucks, I fell completely for his line. And now that it appeared we would soon have a bundle of cash rolling in I went to work with new resolve and before long I had begun to make modest improvements to our "manse," converting a shabby back porch into a rustic den, rebuilding the fireplaces, and restoring an old kitchen that had looked beyond redemption. We added overhead joists from a stack of ancient chestnut beams we had found stacked neatly in the tobacco packhouse. Upstairs, I restored bedrooms for my daughter and two sons. Not bad for a start, even with my uncle sitting at the kitchen table sneering quietly at the great waste of expense and time I was investing in the restoration project.

Well, sure enough, it began to show promise. Not a whit too soon at that. By the time I got rid of all the asbestos siding (hiding from the anti-asbestos police all the while), I was so far in "that," like Macbeth, "should I wade no more, returning were as tedious as (to) go o'er."

One day, not long after my uncle's death, I again set to work with mad abandon, tearing out doors, window frames, wainscoting, mantles, chair rails, shelves, strips of crown molding, thresholds, window casings, porch balusters—you name it—after deciding that all the old paint had to come off of everything. As the pile grew and began to fill half the yard, the laughter from drivers slowing their cars for a better look grew louder and more mocking.

"Old Jacobus, he's sho' gone and got hisself in one more big mess, ain't he?"

I got in touch with a bearded paint stripper from up in the country and described the problem. "Bring your biggest truck!"

Even it wouldn't hold a fraction of what I had torn out. It took a couple of months to get the whole job done. Sure was glad we finished before I learned that my stripper was in fact a notorious thief and cattle rustler. Thief or not, he made me a fair price, and I called on him many a time before our project was complete.

Complete? Truth is, the word is inapplicable when it comes to a house that has lost its will to survive. Such houses remain forever in a state of restoration, impervious to any man's attempt to get the job done in a single lifetime.

Meantime, after our bearded cattle rustler had hauled away the last of the great piles of materials I had stacked in the yard, I went after the rest of the house, wildly, insanely: walls, ceilings, floors, stairs, all the old electrical wiring, until the whole place was little more than a pile of dust and crumbling plaster and falling timber, mostly rotten. That was when I again bumped smack up against my grandfather's internal wall of brick nogging.

I also began to find out something else about the house, about all old houses. Maybe it hadn't had much of a foundation—no concrete footing, nothing but homemade bricks to hold it up and not nearly enough of those, with creek mud and lime to hold them together. But never mind that. In every other way my grandfather and his sons had built for real permanence, inserting between all the studs crosspieces known as "purlins" for extra strength. Damnable purlins! All they did was make it impossible for me to shoot the walls full of insulation, even if all that brick nogging hadn't been in the way. I went to work with mattocks and axes, shaking the whole place like a bag of old bones. Shards of cracked brick everywhere. Creek clay that had deteriorated over the years into thick red dust.

By that time the house was little more than a shell. And it was still summer. Soon now we would be up all night fighting the bats and swamp owls and gnats and maybe even the wolves and cougars that the builders of the warehouses on yonder hill had driven out of their natural habitat. No time even to think about that. First there was the question of all that brick in the walls. Mary Ellen, who escaped to her office each day while I was pounding and battering the house, came in from work one afternoon just as I had about decided the whole place was getting ready to fall on my head. Well, let it fall. Plenty of people had gone through life without seeing Vienna or the Côte d'Azur.

I dragged out a fresh bottle of bourbon and sat down in a heavy sulk, angry at her for spending a long day in an air-conditioned office, while I was busy getting my lungs choked up with asbestos and plaster dust. Might I after all this time expect a little help, or at least a bit of sympathy? Hah! All I got was the sound of her calm and reassuring voice:

"You know, I think we really need professional advice—someone who has been through all of this before, who could tell us how best to proceed."

"Yes. Somebody with a whole helluva lot of money. Isn't that what dear old Uncle Frank kept telling us all the time he was planning to leave his big bankroll to charity? Anyway, where're we gonna find anybody who would touch this job now. Certainly no professional, not for what we could afford to pay him."

"Maybe if we could pay somebody with the new money that's supposed to be coming in from the barn . . ."

"Which reminds me, sweetheart. I haven't seen a dime of that money yet. Besides, it wouldn't make a dent. There's not enough money in the whole Wachovia banking system to induce anybody but a lunatic to come in here and take over this job."

"What do you suggest? We certainly can't go on like this."

"All those goddamn bricks still gotta come out."

So down they came, a great thunder of them hitting the floor day and night and raising a dust storm the likes of which had not been seen since Depression-era droughts in the Midwest. The great whirling red clouds came rolling in over us like those old dust storms Woodie Guthrie had sung about during the thirties. I worked for days, even weeks, the whole summer long—and the days grow short when you reach September—trying to get the brick out of the wall and hauled away by the wheelbarrow load. A tedious and very nearly fruitless task. But one day it was finished—sort of.

Except that now the whole house lay knee deep in thick red dust. Bedrooms. Dining room. Back porch. Every alcove and pantry. It was in your nostrils and your lungs and your veins and your whole being and maybe you would even die from it before you ever had a chance to draw a clean breath again. It lay on the floor and on scraps of old carpet. It lay on the kitchen shelves, on dishes and silverware and punch bowls. It lay on all the furniture that my wife hadn't had time to cover with sheets. Too busy sipping tea in that fancy, air-conditioned office of hers. It lay in the halls and bedrooms, on beds, chairs, and tables. It lay on all my books, including those first editions of *Tobacco Road* and *Gone with the Wind* and *The Rise of Silas Lapham*. The heavy, dry dust of a dying land, and it was all in our house.

Well, not all. Great swirling clouds of it billowed out of the windows and raised a pall of dust over the entire community of Bethania Station. Howls of loud, sneering laughter from the road, where people had stopped for a quick look at my doomed restoration project. For the first time I realized deep in my bones what it must have been like for those people out in Oklahoma trying to get through the Depression— no place to walk, no place to eat, no place to sleep.

We were like pioneers now. Only my daughter's room, which I had redone during a previous "restoration," had escaped the worst of the devastation, and that only because Mary Ellen had remembered to shut it off before leaving for another day of relaxation in her padded swivel chair, amid her glass walls and sales charts and newly purchased pieces of office furniture, blasts of cool air blowing down on her and, in her head, wondrous visions of springtime in the Rockies: "Oh yes, ma'am, a three-bedroom brick rancher—no vinyl, yes, I understand—two baths, a deck and fireplace, with plenty of room for the children to play. I'm sure I have just the thing for you. Worried about your down payment? Oh, my goodness! Let me assure you that we have a uniquely creative financial program, marvelously structured by some of the biggest names in the business and designed to fit almost any budget."

I sat looking as the piles of red dust, emptying another bottle of bourbon.

"How in God's name are we ever gonna get rid of it?" I asked my wife when she came sashaying in that evening, looking all clean and refreshed from her relaxing day in the city. "Can't possibly shovel it all out."

"Never did think we oughta tear out all those walls."

"Well, let me ask you, as a housing expert, how we could ever have insulated properly if I hadn't torn them out."

"How should I know? All I know is that I certainly didn't expect anything like this."

"Gotta have a more powerful vacuum. This piece of junk just won't do the job."

"I'll see if I can pick up something on my way home tomorrow."

Next day she came home with a power vacuum that the man at the rental outlet assured her would suck up all that dust and the whole damn house with it if we weren't careful. I set to work at once. For a long time I didn't know what was happening. I only knew that I was choking on the dust again—nothing like it in all the time I had been working at this hot, nasty business. The rooms still full of it. Shelves, tables, bookcases, chests of drawers, highboys, corner cupboards, first editions—everything still covered with it. A brand new dust storm coming in off the prairie; the sky turned black with it, and there was no more sun.

Mary Ellen had gone out to the vegetable garden, not seeing as how she could do anything to relieve my distress. A moment later, after it had grown too dark to see, I heard her yelling at me from among the cabbages or cauliflower.

"It's coming out the windows! It's coming right out though the cracks in the walls! It's coming out everywhere! Do something!"

Great billows of red dust blowing out the windows, covering the maples and pecan trees, the grass, the flowers, the garden itself piled high with it. A regular carpet in which you could leave footprints an inch thick.

Only then did I finally catch on: the marvelous power vac that was supposed to suck up the whole house wasn't even sucking up the dust. Just the opposite—blowing it all out in powerful swirls and forcing it into places it had never been. We probably would have to throw away all the furniture. Where would we find clean towels, washrags, sheets? Where would I find the horse's ass who had rented this thing to us in the first place? Where would we find anything we needed to survive the catastrophe of the most famous restoration in the history of Bethania Station?

I don't know why, but on this day I had remembered to close off two of the upstairs bedrooms. My wife and little Ellen could take one, the two boys the other. I would make out as best I could in the den that had once been only a back porch. But I'd had enough now.

"No more!" I shouted up the stairs. "Do you hear me? No more!"

After getting no response I went upstairs to explain my plan in more detail. Mary Ellen was already asleep after her hard day at the office, in one of the two bedrooms that weren't a complete shambles. Dances of sugarplum fairies in her head.

Yes, ma'am, we have exactly the house for you, and no more worries about that escrow account!

I shook her awake. "I'll load up the pickup tomorrow, and we'll take what we can and just get on out. California! That's the place for us now. Let them call us Okies if they like. Goddamn them! But at least we can make a fresh start there and put these dust storms behind us forever!"

She turned her back to me without answering, pretending to sleep. I looked around at the house again. Nothing recognizable about it at all. Every piece of furniture, every vase, every trinket, every book and doodad hidden now behind a heavy shroud of dust.

"Maybe I'll just go on out and check the oil now. We can get loaded and start first thing in the morning." The pickup was in good shape. We could make the three thousand miles easy.

"Are you drunk?" she said, without looking around.

"Drunk? Is that all you have to say? You saw what all those poor bastards in Oklahoma went through during the thirties. Now it's happening to us. We couldn't make it with grapes or cantaloupe or peaches, and it's beginning to look mighty like we can't make it with horses, and now this goddamn house has us by the short hairs."

I wondered if any of those "haints" in the attic, or wherever they had fled to, had got choked up on the dust.

"Let me sleep. Tell Ellen to come on to bed."

She got up and slammed the door and left me standing in the hall, ankle deep in red dust. I felt my way downstairs, making a path that blew over behind me like a wind-driven snowdrift, and finally got back to the den where I was finally hoping to get some sleep. Plenty of dust out there as well even though it had escaped the worst of the great storm. I didn't care about that now. I had gone one whole night without sleep. Whatever had to be done would simply have to wait till tomorrow because it sure looked now like I would be making the trip to California alone, if I made it at all.

I cleaned the sofa as best I could, swallowed three of the last five pills left in my bottle of tranquilizers, drank two cans of beer—the large economy size—and lay down. We had worked furiously until two in the morning. I lay there in a half sleep. Nothing else to be done here. Nothing left now but to pack up what we had left, what little was worth saving, and strike out for California. I guess you just couldn't imagine what the fury of a dust storm was like until you had actually experienced one.

Just get everything packed up and hit the long road west and just try not to think about it anymore

I lay there in my house of dust, thinking about the ways I could disentangle myself from the horrors I had brought on myself and my family. Maybe there was an easier way than starting all over again in the West. Or maybe not. My maternal grandfather had tried it as a young man before coming back east and spending his last days trying to support his family out of the sparse earnings of a waterside barbershop.

"Papa always thought he made a mistake coming back," Mother

had often told me. "We should have stayed in Los Angeles. It was such a lovely town in those days."

That was it then. Let everybody sleep for an hour or two and then maybe good old Mary Ellen would see things more clearly. How to get her out of that real estate office? That would be the hard part. We could load up a few pieces of silverware, some coffee, the framed prints—if any had been left unscathed by the dust storm—and what little food was left in the icebox. Enough clothing to get by until I could acquire my own citrus orchard and Mary Ellen her own real estate agency, way out there at the end of the West.

Just as I was about to drift off, with my head full of orange blossoms, I heard a patter of quick, soft, furtive footsteps on the tin roof directly above me. The unmistakable footsteps of our nasty tempered Siamese cat. She had got herself trapped up there somehow, maybe choked with dust, although unlike the rest of us, she was probably shrewd enough to have escaped all that.

You nasty little bastard, go ahead and jump off the roof, goddamn you. Where the hell do you think you are anyway, on the edge of the Grand Canyon? Just go on and get the hell off a there, and go off someplace and die, you miserable little asshole, and let me sleep. Off the roof, goddammit! Off the roof, and be damn quick about it!

The moments dragged on into a heavy silence. I felt myself drifting off again, feeling very comfortable now after slugging down all the booze and tranquilizers. Then it happened: the footsteps again. How did the cat get there anyway? Why didn't it just go ahead and jump off and go on off to the creek bottom and pick a fight with a wild boar or a catamount or something? She had tangled with a raccoon not long before and had come back to lie around groaning with a broken shoulder and a torn eyelid, expecting to be treated like *The Man Who Came to Dinner*. A diet of bread and water is what she got, plus all the medications the vet had sent over. After all that, I knew I'd never find a way to get plumb rid of her. She was in real bad shape, all right. Of course, I never did get a chance to see the raccoon.

I lay there listening to the footsteps. I couldn't remember where I had placed my grandfather's shotgun after I finished firing off a round of buckshot at my last horse thief, but I could see clearly now that I needed to get rid of that cat before morning. Otherwise, there would be one more row if we didn't somehow make room for her on our trip to California.

Shoot her between the eyes, or somehow mount a rescue operation? Not much of either I could do at that time of night. If she could just somehow choke to death on all that dust! Only one room gave onto the porch roof, my office, and that was where we had stacked great bundles of building materials. No way to get through all that junk tonight. Besides, the cat hated my guts. I lay there listening to the footsteps. Nothing. Gone at last. Maybe even to pick another fight with one of the wild animals that had begun to roam our bottom now that the developers had driven them out of their last refuge.

"Please Lord if the cat must die let it be a gentle death." I did not like to think of myself as cruel beyond reason, which is why I lifted up a little prayer in behalf of the cat while trying to remember where I had laid that shotgun. Probably wouldn't fire anyway, not with all that dust in it.

I had just begun to drift off again, scenting the sweet smell of orange blossoms, when I heard the sound again.

The cat had come back.

Well, there was just no help for it.

I went out and shouted a string of wild, unearthly curses that should have thrown the cat into a state of nervous prostration even if it did not drive her off the roof.

A window flew open upstairs. My wife stared down at me with a killing look. Why couldn't she have at least turned it on the cat?

"What in heaven's name are you yelling at? Somebody would take you for a madman. Are you trying to get yourself arrested? Can't you at least try to get some sleep?"

"How can anybody sleep with a goddamn cat walking around on the roof all night?"

"Are you sure you aren't imagining things? I told you not to take too many of those pills. Anyway, I hope you haven't forgotten that it was you who first brought that cat into our lives. And now the children are crazy about it."

"Ellen hates the cat. Blame me for it, if you like, but how in hell was I supposed to know the crazy goddamn beast was possessed by demons?"

"Have it your way, but, please, just try to get some sleep—or at least let the rest of us try."

"Yeah. We gotta long way to go come morning."

I stood outside for maybe another five minutes. No footsteps. Maybe it had finally left forever. As much as I hated the cat, I was not anxious to have it die a painful death. Our old uncle had been fond of bundling unwanted cats into tow sacks and dumping them in the Grassy Fork. I despised him for that. Although "Bama" was a pest with nothing but mayhem in her heart, I just couldn't bring myself to tie her up and throw her in the creek. Not that anyone would have known. The two boys—though not Ellen—would have cried for awhile and then forgot all about it. But I don't know. It just didn't seem right somehow.

I took my last two tranquilizers and lay down again and began to smell the orange blossoms more powerfully now. California would really be nice this time of year. All of the orchards and vineyards would be ready for the harvest. Though my Spanish was poor, if not non-existent, I could always get on as a migrant laborer till something more substantial turned up. Maybe my wife would behave more sensibly come dawn. Anyway, to sleep at last.

Or maybe not. I had just drifted off when I heard it again: the unmistakable sound of those quick, furtive footsteps, resounding through the house like the last sinister gongs of my damnation.

The cat had come back.

I knew it was purely for spite. The cat was not exactly human, but I was sure she had not always been a cat—that she had doubtless had another life as a sorceress or practitioner of witchcraft. Many had noticed her perceptive ways. No way for me to hide my hatred for her—maybe from others, but not from the cat.

I went out and searched around in the dark. No flashlight or lantern, but I found the ladder anyway and set it against the side of the house. I climbed to the edge of the roof, lit a match, and instantly saw the vile creature, staring at me viciously out of the dark. I already had a sawed-off two-by-four in my hand—and a good aim. Two one-hitters during my last high school baseball season. I dropped down a couple of steps and let fly with the two-by-four straight at the cat. I heard a shattering of glass and a great caterwauling, as the beastly animal at last leapt from the roof into some bushes just outside the den.

Upstairs, the window flew open again. "Now what?" Mary Ellen groused. "What have you broken this time?"

"Maybe a window to my office. What difference does it make? The dust storm has wiped us out. We aren't going to be around here long enough for it to make any difference."

"Go back to sleep."

Almost four by now. Little time left for sleeping, what with my need to get out and start packing the truck. I went in and lay down, and then I felt it: glass, great shards of it covering the couch where I had been trying to get to sleep, covering the floor, windowsills, book shelves, cabinets.

No. I had not hit the cat or the window to my office—only the window above my improvised bed. Now what? No more cat, but what about the hoot owls and snakes and foxes and lynxes and bobcats and all the other night creatures that would fly or climb in the broken window and peck at my liver till dawn? What of the cat itself? She could sneak in and strike a certain deathblow at my jugular, which right from the beginning had been her whole aim in life. I thought again about all the chances I'd had to drown her in the Grassy Fork. Entice her with catnip and then toss her into the sack and the sack into the creek . . . let her float gently down to Myrtle Beach. Was it only my conscience that held me back, or was I secretly afraid the cat was much too cunning ever to fall for my subterfuge?

I swept up the fragments of glass, flung them in a box, and tacked pasteboard over the window opening. Still time for maybe an hour or so of sleep before daylight. Or was it even later than I thought? By the time I lay back down, I could sense the first light coming in from the east, over beyond the creek bottom. I found a last good shot of Old Glenmore in the kitchen cabinet, wiped the dust off the top, and drank it down in a single gulp. I shut out the light of the dawn as best I could and was beginning to feel just a little drowsy when I heard it again, the same horrifying sound as before: soft, quick, resounding footsteps above me on the tin roof. I lay quietly on my back listening to the devilish sound, not even caring about it now, knowing it was too late to get off to sleep that night. Why did my wife persist in taking sides with that vicious animal? And how many times had she done so, in how many a fierce engagement? With the dawn now heavily upon me, I got up and went outside and saw the cat comfortably seated on the roof, looking at me, waiting for me to bring the ladder around to accept my offer of a sensible way down or to gather itself for the attack, I was not sure.

Ah, but then I remembered something: the whereabouts of that old 12-gauge shotgun. Right there by the fireplace in the kitchen. If only it wasn't clogged beyond repair. If only I could find some shells! I made my way through the dust and clutter and found it already loaded.

I was no longer worried about what Mary Ellen might say. I had come to believe she might not be sound of mind anyway. Why, for example, had she failed to see any sense at all in my plan to pack up and start out for a new life in California? I got the gun and went back out. The cat was waiting. The roof was quiet, but lights began coming on all over the neighborhood.

Bam!

I knew very well that all my neighbors would be wondering if old Jacobus had come back to plague the community of Bethania Station in death as he had so often in life. *Yeah they're all alike those goddamn drunken krauts.*

A good bunch to talk, those assholes, most of whom had once been Krauts themselves.

Bam!

Now my wife was back at the window. And this time so was Ellen, shouting and hooraying and wanting to know if I had finally shot "that awful cat." I blew imaginary smoke off the end of each barrel. She was gone all right, and maybe this time for good. My wife kept trying to out-shout her, explaining that there was an ordinance against the shooting of firearms in the city and that I would have the law and the neighbors and the church and everybody else on me and that she certainly hoped I'd had sense enough not to shoot the kitty.

"Leave Dad alone," Ellen told her. "I *hate* that awful cat."

"Couldn't have taken that monster with us to California anyway."

"He's right, Mama. I think Daddy has behaved very intelligently about the cat."

Ellen was the only one who had ever understood me. Or the cat.

I began poking about in the bushes and in all the great piles of construction rubbish looking for the carcass. I didn't mind taking the blame. Didn't even mind all the crying. At least now the cat was out of our lives forever.

"Did you really shoot that cat? You know what Bama means to the boys. I really think you need help. I think we should call somebody. This has gone entirely too far."

"Ellen has always hated the cat."

"Just because of a couple of unfortunate experiences."

"Yeah. Like being mistaken for a raccoon that time. Almost got her eyes scratched out."

Now there was another voice at the window: "Has Daddy killed the cat? What's happened to the cat, Mama?" It was the younger of my two sons. For some reason the cat had warmed to him as it had never warmed to anyone else. My older was there as well, not caring a whole lot one way or the other, though perhaps inclined to take the part of the cat, if for no other reason than to aggravate his sister.

"Go on back to bed," Mary Ellen told them. "Everything's all right now. Both of you. Run on now. It's not time to get up yet."

She got them back into the hall. I could still hear them talking out there, mostly in stage whispers, probably trying to decide whether to phone the police or the psychiatric ward at Forsyth Memorial Hospital. Why was Ellen the only one in the whole crowd who understood the logic of my position? Her mother came back to the window.

"You know, I really think you have been working much too hard. Maybe you should just take the day off and get away from all this for awhile."

"Gotta spend the whole day packing the truck. And not a solitary soul here to help."

It would all turn out well enough. I could simply explain to the boys that the cat had disappeared in the night. Possibly had been run over. Or finally bested by one of those wild beasts that had been roaming our bottom. A real shame. A tragedy even. But what the hell: I had often warned them that something was sure to happen to that blasted animal if they did not make sure it was locked up every night. Put the blame all on them. That oughta take care of all the protests.

I sure needed to find that carcass, though, and bury it somewhere or maybe just go on and throw it in the creek. If the boys found it lying crumpled up on the ground all bloody from where I shot it off the roof, I would sure have a lot more explaining to do. I again stirred around in the rubbish. No carcass. I worked my way toward the front, thinking maybe I had only wounded it. By the time I got back to where I started, I knew the terrible truth: my aim had been poor. Without even looking down, I realized the cat was there, meowing softly as it rubbed against my leg.

Damn you, cat! *Damn you!*

Unable to sleep, my wife came on downstairs, worked her way through the piles of dust, and began to make coffee.

"Well, there's Bama after all," Mary Ellen said, bringing me a cup of coffee. She had dressed, although where she found any clean clothes, I don't know, and was preparing to leave for another day of cozy relaxation. She stooped down to pet the monster. "Good old Bama. Couldn't believe you would really shoot the cat when you know how much she means to the boys."

I had just remembered something else: the day a man had come and made a good offer on the pickup and I had turned him down. In that, at least, I'd had a bit of good fortune. Not long since I had changed the oil. Fill 'er up with gas, and I'd be ready for the long trip west.

"So you're leaving now, are you?" I said as Mary Ellen started for the door. "Leaving me to contend with all this damnable mess? Well, you might have a little surprise when you get back. A good thing I kept that truck. I'll be outa here before dark. You think we've even got a chance against these dust storms. Look what happened to all those people out in Oklahoma. These damn things take on a life of their own, you know! Always striking when you're least prepared. If you wanta get away, you'd better just tell your clients to go to hell and get busy helping me pack."

"Where you going?"

"I told you. California. If you don't wanta to join me later, you'll just have to take whatever steps you think necessary."

"Good. I think you need to get away for awhile. I think you could use a nice long rest."

I watched as she eased down the drive and turned onto the main road into town.

Yeah, goddammit, go ahead and make a joke about it and run away while you can, but, by God, you can count on it: I'll be in Memphis by nightfall. Maybe even across the Mississippi.

The Siamese kept a close eye on me as I got the big shovel out of the garage and went inside, and began scooping into five-gallon containers the heavy layers of red dust that no power vac on earth was strong enough to remove. I prayed for a tornado, but it was the wrong time of year, and we were too far inland to hope for much damage from a hurricane.

Just go on, and get out. Maybe I could drive all the way to St. Louis or Omaha or Dodge City or somewhere. Halfway across the continent. Couldn't afford to forget the shotgun. A lot of rough customers out that way. Maybe I could make a name for myself. At least if my aim was a little better. A shootout in the hot sun at high noon. Blow my victim away with a good dose of buckshot, then put my foot on his stomach and look around at the others like Matt Dillon and say, "Some of you men get him outa here."

I looked at the cat. No need to kill it now and distress the boys unnecessarily. Hell, by morning I could be halfway to Denver.

Free at last! Free at last! O godalmighty I'm free at last!

The cat looked at me. I had begun to feel almost kindly toward the critter. Only a matter now of wading one more time through the dust, throwing a shirt and some underwear and an extra pair of slacks in a traveling case, and then I would be gone. I had enough money in the bank to get by until I found work in California and still leave enough for my wife until she sold her next house. She would almost certainly feel obliged to join me when she saw that I meant business. It was a powerful good feeling to look at the cat and the house and the pastures overgrown with weeds and know that soon now I'd never have to think about any of it again.

I scooped out another shovel of dirt and then sat for awhile and smoked a cigarette, breaking a habit of forty years of abstinence, and working out the escape route in my mind. Memphis. Kansas City. Santa Fe. Dry skulls grinning at you from the desert sand. The long road stretching away into nothingness and more nothingness and still more nothingness. A crummy roadhouse that looked like something out of an early Ava Gardner movie.

"Yeah, sure, I'd like to get out," she tells Bogart, while wiping the counter with a damp cloth. "Sure ain't nothin' 'round here for a girl that wants to make somethin' of herself."

More dusty towns, more wayside filling stations, more pastureland withering in the long drought. Albuquerque. Tombstone. Tucson. A saloon like something from an early episode of *Bonanza*. Two drunken malingerers sitting out front, wiping beer suds out of their chin whiskers.

"Nope," says one. "Sho' don't look like no rain today."

"Folks a-gittin' mighty mean with all this here drought. A lot of real thirsty boys gonna be hittin' town after the roundup. 'Spect things could git mighty nasty round here by nightfall."

I picked up the shovel and went back to work. I began hauling bricks to a low spot near the creek. Day was fast going when I realized the house had again begun to look halfway respectable. A few more brick, a few hundred or maybe a few thousand more shovelfuls of dirt, and we could start cleaning out the residue from the walls and packing in the real insulation. Maybe it wouldn't be so bad. After all, my maternal grandfather had lost a small fortune in California. Everything he had saved from a sizable inheritance, he had wasted in foolish investments. For all his good sense he finally had to give it up. He had come back to Carolina broke, disillusioned, angry, forced to live out his life in something almost like ignominy. Maybe it would be the same with me. Plenty of places to lose yourself in this old world without taking the long road to California. The late great state probably would be no more by the time I got there anyway. The big quake was way overdue. Maybe I could make a good life for myself in the Caribbean. Australia. Haiti. I could become a practitioner of voodoo and throw one hellacious big scare into all of these ravenous developers who had taken over my life.

Maybe I would even find inspiration for all those books I had never had time to write.

I shoveled another wheelbarrow full of dust and then another. The place began to look almost clean. But how would we ever get rid of that smell of dust? I looked up at the sky. And the great mounds of red dirt I had hauled away. Dust in your nostrils. Dust in your hair, in your lungs, in your privates. Would we ever be able to get it out of our systems?

"Nope. Sho' don't look like no rain today. Gonna be a lot of mean, crazy folks in here tonight wantin' their whisky, lookin' fer trouble."

I guess I had actually gone a little crazy. No sleep. All those tranquilizers and liquor. A goddamn sulky cat just sitting around waiting for a chance to strike. I sat on the back steps and scanned the west for a sign of rolling dust clouds coming over the land. I guess it was just plain impossible to think about all that dust coming right out of your own walls.

Yup, sho' gonna be a heap of trouble round these hyar parts if'n we don't git some rain mighty soon. Yessir. That's what I say. Mighty soon.

8

My Introduction
to the Sport of Kings

I knew by now I would never truly be able to throw everything over and put all this life behind me. I had also begun to agree with my wife that we would need real first-class professional help if we were ever to get anywhere with restoring the house. I would probably even be obliged to let the cat die a natural death. The question, as always, was money. Where was it coming from? The question Uncle Frank always put to me before deciding not to leave me any.

I had long known I would never make a fortune in grapes or wine. I kept looking at my vineyards, thinking about the great hope I had once had for them only to realize that they were all dying of homesickness. I had warded off every new species of blight or mildew or insect—there seemed to be a new one every year—only to have all my work come to nothing.

As many a vintner wiser than I had now learned, the *vitis vinifere* simply would not thrive on our Piedmont soil. Growers serious about grape culture had been forced to invest in disease-resistant hybrids. The same with me, though with a lot less luck than the others.

Worse, I had about given up on the horse trade. I had gone into the business as one more sure way of saving the farm and getting the money to fix up the family homestead. So far it was just an experiment. A bad experiment. Maybe even as bad as my experiment with grapes, although the whole truth of that was not yet clear.

I would look down at the big barn and think of the hours I had stolen from my work as a roving correspondent for the Atlanta newspapers to get it built. An hour, two hours each day, plus weekends. There was nothing else quite like it in all of Bethania Station. A corridor thirty feet wide. Plenty of room to work the horses. My first overseer was a kind of Snopes-like character, a little too narrow between the eyes, who explained that the barn alone would not pay its way. Nosirreee, we'd sure have to erect a championship riding ring if we were serious about making a name for ourselves.

I stole more time from work to get the ring built while Snopes watched from the shade of the barn. Once I got it done he came out and scratched his head beneath his worn straw hat and said, well, it was a good enough ring for the youngsters; but that I would need a second, much larger complex if we were planning to do any real training. So I brought in the earth-moving machines, flattened some of the terraced land I had created for my vineyards and eventually got the second ring built, stealing more precious hours from my work and more money from my dwindling farm account.

I was about halfway through the project when I realized that Snopes hadn't come there to train horses anyway. What happened was that he'd been turning the place into a haven for drug addicts and alcoholics and figured I was sucker enough not to catch on. I feared the worst: a drug addict making merry with the farm animals while I was on the front porch sipping bourbon and branch water and smoking my fine Havana cigars. Nothing to do but run him off, sneering at his feigned look of innocence.

My second trainer was hardly any improvement: a dowdy little creature, vaguely female, who had spent two years at a community college down east learning how to be a champion horse trainer. Well, she was at the back door every day with some sort of new demand. When was I gonna finish the new riding ring? When was I gonna put in the bleachers? What about the nocturnal lighting system I had promised? What about the fences? Up till now my wife and I had relied almost solely on electric fences. That was all right with Snopes, for whom horses were at best a secondary interest. We had been replacing them a little at a time with sturdy wooden palisades—but not quickly enough to suit my new trainer.

"Them old electric fences are OK for cattle, but horses, why, they'll just run right through 'em."

Not true, first of all. But something for her to raise hell about anyway.

A panoramic view of the farm. Photo by Sid Bost

Author's father, Cletus H. James, seeking his
first term as constable.

VOTE FOR

CLETUS H. JAMES

FOR CONSTABLE

OLD TOWN TOWNSHIP

LIFE-LONG DEMOCRAT

Moravian graveyard whose level gravestones, scorned by Thomas Wolfe, signify democracy in death. Pictured, from left to right, are the author's son, Michael; daughter, Ellen; fire chief and brother, Michael; and son, Lee.

James family portrait. From left to right, bottom row: Effie Belle, Kathleen Grace, Pearl Cleo, Martha Hunter James (grandmother), in perpetual sobriety, Samuel Augustus (grandfather), in a rare moment of sobriety, Ernest Luther. Back row: Gertie Alma, Grady Ruffin, Jesse Frank, Cletus Hunter, Charles Lee, Hettie Jane.

Grandfather Samuel Augustus James, in last years.

Great grandfather Franklin "Old Jacobus" James.

Author, as wine-bibber, snorting first and last glass of Grassy Fork Red.

Author's wife and land-poor Alabama plantation heiress, Mary Ellen.

Sinister devil-cat and James family pet, "Bama."

The restored homeplace.

The barn.

Fire chief Michael James watches the inferno.

An agrarian scene: the James house and lot. Photo by Sid Bost.

Tobacco barn, west side. Photo by Sid Bost.

Pre-Civil War smokehouse with original front. Photo by Sid Bost.

"Why do you keep coming up here telling me the same thing day after day? Everything was all just dandy when you came out here that first afternoon and thought this place was the very thing you'd been looking for. Now every day we've absolutely got to have this, that, or the other to make the place work."

"Horses just won't stay inside of them old electric fences."

I invited her to climb on her prize palomino and ride right out of there if I wasn't doing the job fast enough to satisfy her whims. She went off in a sulk, like always. A day or two later she was back at he house complaining, as she had a hundred times before, that our manure spreader just wasn't sophisticated enough to fit her image of a real first-class horse-breeding operation.

"It's a real old broken-down antique kind of spreader. Don't see how we're ever gonna make use of it at all."

Every day, more of the same. She never seemed to remember that she had promised to pitch in and help with the fencing if I would just give her a chance to lease my "really spiffy barn." She explained that during her last semester at college, she had taken a course that taught her all about fences and that her class had built one of the finest in all creation, and if I didn't believe it, I just oughta go down and have a look. Soon after that, as chance would have it, I was down that way on a news assignment, and I got a good look at her fence. Half of it had fallen down, and the rest was on its way. I was mighty happy I hadn't taken her up on her offer to help erect one of her "really spiffy fences" on our land.

I finally ran her off and was about to close down the whole she-bang when a real slicker showed up and said we had the makings of a world-class horse-breeding operation here on the old Grassy Fork and why not give him a chance to make a go of it?

Boy, he was a slick one all right, a real fancy talker who almost sank us into bankruptcy after convincing us that he was the very man to fill the barn with future Derby winners.

"Name's Jed. Sho' is nice to meetcha. Course, now, you understand I can't work fer nothin'."

"How much?"

"Three hundred a week."

"Can't pay it. Might as well just hit the road."

"Just gimme six weeks. That's fair enough, ain't it? You can afford it fer that long fer the kind of return you're gonna be gittin'. If I can't fill up this barn by that time and bring home a passel of blue ribbons, we'll just up and call it quits. Sho' ain't much of an investment fer what you're gonna be gittin' outa it."

I checked his references. Nothing but good reports from the whole crowd. He must have paid them all off. Six weeks it was, then. And he got his three hundred dollars.

"Sure as hell hope he's worth it. My god, look at what we've poured into this place already. The vineyards, one thing after another on the house, now this." I got plenty steamed up just thinking about it and was getting ready to go out and tell him "no deal" when Mary Ellen stopped me.

"No, we've given our word. Besides, he seems trustworthy enough and seems to know what he's doing. If we're ever to make a go of this farm, we owe it to ourselves at least to give him his six weeks."

It wasn't till I consented to buy him that spanking new dual-wheeled truck—a dooley he called it—that I began to suspect I might be in real trouble.

"Yessir," says he, "I'll sho' fill that barn up, and it ain't gonna take more'n a month to do it neither. Got lotsa contacts. Yessir, I can git those horses in thar, but I gotta have me a new truck."

"We've already got a truck."

It was a three-ton job that I bought from the gas company with the idea of transforming it into a vehicle that would accommodate horse trailers. Not much to look at—half the top eaten up with rust. The running boards coming off. But it would have to do till we got in some of that big money.

The new man looked it over and shook his head in dismay. "Now lemme ask you somethin'. Is this here the kinda image you want the Grassy Fork Stables to present to the world? You want me drivin' up to one of these here big horse shows in this broken-down old piece of junk? Gotta have me a dooley."

"Goddammit, man, the truck will be presentable enough with a little work. And let's stop calling everything I've got around here 'junk.' How does that set with you? OK? Anyway, what happened to all that talk about our starting out on a modest scale? Building the place up and letting the income take care of all our new expenses? You forgot about all that? Nothing was said about me putting out a bunch of cash for a brand new 'dooley' when I agreed to take you on."

Three hundred a week I was paying this character, and still no horses in the barn.

"Image, man. That's what this here business is all about. Gotta go first class. That's how we gonna get them horses in here. Image. All image. Look around you at some of these here other barns. You see one that's even halfway successful, and you know he did it on image, and we ain't gonna git *nowhere* without we have us a dooley. Time we was doin' somethin' about that old manure spreader, too."

"One more word about that manure spreader and the deal's off."

Anyway, he had me. Image. How could I ever become part of the landed gentry without a dooley? I checked the want ads to see what was available. But the new guy—"Just call me Jed"—was already phoning car dealers all over the state trying to find a brand new model with all the latest equipment.

"Goddammit, Jed, I've done told you. You're just gonna have to make out with something less than the best till we get some money coming in. You said you'd have that barn filled in a week. Wasn't anything said about buying a twenty-thousand-dollar truck."

"Look, I thought you understood. Just git me that thar dooley, and I'll have that barn runnin' over with horses in no time a-tall. Just listen to me now. I got contacts all over the South. Fella called me last night from down Georgia way. He said, says he, 'Jed, I got me a couple a new quarter horses, and you're the only man I know I can trust to train 'em good and proper. Why don'tcha just come on down and load 'em up.'"

He looked at my old truck with a sneer. "You see, that's what I'm talkin' about. Image. I go down thar in some broken-down old piece of junk like that and you can jes' imagine how much clout I'd have. Shit, he'd be laughin' at me all the way back to Carolina."

He got the dooley. A real slick job. A good price, too, though still way more than I could afford. Jed? All he could do was complain about the color. "Pale blue ain't gonna git the job done. Black is big this year. Black with a lot of that thar silver chrome on it. And a lot o' them fancy stripes. When people see us comin', we want 'em to know they're dealin' with the best in the business."

"Better get used to pale blue, Jed. Just wait a spell. Pale blue is gonna be all the rage next year. Real big. At least that's what I hear. Anyhow, you got everything you said you needed in a truck. Dual wheels in back. A special attachment for the horse trailer."

Trouble was, I didn't have a trailer, at least not one that came up to his expectations. Only an old farm trailer I had thought would serve well enough until we got some of that big money coming in. Jed looked at it with another sneer.

"That broken-down old piece of junk? We sho' gotta have us a trailer. Reckon what folks gonna think if I come drivin' up draggin' along somethin' like that thar? Look, I'm tryin' to do you a big favor. You buy me a truck and trailer so we can go first class, and everybody's gonna be sayin', 'Now thar's a feller that really knows his stuff.' Got me now? Gotta be thinkin' about image all the time in this here business."

He almost had me again. All that talk about image. Then I got a good sturdy grip on myself.

"No more money for trailers or anything else until we get something coming in, Jed. You hear me? You're just gonna have to rent you a trailer out of that three hundred a week I'm paying you, if you don't figure this one measures up to your 'image.' Meantime, we gotta have some horses in that barn."

He sulked for awhile, reminding me every day that I simply would "hafta git hold of a real first-class trailer" if I ever expected to get anywhere in the horse business. Eventually he gave in and went to work— if you could call it work, him riding around all day in that dooley, pale blue or not, and telling everybody (as I later learned) that he had found himself a real sucker this time. Still, he put up a big pretense. Off he went to Georgia, and back he came with two quarter horses.

"That fella, he sho' gotta a big laugh outa my old trailer. Told him our best trailer was in the shop. No sir. Sho' didn't hear nobody braggin' on it."

Not long after that a third client who had heard about our barn— though not from Jed—brought in another quarter horse. Three horses in a barn built for ten, with plenty of room to expand. It went on like that for weeks. Jed driving around in that new truck and showing up at the barn only long enough to drink half a six-pack and get the three horses watered and fed each morning and evening.

"What're we gonna do about this guy," I asked my wife one morning. "I'm really beginning to have my doubts."

"Well, we can't just keep running people off. Probably won't hurt his reputation, if he has any, but it could sure hurt ours. Besides, we gave him to July. Six weeks. It just takes time. You can see how it might hurt us if we don't live up to our part of the bargain. Anyway, we've got all that money invested in that new truck now."

"Here we are in the middle of June. And before you know it the dog days will be right on top of us. He was supposed to have had the barn full long before now. What gives? Don't you realize that the six weeks we gave him are almost up?"

"Well, I just think we've gone too far to throw it all over. We've got to give him a chance to see what he can do." That same day I went out and talked to him in the nastiest tone I could muster.

"Where in hell are the rest of the horses, Jed? I guess you know the time is about up. I suppose now you're gonna want an extension."

He spoke without looking around. "Tell you what, good buddy, just gimme to the end of July, and I'll have this here place covered up with horses. In the meantime, I tell you what we need to do."

"What's that?"

"We need to buy ourselves a couple o' horses. That's the way to git this thing goin'. Buyin' and sellin'. That's where the real money is in this business."

"Ain't buying no horses. Are you out of your goddamn mind? Buy this, buy that. And now you're talking about a whole extra month and wanting me to finance the whole goddamn operation."

"Takes time. But don't worry. I got the contacts, and I got the word out all over the South. Just gimme a little more time. Three . . . maybe four more weeks."

We drifted into July, out of July, and on into August, and still only three horses in the barn, and no money coming in at all, except from the one renter we'd got with no help from Jed. The dog days *were* upon us. No money, no new prospects.

"Gotta have some money, Jed. That renter you found down there in Georgia, where's his rent? He's way overdue. Three months overdue in fact. And I haven't seen you doing a whole lot of work with his horses either."

"He's good fer it. Believe me, he's good fer it. Been knowin' him as a real square shooter fer a good long time now."

"Time we were giving him a call. Right away, Jed."

"Sure thing, old buddy. Just gimme to the end of the week. He's probably just overlooked it. He's good fer it. Yessir, I'd stake my reputation on it."

Somehow that didn't make me feel a whole lot better. August was getting by in a hurry and another big drought had overtaken the land, and still no money, only the three horses, who appeared to have grown way too fat on all that expensive grain he'd been feeding them.

"When you gonna start working those horses, Jed? Looking a mite overweight to me. Thought you brought them up here for training. When're you gonna get started? We sure can't risk getting those horses floundered. What kind of reputation will that get us? Seems to me, it's time you were parking that dooley and spending more time around the barn. And not just to sit around and spend the whole afternoon swilling beer either."

He explained that he had been out "drumming up business" and that we'd never get anywhere if we didn't "let people know who we were" and that we were looking for "a real high-class kind of horse here" and how in hell would we ever get all his "good contacts" to trust us with their stock unless "they're sold on our reputation?"

"Just get me that back rent. And get busy working those horses."

"It's the heat, good buddy. Hard on them horses to work them in weather like this here."

Maybe he was right for once. The summer of '86. One of the hottest on record. Nostradamus had seen it coming. No rain in months, and none in the forecast. We were luckier than most; we managed to produce a good crop of fescue along the damp reaches of the Grassy Fork and were selling it for two dollars a bale. I had even turned down offers of two-fifty and three dollars. Nobody could remember a drought like this one, and nobody but Nostradamus could have foreseen how destructive would be its impact.

"Just get me all that goddamn back rent."

"He's good fer it. You gotta trust me on this one. I'll give him a call toward the end of the week."

September was coming fast. Jed had been gone every weekend, off to some horse show or other. No blue ribbons, though. Nothing but one lousy faded pink ribbon so far. Last place in something. I don't know where he got the nerve to put one of those fat quarter horses on show at all. Getting in and out of that trailer was about the only training those two "show" horses had ever had.

"Gotta let him go," I told Mary Ellen. "He's letting both those horses get floundered, and where in the hell is the rent?"

"We've too much invested now. At least give him till the end of September."

I had been all around. I thought I had learned enough to spot almost any kind of shyster, but maybe not. Those horse people were a special breed. Sometimes I longed to have Snopes back. At least he stayed drunk all the time and never bothered anybody and was never behind with his meager rent.

Our new man had finally put on a show of training the horses—walking them around the ring, and that was about it. He had once boasted of a career in the state patrol. Bragged about being in the special service of the governor. Why had he quit? Was it just another of his lies? Had the authorities discovered he was a common thief and thrown him out? Had he tumbled the governor's wife in the back of his car? Did he really know anything at all about horses?

"Gotta get rid of him."

"I still think we need to give him every chance to make good."

"September, goddammit, and that's it."

September came and went. No more horses, no money, not even from the guy in Georgia. Almost three months we had been keeping up his stock, and so far not a dime.

"He's good fer it," Jed kept saying. "I'm telling you he's good fer it. You can count on it as money in the bank."

"OK," Mary Ellen said. "A couple more weeks. Mid-October, and then you can do whatever you like."

"I think I've figured out what it is with this character. He comes from a real bad part of the mountains. Grew up back in one of those hollers where there's a lot of inbreeding."

"He doesn't look inbred to me. You were always saying the same things about Snopes."

"Same for them both. All those bad genes come out in different ways. I figure this character is bound to be a product of incest. Grew up on a diet of pork rinds and corn liquor. The kind of whopsided-looking people you used to see working in some of those cotton factories back in the hills."

"Well, as least he isn't whopsided. And he does seem to be doing some work for a change. And in all this heat, at that."

We still had good hay in the lower part of the bottom, along the Big Grassy. Trucks were still coming onto the land and hauling it away at two dollars a bale.

"Some of the richest land I've ever seen," one farmer told me. "Hard to believe you're getting real quality hay in weather like this."

We sold an awful lot of it. Why not? Our champion quarter horses, whose owner's name I didn't even know, had put on so much weight that we would have more than enough to see them through the summer, along with any others that might accidentally appear.

"What about it, Jed? Got any more horses lined up?"

"They're gonna be comin' in droves. That's right. Fall's the big season. Why, by Thanksgiving we'll have this barn crammed full and people clamoring away for more space."

"Yeah? Well, that big-timer from Georgia still hasn't paid us a cent."

"I keep tellin' you he's good fer it. I just been so busy out scouring up business, I ain't had no chance to give him a call. Got a lot of solid promises, though—a lot of good prospects for the fall."

By merest chance, Mary Ellen found the name of the man we suspected of being our Georgia client on a scrap of paper in Jed's office. No telephone listing or address. Yet somehow she managed to get him on the phone. I came in about the time she was ready to hang up. I watched her as she cradled the phone.

"Well?"

"OK, I admit it, you were right and I was wrong," she said. "It looks as though we've really been had."

"What did the fella say? Who is he anyhow? Is he sending a check?"

"Just as nice as he could be. He seemed genuinely surprised when I told him the whole story. You see, Jed never did tell us the truth about his arrangement. The man actually didn't want to let the horses go. But Jed—according to what the man in Georgia told me—begged and pleaded with him to let him have them on a trial basis and even promised to keep them for nothing. Just so it would look as though he were getting business for the barn."

"Wonder how long he thought he could get away with that?"

"He certainly got away with it for long enough. And I'm more than willing to take my share of the blame."

"All of it, you mean."

"OK, if you want to be ugly. Anyway, Mr. Smithwick—that's the fellow's name—says he's coming for the horses this weekend and will pay us all the back rent."

"Time I was going down and having another little talk with Jed.

You know, I don't think he knows a damn thing about horses. I guess he thought he could get away with the sham after he found out that we knew even less. He's a tough one, though. Saw him stagger one of those horses one day—almost knocked it halfway across the stall—with one slap of his hand. That's when I really began to feel that he had no feeling for them at all."

"Well! I certainly never knew that."

"I told you all along that he's a product of incest. Sometimes it can strengthen as well as weaken the breed. Weaned on corn liquor, like I said. Yep, incest is a funny thing. Sometimes it makes you skinny and good-for-nothing, with a cleft palate and no chin and eyes sunk way back in your head. Sometimes it just makes you stout and mean. A real tough bastard, this one is. Probably a professional eye-gouger in another life. And all that stuff about the state highway patrol. Nothing but just a lot of lies."

"What are you planning to do?"

"Tell him to get the hell off our land."

"A man like that? After all you've said about him? I'm calling the sheriff."

He was gone by the time I got there. That had got to be a real habit with him. Disappearing in the middle of the afternoon, complaining about the heat, leaving the horses unfed and unwatered, leaving beer cans scattered all over the place. Lucky those horses could afford to miss a meal now and then.

"Too hot to work 'em today," he would say, going out and scanning the sky like some dusty gunfighter in an Old West movie.

He was still commuting between our farm and his home in North Wilkesboro. Some town, North Wilkesboro. Moonshine Capital of the World, as it was known in my early days. Known more recently for its marijuana production and for a whole generation of stock car drivers who had got their training on night runs between Wilkesboro and Winston in the days before our town had voted in ABC stores. A real rough place, that old town, though probably nothing to compare with Jed's original home, way back up there in one of the deepest hollows of the Great Smokies.

I got down to the barn as soon as I saw him drive up next morning and before my wife had a chance to call the sheriff. Every time I thought about how he had halfway knocked that horse to its knees with one slap of the hand I was a little sorry I hadn't planted my old double-barreled shotgun down there. Just in case.

"Better just go on and hang it up, Jed. We know the whole story now. Everything. Just pack up whatever you've got, and get the hell on out."

He flung around at me wildly, fists poised to land a real haymaker, his eyeglasses flying off across the corridor, and him looking like one of those old posters of Gentleman Jim Corbett ready to come in swinging. I went through the whole story. By that time, he had dropped his hands and most of the color had drained out of him and he had gone over to pick up his eyeglasses.

He came back and got right up in my face. "You callin' me a liar?"

"You're goddamn right I'm calling you a liar!" I stood my ground. Not out of any show of bravado, but only because I knew I was on home territory and that even a lowdown thieving bastard like Jed would know better than to attack a man on his own place. I also figured my wife had called the sheriff by now.

He stepped back a ways, took off his glasses, and raised his fists again. "By god, you just let me hear you say that again. Callin' me a goddamn liar."

"You're a goddamn liar, all right, and a son of a bitch in the bargain. Guess it's all those old bad genes coming out. So, just go on. Scat! Get moving. Take your stuff, and get on out."

Just as I thought I was in for a real fight, after which I would be certain to end up in the emergency ward at Forsyth Memorial, he dropped his hands and walked away. I guess he had finally figured out that legally, the odds were all against him. Then strange as it seems, he put on his glasses and calmly began to feed the horses.

"Gotta keep these here horses on the right diet. See that they've got plenty of water in this kind of weather."

"Not your bother now. I want you out now. Not in some grandly undefined tomorrow."

He ignored me and methodically went about his chores, as though nothing had been said about his leaving. First time I'd ever seen him so solicitous about the horses.

Mary Ellen appeared at the door without the sheriff, quietly explaining all over again that she had talked to the owner of the horses and that he, Jed, really would have to leave.

He nodded angrily toward me. "Just git him outa my way. Me and you, we'll talk. Ain't got no more to say to him. Expectin' me to make somethin' outa this place with nothin' to work with 'ceptin' a broken-down old manure spreader and horse trailer."

She started for the house, and he fell in behind her. I watched them moving across the hot grass in the sun. I got to the house as he was coming out and going for his car.

"What'd he say?"

"Not much. Only that I seemed like a very nice and reasonable person, but that he sure didn't have much use for that husband of mine. It's hard to imagine, but I suppose he thought I might actually invite him to stay. Now, if our Georgia *client* will pay us even part of what he owes, I will certainly feel a whole lot better about this whole ordeal. Were you really going to fight him?"

"If it came to that. Mainly I was banking on him not fighting me. I guess in one of his few lucid moments, he realized it wasn't the best idea for him to attack a man on his own property."

"What should we do now—other than try to sell that truck for something close to what we paid for it? Get Snopes back? Advertise? Or maybe just close down the whole operation for awhile?"

"Dunno. Sure don't. I can't count the number of people who've come out here and told me there is real money in horses. 'Build you a real nice barn down here, and you'll be set for life.'"

"It was the same with the grapes."

I looked up the hill at the withered vines, the black rot, the powdery mildew, a dozen other splotches of disease that so far didn't even have a name. "Maybe we oughta just go on and get out. Find us a small place in town or out on the river or at the beach, and try to get some sanity back in our lives. The Virgin Islands would be really nice."

"You know you don't mean that. Four generations of your family have lived in this house, and now we have a fifth coming along. More than a hundred years, your people have been here. I don't really think you are ready to turn your back on all that."

"How're we gonna keep the place up? Just look around. The city moving in on us all the time. Won't be many years before they'll have the whole place in the corporate limits. How're we gonna pay all those taxes? Tobacco is on its way out, thanks to those meddlesome bureaucrats in Washington. And all those developers channeling water into our bottom, turning half of it into little more than a godforsaken quagmire. No money in corn, no money in grapes or horses, and nobody left but Orientals and Bulgarians to smoke cigarettes anymore. So you tell me. How're we gonna make the place work?"

"I think something will work out."

"You always think something will work out."

"I just can't believe that you're ready to turn your back on one hundred years of family history—a lot more than that when you consider that this was the very first site worked by the Moravians when they settled Bethabara way back in the middle of the eighteenth century."

One afternoon not long after that, a knock at the back screen roused me from my gloomy reverie. I looked up and saw a mangy looking little character in a dirty T-shirt. Snopes all over again.

"Say, feller, I hear you gotta a horse barn to rent."

I looked at the man. "Would you wait right there, sir? I shall be back momentarily and will be most happy to be of service."

I made straight for the closet where I had hidden that old shotgun, which I kept loaded in spite of my wife's remonstrances. I grabbed it and got back to the door in a hurry. The stranger was just lighting up a cigarette when I kicked open the screen and put the gun on him.

"You goddamn horse thief! Get the hell off this property, or I'll fill your ass so full of lead, you'll think the crows had mistaken you for a bag of chicken feed. Just get the hell on outa here, and be quick about it!"

I emptied both barrels over his head. He didn't stop running until he was at least half a mile down the railroad. I started to reload, feeling cocky. "Where's that evil Siamese cat?" I asked myself. "I might as well go on and finish the job." The man who moments before had been at the screen was now climbing up the other side of the railroad embankment and leaping for safety into a drainage ditch at the foot of the hill. Before I could look up a second time, he was completely out of sight.

Mary Ellen came screaming up from the hall. "What in heaven's name are you doing now? Have you completely lost your mind? Are you trying to get yourself thrown in jail? Do you think this is still 1933 and that you can still shoot at people and figure you can talk about it to the sheriff over a game of cards? What do you want people to say? That there's that old Jacobus all over again?"

"It's an old and honorable family tradition. Anyhow, I shot over his head."

"Maybe next you'll fill yourself with liquor and go up to the church and take over the pulpit, and start shouting out all the community dirt. Don't you realize that we are on the verge of a new century, and that the Depression and Herbert Hoover and Reconstruction just don't matter anymore? Please promise me that you won't do anything like that again."

I went back and set the gun down, though not before making sure it was reloaded.

"I just hope that man, whoever he was, doesn't call the law. My word, what will we do then? As if we didn't have enough trouble already."

"I already told you, I shot way over his head. Probably a mistake I will live to regret. My grandfather shot one of those carpetbaggers right through the door of his bedroom one time. So they tell me. Couldn't even see the guy. Just heard his voice. As you know better than anyone else, we've still got the hole in the door to prove it. Patched it over with a big piece of tin. Just thought I'd leave it there. Part of the old family tradition we're trying so hard to preserve."

I went outside and sat on the stoop, Mary Ellen beside me. "I wonder how long it will take for this to get around. Why, it will be all over the church Sunday. What am I supposed to tell my Sunday school class?"

"Tell 'em that old Jacobus has come back from a sojourn in Transylvania. Like the ghost of Hamlet's father. Doomed for a certain time to walk the midnight and settle old scores with all of these lying, thieving, incestuous bastards. I reckon we just got too many of those bad Moravian genes. You could tell them that. They've always thought those Moravians were kind of a snooty crowd anyway. Look at Mr. Will and all the trouble he caused. And look at all their church leaders. Too good to sit down and take a good honest drink with you anymore. Not like the old days. Why Cornwallis marched all his troops right through these parts during the Revolution, knowing he could count on those old Moravians to provide him with plenty of liquor for his troops. Yeah, they're holding themselves mighty high these days, those old Moravians, but, listen dear, they're just like the rest of us and don't even know who they were to begin with. Boy, those damned Baptists will get you every time."

"I don't think I want to get into all of that. I think what we need to ask ourselves is how we will ever get anyone decent and honest to run the barn if they've got to spend half the time wondering whether they're going to be shot or not. Why, you didn't even know that man! Couldn't you at least have treated him with a certain amount of civility?"

"Too narrow between the eyes. Just like all the others. That's right. They're all alike. Too many years of living off pork rinds and corn liquor. Maybe I haven't learned everything, but at least I've learned to judge a horse hustler when I see one."

"So you really do think you're living in the old days and that you can get away with the kind of ridiculous nonsense that your grandfather did. At least he had a friend in the sheriff. And you didn't even vote for the man who's in office now. You voted Republican last time. You know you did. How would you like for *that* to get out in the community?"

"Times are changing. This is getting to be real Republican country now. Just said so yourself . . . how all that old stuff doesn't count anymore."

"I expect it would sure count with your grandfather."

"Dunno. Hard to imagine what he would make of this new generation of Democrats. Pornographers, welfare quacks, all these whining women getting above themselves. Self-righteous neo-Abolitionists pissing all over themselves trying to find a Cause that will force the rest of the population to adopt their notions about how you're supposed to live and think. I expect he'd be in quite a quandary, although I doubt that it would change his mind about Mr. Will or about that carpetbagger—whoever he was—that he shot through the door without anything to go on except the sound of his voice."

Mary Ellen went in to answer the phone. She came back moments later to explain that it was one of the neighbors who thought she'd heard something that sounded like gunfire from down this way and wanted to know if anybody was hurt.

"Didn't think it would take long for the news to get around. I simply had to lie and pretend that I'd heard nothing. I'm sure she didn't believe a word."

"You'll feel OK after a good night's sleep."

"If you say so. But what if that poor fellow you shot at or someone else takes it in his head to call the sheriff?"

"Not a chance. He knows he was in the wrong. Believe me, everything will look a whole lot different in the morning. We'll both be able to see things a lot more clearly."

"I just hope it isn't that little patch of blue that prisoners call the sky."

9

"The Old Ways Are Allus the Best"

We must have worked for another two years on our neo-Victorian "manse," as we now called it, before I had a chance to turn my whole attention to the land itself. I was long finished with being a wine snob. I'd had enough of the sport of kings. I still had my books and word processor and I guess that was all I really needed. But we were also in the business of growing hay for the commercial market and not doing too badly at it.

I looked down at the empty horse barn and then around at the dying vineyards and wondered vaguely where I had gone wrong and whether a fresh start would bring more positive results. Mostly though, I tried not to think about it at all. I just worked the bottom and the upland pastures, hoping to improve my field of fescue, and watched the sky for signs of rain.

Every year there was a little less of the bottom to work. The highway people had come along and erected a curb and guttering system that effectively dumped great batches of water onto our property, transforming a lot of our good pastureland—"floodplain," to the zoning bureaucrats—into a varmint-infested swamp. Nobody had thought about arranging for a drainage system that would channel the water onto a lower part of the floodplain and from there into the creek.

By the summer of 1990, or thereabouts, it had become a constant and well-nigh impossible struggle to keep the lower third of the bottom from being overrun by an impenetrable morass. Protests meant nothing to those highway people. Ring them up, and some anonymous voice would say, "Yessir, we'll git right on it, soon as I kin git in touch with the big boss." If you ever managed to get hold of the big boss, he'd say, "Well, hit's the law. That's all I kin tell you. Talk to the boys down at the planning department. That's right. The law says you allus got to let the water seek its natural level."

"So you plan to do nothing. Is that it? You aren't gonna do a goddamn thing about it at all?"

"Reckon you'll just have to talk to the appropriations people down thar in Raleigh 'bout that."

To get rid of all that water, we would have to dredge a one-thousand-foot drainage ditch from the back of our property to where the land dropped down to meet the Grassy Fork. But before we could do that, we had to get rid of all the dense growth that had sprung up in the last couple of years. For all I knew, the bobcats and catamounts had come back by now. Bears and wolves on the prowl. Not that they necessarily would be pleased to call it home; it was in better shape when the Cherokees had it. As it was now, you'd be crazy to think about going in there unarmed. Anyway, I at last hit upon what seemed at least a partial solution. I would wait till the driest part of the winter and then burn off the whole place. The best way I knew to reclaim the swamp, and besides, I knew from my younger days that the surest way to get a good stand of fescue in the spring was to burn off all the old growth in the dead season.

It was mid-March by that time—probably a little late in the year to start that kind of fire—but I'd wanted to wait until the land was good and dry. So why blame me if things got a little out of control? How was I to know the fire would get into the woods? Or across the railroad tracks? Or into old man Washburn's hay bin and corncrib half a mile away?

The fire started out as what we true agrarians call a "controlled burning." You set it late in the season not only to burn the dead grass and weeds out of the pasture but also to infuse the soil with nitrogen. Nothing is better for the land or the fescue. A common practice in the old days. And, as I said, the only way we could get in there to fight that swamp. It just happened that at the time of my "controlled burning," we'd had no rain for weeks. Exactly the way I wanted it. I figured it as a real lucky turn of events. Finally, a chance to practice the true agrarianism I had so often celebrated when I was writing newspaper editorials.

Back in the old days, Uncle Luther would burn off more than a hundred acres to get the pastures ready for the next haying season. We still had more than fifty acres in pasture, and even though everybody kept warning me that it wasn't the old days and that we were almost in the city now, I knew no one could legally stop me from burning the place off, as long as I kept the fire outside the corporate limits. Every day a bunch of city firemen would come there wanting to put it out. Then I would have to go tearing off to explain that they were out of their territory now and to just keep their damned hoses out of my controlled burning.

Along about the third day, one little squirt wanted to get real nasty about it. "I wish you had to sit up there and answer that phone and listen to all them complaints that's been coming in. The smoke's gettin' inside their houses and tyin' up traffic on the highway. Shit, mister, you need to put this fire out. You never can tell which a way the wind is gonna carry it. You gotta be mighty careful with a fire like this."

"I broke any laws?"

"Can't rightly say that, but you let it get across that city line up 'air and there's gonna sure be hell to pay."

I watched them drive off. They went up the back road through a new, heavily wooded subdivision that surely was the source of most of the complaints.

Like I didn't have sense enough to keep the fire out of the woods! I had started the first blaze two days earlier. Everything had gone well. I would watch the fire all morning and afternoon as it slowly burned its way across the high ground beyond the hay barn and on up toward the Baptist church, leaving behind the covering of charred grass that would vanish with the first rain and give way to the lovely crop of new fescue. The wind was with me, and I managed to keep the fire contained within a nine-acre field behind the church. I knew even then that all the residents of those new subdivisions would be on their phones whining to everybody in City Hall. Well, let 'em holler. A man willing to stand up for his agrarian principles still has some rights in this goddamn country, doesn't he?

I had plenty of encouragement from my brother, and a good thing it was too, since he was, after all, chief of our rural fire district. Each year the city hall bureaucrats had eaten away at a little more of his territory, and we both knew they eventually would have it all. "Go ahead and burn," he told me. "You're within your legal rights as long as you stay in the county. Gotta be careful, though, with the city squeezing you on every side."

"It's the only way to get a really good stand of grass," I told him. "Like our father always said, 'The old ways are always the best.'"

On the second day, the chief came out to help start some of the fires and, with the wind beginning to stir, had stayed to watch for awhile, maybe only to convince himself that I had heeded his advice or at least had sense enough to keep the blaze confined to one section of the field at a time. I guess I didn't have sense enough after all. First thing I knew the flames were shooting up everywhere and, sure enough, before I realized what had happened, we were both fighting like crazy to keep it out of the woods.

It was all right. We soon had it back out in the field where it belonged, and he looked at me and lectured me gently about the need to "stay with an orderly established pattern." I guess after that he thought I had learned my lesson. Mighty slow taking his leave, though. He was out there most of the morning. By the time he did leave, we had finished burning off the upper field behind the house and barn lot as well as another two or three acres of good pastureland separating the church from the nearest subdivision.

"Thought I'd start in the bottom tomorrow," I told him.

"Just remember, it can get ahead of you before you realize it. But I guess you've learned your lesson by now." He looked at me as if he still wondered, but he had a lot on his mind without having to worry about the quality of my new crop of fescue. "If you start down there in that bottom, just be mighty, mighty careful. I won't be able to get out here until late tomorrow."

"Don't worry. I've learned my lesson real good."

That's what I kept telling myself anyway. Same thing I'd tried to tell all those city firemen. You'd think even they would have some respect for a man who was only trying to practice sound conservation principles. But I knew they had their eye on me now. Let that fire crawl over the city line by as much as a foot, and I knew that the little guy who wanted to start all the trouble would be right back down there, waving his hose in one hand and a court order in the other. *I done told you, mister. I done told you now. I told you to put out this goddamn fire, and now we're gonna have your ass. That's right, mister. We'll see how you like talking to the judge.*

Then see me in durance vile for the rest of my natural life. Well, let him smart off as much as he liked. Everything had gone fine so far, except for that little scare we'd had the day before. But it was that same day—the third day, the day I began to burn off the bottom—when all the trouble started.

That morning I had started over where the dry land met the new swamp, watching carefully to make sure none of the flame jumped over into the city. The city line ran straight behind our house; we had been shamelessly gerrymandered into the corporate limit that same year just so the aldermanic board could saddle us with a big boost in taxes. Another two or three years, and the board would be ready to snatch up the rest of our property. I could just imagine all those guys sitting around in the fire stations, impatiently tapping their feet against the day when they would have a right to come swaggering onto the place and stamp out my last spark of flame, giving me the finger and saying just kiss our ass if you don't like it, mister!

After an hour or so, I looked at the blackened lower end of the bottom and had a brand spanking new idea. Since I knew the fire could not burn back over itself, I realized I could finish the job a lot more quickly, and without the slightest risk, by starting other fires in various parts of the field. Although the chief had warned against it, I could see there was no way for the fire to get out of bounds. The railroad would stop it on one side, the creek on two others.

So it would be all right. I went up and down the bottom setting fires and spent the whole morning watching them burn into one another, slowly working their way north toward the city. By mid-afternoon the whole bottom had turned to charcoal, a sure sign that I would get a good stand of grass in the spring. I figured the time had come when I could go upstairs and put in a little work on my manuscripts. I would be able to keep an eye on the fire from my window as it slowly burned itself out. Anyway, the chief had given me his private telephone number, just in case.

I gave up on the word processor in almost no time and went over to lie down for awhile. I had barely done so when I heard the first screams.

"Oh my heavens!" Mary Ellen was shouting. "The woods are on fire! Did you know that the woods are on fire?"

I shook myself awake and went to the head of the stairs. "It's nothing," I explained.

"Nothing? Are you crazy? I'm gonna call your brother and tell him to get over here!"

"Just hold on. We've got plenty of time."

"I'd better go on and call. The wind is really picking up now. Why did you just walk off and leave it? You promised him faithfully that you would keep close watch on it, and he'll want to know why you left it to get out of control."

"Just don't call him yet. It's just a lot of smoke. Wind and smoke. That's all. Looks a whole lot worse than it is."

"All the same, I'm going to call."

"I tell you, it's nothing to get excited about."

"You'd just better get on down here. Those firemen are going to need all the help they can get. He told you a hundred times that if you once let that fire get out of control, the county fire marshal would want to get into it, and then there would be real hell to pay. Perhaps the U.S. Forest Service as well, and the Lord knows who else. We will be laughed right out of the community and the church and the Farm Bureau. Do you think we'll ever be able to get another dime's worth of insurance after this?"

"Let me get my shoes."

"Hurry!"

"Hurry. Yes, by all means. But I tell you that it is nothing to get excited about. It's the only way we're ever gonna get a good stand of grass and get rid of that damn swamp. Those city bureaucrats have nobody to blame but themselves anyway."

"Did you not hear anything I said? I said the whole woods are on fire!"

"I can take care of it easy. Just let me get my shoes." I knew it was nothing. Just a lot of wind and smoke. "We've got plenty of time!"

Yes. Hurry. But it was plain as anything that the fire had long ago burned itself out.

"Are you coming?"

"Calm down, will you? I told you I'm coming. Just don't touch that phone until I get there."

About that time my sock feet went out from under me, and I was on my way down the steps head first, all the time telling myself, "Don't panic. There's nothing to worry about. Just stay relaxed, and try not to break anything." I realized even as I was falling that my wife had gone out to the back porch to take another look, her voice mingling with the loud crackling of the flame.

"Just please, please hurry!"

I was making record time, head first. "You just keep your hands off that phone!" I was still falling, faster now, my whole sorry life passing before my eyes. The steps were quite high and steep, as they often are in old houses, and I took a real pounding as I went down. I finally hit bottom and lay there crumpled up like a piece of discarded note paper. Falling down the steps head first does have one advantage: it gives you a little extra time to get your thoughts in order. Not that I figured the fire was any kind of crisis at all.

My wife came running back in, shouting for me to get out there so I would be ready to show the firemen the best route into the bottom.

"I don't think I broke anything," I said.

"I love you dearly, and I really don't regret marrying you at all, but sometimes you act as if you don't have half sense."

"I can still see it," I said.

"What?"

"My life. My whole sorry life. That's how close I came to death, and then you would have been forced to have the funeral on the very day you were planning to show houses to the new couple from Bridgeport. My whole life just flew before my eyes, and yet I am not dead. At least I don't think so. Of course, they say you can be dead for days—even weeks sometimes—without knowing it. Did you know that? I read about it in one of those books on the occult you're always bringing home."

"Will you stop talking nonsense and get on out there? Are you sure you're still taking your anti-depressants? Sometimes I can't make half sense out of what you are saying. I don't know anything about being dead and not knowing anything about it. All I know is that we're all gonna be in jail if you don't get out there and do something. It's completely out of control now. I'm going to call."

I finally got all the way up and limped out to the porch. I couldn't see anything for the flame, and not much of the flame for the great whirling billows of smoke. Strange. There was hardly anything left burning when I lay down.

"I'd better get your brother on the phone."

"Wait a minute!"

"No, there's no time to wait! I'm going to call! You can't stop me now!"

"Just hold on for a minute! A good fire is the only way to get a good stand of grass. That's the way we always did it in the old days. Like I say, 'The old ways are allus the best.' So just hold on for a second, won't you?"

I just didn't like the idea of my brother knowing I was a fool, and I didn't like the idea of him bringing all those firemen onto the property and then having to explain that his own blood kin had set the woods on fire. I didn't like the idea of the sirens. I didn't like standing there in my sock feet, knowing the fire trucks were on their way to my house. I didn't like having to worry about all that while I was trying to feel around to see if I had any broken bones. I didn't like the thought of all the children in the neighborhood running up and down the drive and pointing their fingers at me: "That ignorant old red-headed dunce set his woods on fire! That crazy old man set his woods on fire!"

"I'm going to call," Mary Ellen said.

"No. Its all confined very nicely in the bottom. It only looks worse than it is, all that smoke and everything. And all those busybodies complaining, when there's really nothing to complain about. I'm telling you, it will burn itself out and everything will be fine."

"I'm going to phone him this minute."

"No!"

"Yes!"

"Wait!"

She had barely got the phone off the hook when we heard the sirens bearing down on us now. Loud and wild and crazy. And the mad shouts of villagers who had gathered in the road in front of the house to watch. Even the rescue squad was there. Then came the sheriff and half of his deputies. I hadn't seen the fire marshal yet. There would sure be hell to pay if he got into it. All I could get out of the onlookers was that there had been reports of a forest fire raging out of control all up and down the valleys of Bethania Station, driving people from their homes, frightening the farm animals, setting all the dogs to barking.

Some of the volunteer firemen came barreling up the driveway in a jeep equipped with hoses and a tank of water, yelling for me to show them the fastest route into the bottom. I hated to have to tell them that we'd had no real access to the bottom for three of four months now, ever since the heavy rains of late winter had washed away our last good bridge.

My brother came around the corner of the house about that time, being very understanding about it all. "Can we drive into the bottom? Is the bridge still strong enough to hold?"

"We don't have a bridge."

"Where is it?"

"Probably down about Salisbury by now. Maybe at Myrtle Beach or some place like that. I guess it wouldn't do us much good even if we could get it all back."

"You mean the bridge is washed away? There's no way into the bottom?"

"I'll show you where you can ford the stream."

By that time the men in the jeep had found the ford and were roaring off across the bottom toward the distant fields. Somehow the fire, against all known laws of physics, had jumped all the way back across itself and into the woods.

One of the firemen, his face charred black, came running back into the yard. The news was getting worse all the time. "It's jumped the railroad and gotten all the way over into that big stand of timber over there! Just ain't no way to get to it. Might haveta call in the people from Rural Hall."

That was the part the chief hated most of all: the idea that he would have to call in firemen from another department to help him put out a fire in his own district. Having to confess that it was something he and his men couldn't handle themselves. But maybe he wouldn't have to call. Maybe by now it was all the way across the line into the Rural Hall district, which would mean there was nothing he could do to keep the "enemy" out of it anyway. Nothing to keep all those Rural Hall firemen from laughing at him up their sleeves.

"Sounds like sirens coming down the other way," I said.

"Rural Hall," the chief said.

"Do you think it's burned up the whole town. I just don't see how it could have got that far out of control."

"I guess we're going to have to answer to the fire marshal now for sure," Mary Ellen said. "We'll probably have to pay a big fine even if they get the fire out and even if they don't haul us into court."

"I still say it's worse than it looks."

"Hahaaahahahahhaaa!"

My brother's laugh had taken on a strangely sinister quality. I watched the firemen coming back out of the bottom and parking their jeep out along the railroad and then getting out and running like crazy down the tracks, maybe hoping to beat the people from Rural Hall to wherever the latest crisis was. I couldn't see anything for all that smoke.

Two fire trucks had come, but how were they supposed to get down across the tracks and back into the woods where the real inferno was? My brother was out talking to one of the drivers, his foot on the running board, pointing up toward Rural Hall and the mountains. The driver would have to go back up that way and then cut back down across a wide swath of pastureland thick with grazing cattle—unless they had been driven out by all that smoke—and on to another set of woods where there was an old logging road that would provide access into the big timber.

Well, maybe it would and maybe it wouldn't. It had been left unused for so long that in all likelihood it was no longer passable. Maybe they would just have to build their own road. It's just that there was so much smoke, you couldn't even see the fire, much less a road or even the best part of the forest.

I watched as the other truck abruptly backed out of the yard and went roaring off up the road past the Baptist Church toward a new outbreak of flames. The driver of the first sat waiting further enlightenment. A moment later, as he backed off down the drive, he still looked mighty confused. I don't think he ever did find that old logging road.

Presently, the chief came back, not smiling yet very much in control of himself. That was just his way. He had taken after my father, who had never let himself get carried away about anything. I had inherited my mother's nerves and penchant for hysteria. It was just that I was trying not to show it now. Meantime, the men who had come in the jeep were way off down the tracks. With the portable water tanks on their backs, they looked like men from outer space, leaping maniacally from one side of the railroad to the other. My brother stood there, being very understanding.

"I guess we'll be hearing from the fire marshal next. He'll be wanting to levy a mighty big fine, I imagine. I'll have to talk to him."

"What about the Forest Service?"

"I think they're all busy out at Yellowstone."

"Think you can hold off the fire marshal?"

He shook his head doubtfully. "We'll just have to see. Are you going to start any more fires?"

"This was the last."

"How about next year?"

"Haven't thought about that yet. I still say it's an awfully good way to get a good stand of grass. You remember how dad used to do a lot of burning every spring? You probably remember what he used to say, 'Well, boys, don't let anybody kid you now: the old ways are still the best.' Always were. Always will be."

"But this was all country then. Not like today."

I was wondering, too, about the possibility that some know-it-all would force me to endure a sanity hearing before the magistrate. I wouldn't mind it so much for myself, but I knew it would make the family look bad. How would my wife ever again face her Sunday school class knowing her own husband was in a lunatic asylum? How would my brother explain it to all the people at work? That would be almost as bad for him as having to call on all those other fire departments for assistance and having to explain to the marshal that his own brother had set off the biggest fire in the whole known history of Bethania Station.

"Can you go easy on him this time? He's given me his word that it won't happen again."

I figured that was the way he would have to try and talk him out of the big fine. Everybody liked my brother. If anybody could get a favor out of the fire marshal, he was the very one to do it. So maybe it would be all right. He had done a lot for the county. Everybody admired the discipline he had brought to his department. His men were all well trained, aggressive, energetic, and young, and they loved a fire better than almost anything. Of my brother, we'd always said that if he couldn't have been a firefighter, he almost certainly would have been one of the world's great arsonists.

"It's just that everything's got so built up around here," he said. "It's not like you're in the real country anymore. All this smoke blowing into people's windows. I mean, you're still within the law as long as you stay on your own property. I don't know what happens when you let it get out of control like this. But at least so far we haven't let it get into the city. We'd have real hell to pay then. All they're looking for is a reason to eliminate the rest of our fire district anyway."

I explained that I was sure apologetic and would try to make it up to him, and that maybe I just wouldn't start any more fires if it meant causing him all this kind of trouble.

"We're just so close into the city now. The countryside is so built up. All those people calling in and complaining. That's what's causing the problem."

By that time the people from the city fire department had come. I watched my brother go out and try to explain that everything was under control. I didn't see the guy who had tried to cause all the trouble on the first day of my controlled burning.

The chief came back.

"What did they say?" I asked him.

"They say they're gonna be watching it. We may have to call them in too. The city, I mean."

"Do you think its completely out of control?"

"Dunno. Looks pretty bad."

"Well, I still say it's the very best thing for the pasture."

"Not quite as good for the timber, especially since a good part of it belongs to somebody else." That was about as close as he ever came to sarcasm. But he was still quite understanding about everything. "Like I say, it's just that we're so close to the city. I guess we have to take that into consideration."

"We shoulda never sold those woods anyway."

At that moment I turned and saw three children, not yet of school age, running up the drive, exactly as I had anticipated. The little schmucks. One of them came right on in the yard.

"Mister," he said. "How come you set your woods on fire?"

"Turn the hose on that little fart," I said. "You kids just run on home. Everything's under control now."

Later I saw him and the others off in the corner of the yard talking among themselves. Every now and then one of them would nod and look up toward where I was standing. Then the others would look up at me and nod. Then they would all start laughing again. But what could you expect? The new generation knows nothing about what it means to respect the land or to observe sound conservation practices. There's nothing better for pastureland than a good fire. Anybody who grew up in the country knows that. All these new people are worried about is whether they might get a little smoke in their eyes.

The firemen fought the blaze until almost dark. As soon as the smoke began to clear, I could see them again, way off beyond where they had started, still leaping from one side of the tracks to the other with those heavy tanks on their backs. I wondered if they would have to chase the fire the entire five or six miles to Rural Hall or if the people from Rural Hall would get to it first. *You mean your fire chief's own brother set this fire? That skinny old red-headed Kraut? Jesus!*

As soon as they knocked out one blaze, I could see another flowering anew way out in front of them, first on one side of the tracks, then jumping to the other. I realized then that a fire has its own ideas about how to burn itself out. Finally they went around a curve out of sight, so that all we could see then were the towers of fire, always out ahead of them. Now and again the chief went out to his truck and talked to them by walkie-talkie. He would come back and say, "It's still touch and go."

"How far are they now?"

"Couple of miles. If they keep on much further, they're gonna be right smack in the middle of the Rural Hall Fire District. They'd like nothing better than to come and put it out for us. If it comes to that, it's gonna be hard to keep the fire marshal out of it. He's already wanting to levy a $50 fine, and that's just for starting the fire in the first place."

"Fire's a mighty funny thing," I said.

The jeep had followed the firefighters part of the way, and would periodically come back up the tracks to refill its tank. About dark the truck that had gone rushing up toward the church came back, the driver waving at us triumphantly. My brother rushed off to get a report.

"It's OK," he said. "Looks like we've got everything under control on this side of the creek."

He went out to talk to some of the other volunteer firemen and was gone for half an hour or more. "Well," he said as he came back into the yard, "I think we've about got a handle on it now. Just wish we could have done it without having to call Rural Hall in on it. I reckon they'll have a mighty big laugh outa this."

"Fire's a mighty funny thing for sure," I said.

"Gotta watch it every minute."

"Sometimes you think you'll never get it started. Then just as you're about to give up, it takes on a life of its own."

"Can't risk taking your eyes off it."

"I just thought I had it under control. Couldn't see a spark anywhere when I went to lie down."

"Well, like you say, fire's a mighty funny thing."

"Sometimes, it's like . . . well, it just appears to defy all the laws of physics. You think that's what happened today?"

"Maybe. Just hope we can make the fire marshal understand that."

"What am I supposed to tell everybody at church?" my wife wanted to know. "Why did you have to wait till Saturday and me with a Sunday school class in the morning?"

"Well, they know I've been on a lot of medication. Maybe you could mention that."

"Or maybe you can tell them that this was one of those times where the fire simply violated all known laws of physics," the chief said, beginning to laugh a little as he turned away and signaled for the two big trucks to head back to the station. He would stay there with the jeep awhile longer. Just to make sure.

"Yup," I said, looking off toward old man Washburn's parched farm buildings. "Mighty funny thing about a fire."

The firemen had got there barely in time to keep his whole place from burning down.

"Well, at least you've got a nice clean pasture out of it."

"Mighty surprised we haven't heard from old man Washburn."

"What's he got to complain about? He's got roast'n' ears ready for the table. He oughta call you up and thank you."

Maybe so. But I kept waiting for him to show up with a gun and demand that I get over there and do something about the damage. Well, maybe I would do that anyway. Just as a Christian gesture, if for no other reason. He hadn't actually suffered that much damage. At least his house hadn't burned down. Scorched in a couple of places. A corncrib and tool shed gone. Nothing else to speak of. Probably a big improvement, if anything. Anyway, I hoped he wouldn't develop a really bad attitude about it. Even he would have to agree it was a trifling enough loss compared to my gain. Why, my pasture would be in the best shape it had been in since my grandfather was alive!

Even my brother had to admit that the pasture looked better than it had looked in years. In another two weeks it would look even better, with all the new grass coming up rich and lush and green. You never could tell: the UFO people might find it so inviting that they would even decide to make a landing there. I guess that was my secret hope, but I didn't want to say anything about it right now; everybody knew about the pills I had been taking. We hadn't even heard from the fire marshal yet, and I sure didn't want to push my wife into calling for a sanity hearing.

"Mighty funny thing, a fire is," I told him.

"Just got to keep your eye on it every minute. Never can tell when it might take it into its head to violate all the known laws of physics."

It was a long time after dark before all the firemen left. Or the sheriff and his deputies. Or the rescue squad. But at least the fire marshal did agree to forego the fine—all my brother's doing, I'm sure. At least he could understand that I had never at anytime wanted anything except to practice sound conservation principles and reclaim all that good pastureland we had lost to the swamp.

"Yup. Fire can sure be a mighty funny thing. But it's like I've always contended . . ."

"Yeah," the chief said, "the old ways are allus the best."

10

Little People
with Fur Coats

We would first see him on a morning in early autumn. He would come slogging down through our bottom and make his way along the Big Grassy Fork, always in that purposeful way of his, anxious to relieve his traps of their prey and the prey of its fur—and to fill his pockets with money.

He was already old before I knew him and had been coming to the farm for many years to set his traps. There would always be a paper to sign; it would be the same paper he had brought the year before and the year before that and maybe ever since he had first found our bottom to be a marvelous trapping ground for mink and otter and raccoon. So you would take the paper and try to find a new place to scratch your initials.

Quite a disarming fellow, the trapper was. He had been a biology instructor once, at a small college somewhere in New England and was always very cheerful and articulate as he talked with us about the roles of Man and Nature in the universe.

On the day when he came by to get my signature on his worn-out piece of paper, he would always hang around to talk for awhile. After that, I saw him only when he was out checking his traps. Then I thought no more of him until the next year when he would rap again at the back door and hand me the moldy old piece of paper. I would always sign the release, trying not to worry about all the furry animals he was snaring out of our bottom.

It was from him, in fact, that I first learned of our vast resources in mink. I had always thought of mink as an exotic species found only in the Yukon or in the deep mountain hollows of the Northwest wilderness. Not at all, said he. The Grassy Fork was the home of many a fine specimen, not only of mink but also of many other forms of wildlife that I had perceived as much too exotic for our bottom.

Once, in the night, I had allowed campers to use the farm. About midnight I heard a mad caterwauling out in the pasture: headlamps piercing the dark, loud shouts filling the night as the campers came clambering onto our porch.

"A wildcat," one said.

"A cougar," said another. "They were once native to these parts."

"No," I said. "Just can't imagine that. Not here. Why, we're practically in the city now. The last cougar disappeared in the eighteenth century. Can't imagine what it was you thought you heard."

"Wildcats," the first man said again. "Heard them once in the mountains, and once you hear a sound like that you never forget it." He couldn't stop shaking until I brought him a little shot of whisky. "Must be a whole den of them down there someplace. You sure wouldn't expect to find them this close to the city, but there's still a wilderness area over there next to the railroad. All I know is that once you hear it, you'll never forget that sound."

Later, when the developers began to put up their office buildings across the creek, I began to notice other alien forms of wildlife emerging from the wilderness: gray foxes waiting in the driveway each morning as I started off to work, a deer skirting into the brushwood way down at the end of the pasture, and, at least once, a really big cat, maybe even a cougar, slinking into a huge drainpipe down next to the railroad. Maybe the bulldozers and jackhammers were driving all the wildlife into our part of the bottom and on up into the yard. Next thing you knew, we would have foxes scratching at the back door, wolves lying in wait on snowy nights every time I went out to get an armload of firewood. Yes, and probably wildcats as well, except that they wouldn't have wanted to get anywhere near our Siamese.

I'm not sure when I first began to feel a certain resentment toward the trapper. It must have been about the time that I fell in with some New Age people who had voted for Gary Hartpence and had come to believe in the sacredness of all life and were now worried that my karma would take a terrible beating if I kept letting the trapper come on my land and destroy the unique ecological resources that had made the Grassy Fork one of the last natural habitats for wildlife in this part of the world. I tried to argue that the trapper was actually doing no harm—that he was only snaring the big, cumbersome falling-down kind of mink that didn't have much time left on their clocks anyway. So naturally I kept right on signing the release, and the trapper and I always parted on the best of terms. Still, I felt the resentment building. I just didn't like thinking about it anymore—the idea of him taking away all of our fine mink and otter and enriching himself on the proceeds that came from the sale of their fur, though naturally he always insisted that his was only a marginal existence, at best, and that his work was nothing more than one more small contribution to the preservation of the balance of nature.

Each fall I began nervously to await the ominous coming of the mink killer. He would hand me the paper, and I would sullenly inscribe my initials and try to hide all my resentment behind a big, phony smile. I would see him out looking at his traps. Once I even fell in behind him, at a good distance, and when he was out of sight, I assiduously investigated all the places where I had seen him poking around with his stick. I never found anything.

No traps, no mink. Nothing. I couldn't figure it. How could he camouflage his insidious enterprise so deftly that even I couldn't find the evidence? No matter how often I retraced his steps, I just never could find out where he was setting all those traps.

I would resent him all through the winter, every time I saw him out walking the creek banks, wondering why I couldn't find his ingenious little network of traps, why I never saw him driving off with huge bags of prey. I had gradually come to think of the mink as belonging to the place, an indigenous inhabitant that no man had a right to disturb. I began to run over in my mind how next season, when he came with his little paper, I would break the news to him that he would no longer be able to set up his traps in our bottom.

Still, he was a likable enough fellow. What could be done? With the approach of the autumn day, a Saturday, when he would almost certainly appear at the door, hat in hand, and ask me to sign the release, I began to search ever more frantically for some diplomatic means by which I could run him off the land.

Like a prize fighter preparing for a big bout, I felt that somehow I had to work up a livid hatred for the old man. I had come to think of him as secretly vicious and conspiratorial, and often practiced how I would break the news: "Now look here, old chap, we just can't have it anymore, can we? We really can't. Just take your traps and be gone— gone I say, and be quick about it! Sorry for the inconvenience, old boy, but we just can't allow this sort of desecration to continue unabated." I would go on to explain that as a New Age ecologist and militant agrarian of long standing, I could no longer compromise my higher principles by allowing myself to serve as an accessory to his devilish activities.

The inevitable day came. Along about mid-morning he appeared at the back door and knocked gently, a good old man and very gentle, always careful not to offend. This time he had brought three fresh ears of corn from his garden and a box of candy. I went to the door thinking about how he had explained that he was merely doing his part to promote the balance of nature. Even as I opened the screen and invited him in, I remembered how, some two years earlier, he had mistakenly got the impression that he was no longer to have access to our bottom. I remembered how broken he was, how apologetic, when he called one evening to say he would have his traps out of the bottom by first sun.

I had told him, "No, there's been some misunderstanding, that's all." Certainly he would be allowed to leave his traps as they were. Quite so. Sorry for the inconvenience.

I thought of all that and more as he came in and laid the corn and candy on the coffee table. I was afraid I might weaken. Then I thought of all those mink that had never harmed anybody and him hauling them all away and yanking their fur off, like so many suits of dirty underwear, and making a fortune in the city—the big rich trapper come to town, with his trunk full of mink and otter and raccoon out of our bottom. No, I would not weaken. I would tell him straight out how it was: "Now, look here, old boy, old scout, you're just gonna have to get those traps out of there. And not a minute to waste! Do I make myself plain?"

He sat down and talked for a long while. He went on at great length about how much the recent rains had revived his garden and was only hoping that his corn offering would make a nice little dish for our supper table and that we would enjoy the chocolates. No, it wasn't much, but he did want us to know he had been thinking of us and the big drought of the year before, when our whole garden had dried up, all the grass except for the good rich stand in the bottom. He still sat there. He hadn't taken out the paper yet. He asked instead about a particular book he had spied on my shelf. He said he had the very book and a first edition at that.

"Is that so?"

"Yes. A very old copy."

He asked about my family and about how the writing was going (not very well, I assured him) and about all my plans for the future. Yes, and he was sorry to hear that Gary Hart—or "Hartpence," as he had just learned—was running for president. There'd always been something about that fellow he didn't quite trust. I looked at the trapper, wondering how he had guessed at my own distaste for Hart. Was that why he had brought it up, or was it only a coincidence?

"No," I said, "don't much care for him myself. Something about his eyes, I think. That harsh, fixed smile. Not a fellow you would want to trust with the presidency."

For the first time I realized that I really cared a whole lot less for Hart than I had originally thought. I resented the possibility that I had been influenced too much by my friends of the New Age. I had never thought much about Hart one way or the other until the day I met him at a political rally in Atlanta. I think it was then that I first developed a real disliking for the man. Not only because of the grin, but also because of that phony way he had of imitating Jack Kennedy's mannerisms, a certain irritability that always manifested itself when he found himself in an exchange with political reporters.

Now I realized that my disgust had turned to pure unadulterated hate, so much so that my karma had probably been set back at least a dozen lifetimes. His arrogance, his contempt even for people who were supposed to be his political allies, or at least for those who had professed to be on the side of modern liberalism—which is to say, the press, or "media" as it had come to be known. All this was quite a long time before a couple of reporters from the *Miami Herald* caught him shacked up with a South Carolina beauty queen.

"No," I told the old trapper, "we sure as hell don't want Hart."

I sat there thinking about all the times I had met with the New Age people and realized, with new disgust, that they were all solid for Hart. I also realized that they probably would not invite me to any more of their parties. I had made a terrible mistake at their first *weinprobe* by admitting that I had been turning our bottom over for many years to a mink killer and that I was a little concerned about how to get rid of him. Now, if I were to own up to my true political feelings, I would be of no more use to the society, and my name would be forever stricken from the membership rolls.

Maybe it already was. At a meeting not long after that, a New Ager wearing a linked gold chain that hung almost to his crotch brought up the subject again, looking at me with a mixture of arrogance and disdain, "You still letting that trapper onto your place?"

I explained that he was quite a nice old gentleman and that it was difficult to inform him tactfully that he would simply have to give up his insidious traffic in doomed animals.

"Oh, my goodness, that's simply awful," said a spiffy young brunet who wore a sweater inscribed with the words "ANIMALS ARE LITTLE PEOPLE WITH FUR COATS." She looked at me, her boobs pert and disdainful behind the garish red slogan. "You're still letting that criminal come onto your place and take all those precious little animals to the slaughterhouse? You should be ashamed of yourself. You really should."

"It's the last year. Next year I'm asking him to leave."

The environmental talk had become quite intense. I tried to think of something positive to say about Jesse Jackson. It was no use. The talk had dropped almost to a monotone, little more than a murmur, after I admitted that I had let a whole year go by without doing anything about the trapper.

The brunet, who also did seances and investigated past lives, had been talking about the rise of the Lost Continent of Atlantis, as predicted by our great seer, the immortal "sleeping prophet" Edgar Cayce. Atlantis had not yet risen but was expected at any hour, along with monstrous earthquakes in California, tidal waves, volcanic eruptions, floods, fire, and the discovery of arcane writings that would explain the secrets of the Great Pyramids.

Even with all of his marvelous prophetic gifts, Cayce, who died in 1945, apparently did not foresee the coming of the New Age and its fastidious ways. I believe he would have scorned the whole crowd. Cayce ate as he pleased, smoked cigarettes with abandon, and, for all I know, enjoyed a good stiff drink of moonshine whisky before dinner each evening. (New Agers, at least those I have encountered, drink only wine, under the curious impression that, unlike other spirits, it is a wholesome and natural drink and that, if you can tolerate the headaches, you can consume almost unlimited quantities without suffering any of the usual debilitating effects of alcohol.) Despite his "hedonistic" ways, Cayce was almost wholly responsible for all the great prophecies that govern the ascetic philosophy of the New Agers.

My hostess looked at me, thinking, I suppose, that it was only my little joke, that I would certainly not allow foragers of fur to come onto my land and cart off huge wagonloads of lovely, young animals that had no way of defending themselves. She had just come back from filling her glass with a very dry and tasty Chardonnay. She rested her elbow in her hand and gazed at me with new intensity.

"You know what we say, don't you?"

"What?"

For an answer, she drew her hand across her breasts and the garish slogan. "Yes, we really do like to think of them that way. Animals, I mean—as little people with fur coats. We like to think of it as a really neat way of getting our message across. We will soon be getting in a whole shipment of bumper stickers, license tags, and other pertinent materials making the same point."

"Very apt," I said, feeling a little embarrassed. More than just a little embarrassed, to tell you the truth. "Quite to the point."

"It's our way of trying to get across the terrible crimes being committed against the environment. We have already received a few samples of the license tags. Have you seen them? They are really neat. Would you like to borrow one until the shipment comes in? Maybe it would help your trapper friend get the point."

She turned abruptly and left the room. I made for the Chardonnay and poured a double portion. By the time I turned around, the girl was already beside me, holding one of the new tags. *Animals are little people with fur coats*, I read to myself.

"Why don't you take this one, at least temporarily? I just happened to have an extra."

"You put it on your car?"

"Oh, yes. We all plan to do so. I think, really, that it's the neatest idea. We think the bumper stickers will go over really well. We plan to hand them out at all the shopping centers. I don't think there is any question but that members of the general public have grown much more environmentally conscious. All that's lacking is a way for them to express themselves effectively."

I felt a little faint and again a horrible flush of embarrassment stinging me all up and down inside my clothes. I just hoped it wouldn't show. I looked deep into my glass of wine and tried to think of a way to change the subject. A fringe of sweat had broken out on my forehead, and I felt that I simply had to scratch myself from top to bottom all at once. Not long before, I had seen a car with one of the idiotic slogans plastered to its rear bumper. I hadn't given it a whole lot of thought at the time, other than to sneer quietly at it as just one more sign that the New Liberalism had utterly taken leave of its senses.

Now I began to wonder, despite all the embarrassment, if I had it all wrong. The New Agers were only practicing a kind of "neo-agrarianism" that I had once preached with much self-righteousness in newspaper editorials and had even attempted to practice, after a fashion, on my own land. Somehow, though, it just wasn't the same. The same slogan that had only slightly embarrassed and irritated me the first time I saw it embarrassed me all the more now that I was hearing it spoken aloud. I even heard myself speaking the words, as though from a great distance. I kept looking at the girl's breasts, wondering if she'd had them pumped full of silicone. Except that that would have been altogether contrary to her environmental philosophy. I supposed it was all right to stare because of the slogan. Still, it was a little hard to imagine that somebody would actually walk around in a sweater like that.

Was she secretly trying to draw attention to her lovely body? I wiped my brow of sweat, but all that itching just plain wouldn't stop. I was trying to take it all in, realizing that, for all my embarrassment, the "really neat" slogan had now become an aphorism for all New Agers to swear by. I would have to plan to be out of town on assignment when they called a meeting to start passing out bumper stickers.

Tree huggers. That's what we call them now. Was this indeed the ideological stomping ground where the New Liberalism crossed paths with pre-industrial conservative thought? I held the bumper tag at my side, hoping I would remember to get rid of it before going home.

"Well, we've been needing something like this for a long time," I said, embarrassed again, this time at my own monstrous hypocrisy.

I have to confess that I had begun to feel a little ambiguous about the New Age people even before they had made an issue out of my friendship for the mink killer. I guess I'd heard them speak once too often about the New Liberalism and the growing "feel good" movement of the late eighties. On this night it was different; I felt a great sense of relief when the conversation turned to all the old familiar themes—and then immediately found myself in new difficulties when the question arose as to whether all men were potential rapists.

"I guess that would include Hartpence," I said.

Again the nasty stares, the sudden coldness, as though our hostess had called upon unseen spirits to witness my ridiculous apostasy. I knew it was a mistake to say anything. Always before I had fallen silent during such discussions. I personally would have found it impossible to rape anyone, not because it was against my inclination so much as because I knew I would never be able to concentrate properly and would be certain to make a shameful botch of the whole affair. And then get thrown in jail for a crime I was not even able to commit.

I took a good long look at the room, at all the plush Victorian surroundings, and wondered if it was my last night there. I decided just to keep my mouth shut. The only safe policy with those kind of people. If I couldn't think of anything constructive to say about Jesse Jackson, I would at least try to avoid saying anything detrimental about Hartpence: I hadn't completely decided whether I was ready to be kicked out of their society. One more nasty word about Hart, and they almost surely would decide the issue for me. They would be unable to conceive of my dislike for a politician who, above all others, would support sweeping constitutional safeguards for unprotected wildlife. In the end my resolve gave way.

"I've heard some pretty unsavory stuff about this Hart."

A gruff and expectant silence fell about the room.

"You don't care for Hart, do you?" said one, siphoning off the last of his Cabernet Sauvignon. "As a newsman, you get around a lot. Maybe you could tell us your side of it."

"Well, for one thing, I understand him to have said that all women were potential sluts."

It was all a lie. Maybe I hoped they would take it as a joke. Maybe I wasn't sure how they would take it. Maybe I only wanted to get a laugh and had forgotten that, almost without exception, the people of the New Age have little sense of humor. That's a little funny in itself. Maybe it's never occurred to them that their hero, Cayce, had an excellent sense of humor.

Cayce took life as it came. He cared little for politics and no doubt would have been greatly puzzled—and almost certainly a little amused—at the sensitivity of most New Agers toward the liberal issues of our day. What would he have made of the bitter and often frenzied outcry of environmental extremists, of subversive condom-pushers and bloody minded abortionists, of big government zealots, of one-worlders, multiculturalists, neo-interventionists, and frantic espousers of political correctness? What would he have made of Hart or Ted Kennedy, who I am now told is stalked night and day by the ghost of Mary Jo Kopechne?

Old Cayce did not believe in a perfect world. As a reincarnationist, he probably believed in, or at least accepted, a very imperfect world, a place where a man or woman with bad karma could always come back and get himself straightened out in his own good time. The way he looked at it, the spirit world never gave up on anybody, not the most bloodthirsty desperado, not the most insensitive wife-beater, not the most depraved pedophile, not even on people who believe that killing is a very healthy thing when done in the name of abortion-on-demand. It presumes a lot, of course, for anyone to say for sure what Cayce's political beliefs might have been. Or whether he even believed half of what he foretold in the name of "prophecy." He gave all of his famous "readings" while in a deep trance and never had the faintest idea of what he had said until he woke up and read his transcripts.

"I'm not sure what to make of all this," he once told a close follower who had benefitted from one of his cures. "I just hope that something good will come of it someday."

You just have to believe that a guy like that would have got a real big laugh out of some of the ideologies now being put forth in his name.

Anyway, I got out of there without finishing my wine and never did go back to any New Age meetings and conscientiously burned the bumper strips that began to come in the mail.

Now, sitting in my den and listening to the old trapper, I was surprised to learn that he shared my feelings about politics and that he was much given to reading books I had scarcely heard of: Cicero, Tacitus, the Younger Pliny. It was a little embarrassing. I promised myself I could no longer put off fulfilling my vow to finish the last volume of Gibbon. I kept wondering if I was truly a committed agrarian after all. All I knew for sure was that I would not allow myself to get caught up in any more of those New Age parties.

The trapper, in short, was making it awfully difficult for me to keep up those intense feelings of anger and disgust I had reserved for him and his kind. Why was I letting the old guy control the direction of the conversation? Just because he had brought three ears of corn and a box of candy and felt terribly hurt about last year's drought? I could not allow his wheedling tone to throw me off. Not this time. And, oh yes, what of that card in my wallet and its Old English wording? *"People for the Agrarian Way. Lifetime member."*

The one thing I probably shared with Gary Hart: a charter membership in the *People for the Agrarian Way*. Goddammit. I bristled inwardly as I prepared to tell the old fellow to remove his traps and that I was very sorry but I would not be able to sign his paper this year. None of his business to be sounding off against Hartpence anyway.

Get off this land and stay off, do you hear me, old man? Do you hear me?

I would put it much more diplomatically, of course. I asked myself again why after all this time I had never seen any of those mink in our bottom. Was it all a ruse of some kind? All I'd ever found were copperheads and, sometimes, now that industry was ravaging our forests, an occasional pack of gray foxes, raccoons, and such. Otters? Cougars? In our own bottom? Surely he must be mistaken. Why, we had seined the creek for years in my younger days and had never seen the first sign of a mink or otter. Maybe I resented that in him too—his ability to ferret the secret wildlife out of our bottom and claim it as his own only because I had signed a ridiculous piece of paper. There just wasn't any way around it. I would simply have to tell him to get off the land and stay off.

You hear me, old man? You better hear me good now!

I would explain that I had gone along with him all these years because—well, he had been coming there and setting his traps long before my wife and I had returned from Yankeedom and he had always been very kind and decent about everything, but that now, well, on the whole, it would probably be best for us to make other arrangements before the Sierra Club and the People for the Agrarian Way found out about my apostasy and made a *cause celebre* out of it. Surely he could not argue with that. The country was getting so built up that he couldn't depend on much of a yield, anyway. I hoped that we would even be able to shake hands and remain friends and that he would still come by sometimes to talk about the balance of nature and how the country would be doomed to an era of total anarchy if ever we were to let these feminists and New Age people gain control of the White House.

At last he fumbled around in his jacket and brought out the release. The same piece of paper he'd had these five years past, crumbled and brown and stained with sweat from where he had been carrying it in his coat pocket all that time, and where in god's name would I find another place to scratch my initials? I was preparing to give him the bad news when he abruptly informed me, for no apparent reason, that he had once read Herodotus in the original. Not long before, I had been overcome simply trying to read him in translation. Now, here was a fellow who had read all that mass of material in the original? How could I bring myself to treat him so cavalierly?

"That must have been quite a job."

"Well, there was a time when I was very good with Greek. Not so much now, I'm afraid. You get rusty, you know, unless you keep after that sort of thing."

I looked at him as he brought out the paper, exactly as he had all those other times. I thought about all those other years, how he always brought it out and spent a few minutes more each time looking for a place for me to sign, whereupon I dutifully scratched my initials and the date on some forlorn spot of the ragged paper. Then we would go on talking for awhile, all very congenially, until he rose to take his leave—and in so friendly a fashion that it was really hard to go on thinking of him as an unfeeling mink killer.

I took the release. It would be different this time. I was still working myself up to explain that we didn't need him anymore. Perhaps I could simply inform him that we were preparing to re-seed the bottom and would undoubtedly interfere with his traps. But he would have an answer for that. He had an answer for everything. Just like all professors.

I initialed the release and put the new date on it. He seemed most gratified. I cleared my throat and said, as though discussing the politics of a foreign country, "Some of my friends—you know how these environmentalists are—wanted to make a big thing out of it. That's right. Thought it might be best that we give up trapping all these mink, so to speak. But I assured them that you were only taking the old mink that were ready for the grave anyway."

He laughed an enormous, slightly maniacal laugh that was a little unnerving. No, he said. Not so at all. The very young mink as well. Yes, indeed. "Young, old, in-between, quite a crop of them, my lad." Then he went on to say something about all the money he had made from the fur of the young mink, of which we appeared to have an unusual abundance, and how grateful he was that I was allowing him to continue as before.

"Think nothing of it."

"I do want you to understand that I am most grateful."

"Quite all right. Quite."

He turned with a tilt of his hat and went off through the yard, turning once more to explain that he had picked the corn that very morning and that it would be much more palatable if we were to eat it while it was still fresh.

"Yes, by all means. Do enjoy the corn."

"Oh, yes indeed. Never fear. I'll have it turned into liquid by nightfall."

I watched him as he went on up the drive and thrust the release in his pocket, wondering how he managed to hold on to such a scroungy looking piece of paper year after year. I realized I would have to wait another twelve months before flat-out running him off the place: *Listen, old fellow, I've been mighty patient with you. But you're just gonna have to get those traps outa there in a powerful big hurry. No more dilly-dallying now. We've had quite enough of this nonsense . . .*

But how could you talk like that to a man who had read Herodotus in the original? Was it possible that he had read Xenophon as well. Thucydides?

Mary Ellen came up behind me. "I'm glad you didn't refuse to sign. It would have hurt his feelings terribly."

"Think about all those mink down there. We once had a great idea of saving the land and making agrarianism a reality instead of just something to talk about at lofty seminars."

"Do you think there are really any mink down there?"

"Why, he says he's making a fortune off the fur."

"I wonder."

"Well, I suppose he hasn't actually said that. He couldn't afford to let us know the whole truth. He might be afraid that we'd want to take over the operation ourselves. I wouldn't be at all surprised if he is making quite a bundle despite his insistence that he's in it only as a hobby."

"Well, he's old and lonesome and obviously wants friends. Maybe he really is doing it for that reason and doesn't want anybody to know that there isn't really anything in those traps. I've seen him down there dozens of times, going and coming, and I've yet to see him leave with anything that looked like a mink. Or like anything else."

"You mean he's always empty-handed?"

"Every time I've seen him."

"Well, nothing ever goes the way you plan it."

"What do you mean?"

"I mean, if I couldn't run him off, if you weren't going to let me run him off, I thought we might at least have a right to share in the proceeds."

"Don't be silly. You know there isn't that much in it."

"Well, there's too much work in it, tramping through all that ice and snow, for him just to be doing it for nothing. If we can't get rid of him, the very least we might expect is a decent percentage of the receipts. Twenty or thirty percent ought to be about right."

"How high-minded of you! I'm sure your environmentalist friends would like to know how cheaply you would sell out. Anyway, he's an old man, and I still say its nothing but a hobby for him and I really don't think he's getting anything out of it at all. I doubt that you'll have to worry about him for too many more years. I feel really sorry for him in a way. Sometimes, I wish he could really strike it rich in mink."

"I'd be laughed right out of the Sierra Club."

"Who cares? All they want is your dues. I just think we ought to leave the old fellow in peace. Why, I'll bet it's been twenty years since he got a mink out of that bottom. I think he's only living out all the dreams of his youth."

"Maybe you're right. I guess I just hadn't thought of it like that. Did you know that he once read all of Herodotus in the original?"

11

The New
Patriarchs

I'm not sure when I first realized the trapper was not coming back. It must have been some time in the fall of 1988 or 1989. All I remember is that the cold weather was suddenly upon us and that he had not come around with his little paper for me to sign. Had he somehow guessed that we no longer wanted him on the property? Had he heard talk? Perhaps he was ill. Maybe he had even died. I could not find out because, as it happened, I had forgotten his name, if indeed I had ever known it at all. I guess it was instinct or something; but whatever the reason, I knew I would not be seeing him again; and I guess I must have realized something else at just about the same time: that in all the years the trapper had been coming to the farm to get his little paper signed we had been losing something infinitely more valuable than any small game he might have been taking from our bottom.

Or maybe I had known it a long time before that. I first saw our way of life coming to an end one July afternoon when I went out to weed my sickly patch of vegetables. I had just made a couple of rounds with my tiller and had paused to survey, a mite sadly, what was left of my once-proud vineyard when two men came into the yard. I swung the tiller around and saw them standing down at the other end of the garden, holding their charts and maps and all the other ominous blueprints of our destruction.

One stood with his sleeves rolled up, bent forward slightly, sweating in the hot sun, a lean balding fellow with a kind of intensity born more of inner fires than the heat of the July afternoon. The other was fat, not sweating at all, even though he was got up majestically in black tie and freshly pressed suit. He stood a little back of the other, as though he were not quite real, like a prop from some old vaudeville show. Or as though he had been dragged in from a wax museum for nothing more than decoration . . . except he wasn't sweating the way wax would have sweated. Real or not, I knew—again, I suppose, by instinct—that he was there for some genuinely evil purpose.

Maybe it didn't hit me all at once, but on some level I must have realized that the best we had known of this life was gone forever. I saw everything in an instant and knew I was finished—me, the land, the whole tradition of the land, everything—before I had taken half a step behind the tiller down the long corn row.

I couldn't help asking myself what old Jacobus, my great-grandfather, the stormy giant of a man who drank and fought like a demon and never allowed even his friends to call him by his German name, would have had to say to these characters. I wondered what those old Moravian settlers would have said. I thought about all the Indian tribes that had roamed the creek bottom, burning off trees and brush so as to drive the deer and other small game into ever smaller patches of undergrowth, setting them up for an easy kill. I thought of all the other men who in the two centuries since then had worked or grazed the land, the good lush bottom that seemed almost to welcome the coming of the railroad back in 1893. Way back then, no one could possibly have guessed that the great event was merely the first hideous and portentous symptom in a long, drawn-out death, which finally caught up with me on a hot July afternoon in the late 1980s.

I thought about all that and a lot more as I walked across the garden to shake hands with the two men and listen to their slick presentation of how they were planning to destroy not the bottom exactly, but all the land for miles around it. They actually were somewhat critical of the bottom, not wanting to buy it at any price. I did not realize until later that I had been roundly insulted.

"Lies too low for doing any kind of building on it," said the skinny, intense fellow.

"Not for sale anyhow," I said, adopting a self-righteous tone.

He kept wanting to explain all the details, where everything was going—the new factories, the shopping centers, the apartments, the warehouses.

"What warehouses?

"Why, the warehouses I been telling you about. They're gonna be built right across the bottom yonder, just beyond the railroad. Won't encroach on you one little bit. Why, you'll hardly even know they're there. That's right. Gonna all be built of the very latest in vinyl and baked-on metal. A real cool green in color. Yessir, the very latest thing—made to blend right into the landscape. Why, it won't be no time a-tall before you won't even know they're there."

I hadn't even started listening to him yet. I guess I was hearing him, all right. It was just that I didn't want to take it in. I was still trying to hold on to the thought that the two men were merely phantoms from outer space if not from the wax museum and would both soon vaporize or melt and be gone from my life forever. I looked up the hill with my hands still on the tiller and saw over the top of the corn rows the high grassed-over hillside that was once to have been the site of the vineyards that would produce my fine Grassy Fork Whites and Grassy Fork Reds. Now there were to be no fine wines. Maybe before long, there would be no Grassy Fork either.

"What goddamn warehouses?" I asked him again.

He looked at me a little strangely. "Well, like I was saying, they'll be built right across the stream yonder. Just across your bottom where the land rises. Across the railroad just over yonder."

"You mean you came all the way out here just to tell me you're gonna build warehouses up there?"

The vaudeville nude—I knew I had seen someone who looked exactly like him in a comedy routine somewhere—shrank back as I moved toward them. Old Jacobus had been one of the finest eye-gougers in the county, and I wondered if I had inherited any of his skill. I wondered if it would all come out now as I moved in for the attack. I could readily imagine the two of them bloody and groaning on the hot wiry grass, charts and maps strewn from here to yonder and no more silly blasphemous talk of warehouses either.

The fat man still didn't say anything. He just stood there looking me over. I later realized that he was the important one, the man with the cash, the most feared man in our county, it was said, because he was something of a parvenu, unafraid to use his wealth in ruthless ways if necessary, not like the old tobacco families whose paternal instincts were still strong.

"Warehouses," I said, incredulously. "The bottom will be worth nothing after that. The land will be worth nothing. Nothing will be worth anything except for more and more of this rotten development."

The fat man stood there, still not sweating, not smiling, not even showing his teeth. The other began unrolling his charts and maps to explain in that smoothly beguiling way of his that them there warehouses won't hurt you one tiny little bit.

"Like I was telling you, we got this new green vinyl material that'll blend right into the natural environment. Believe me, it's the very latest thing. State of the art. Be mighty proud to have one of them on my street."

The fat man with all the money (although I didn't know that yet) still stood there not sweating, not saying anything. But I knew now that he was real enough. Wax wouldn't have lasted any time at all in that sun. He just kept looking at me, his bland, somber expression hiding every dastardly thought in his head.

I just stood there holding my tiller and staring him down. Only gradually had it come to me who he was. He and his brother were partners in a giant corporate scheme to transform the rolling countryside north of the city into a land of asphalt and executive office parks—and warehouses. They liked to think of themselves as self-made men, and I guess they were. They had started out building cheap houses back during the boom times of the late fifties and early sixties, learned how to build fast to meet a growing demand, and had hit it big. Now, tired of enriching themselves from housing developments, they had turned their attention to more important projects.

They were really big now. The elder served on the State Highway Commission and had got roads built at the right time into all the right places. Sometimes into a lot of low swampy places where no one had thought a road rightly ought to go. But that was only after he had bought the swamps at giveaway prices and drained off all the water. They had already built the first phase of a massive executive park out along the new University Parkway, across the ridge and out of sight of our farm, over beyond the textile mill that years ago had represented the first deadly urban intrusion into our part of the county—if you didn't count the railroad.

I had always hated the mill. I remembered it as the site of the county farm, a complex of white silos and farm buildings where, as a boy of eight or nine, I had once gone to watch the farm agents breed their bulls.

The fat man spoke for the first time, "You see, the mill can't afford to hold this land any longer now that the city has taken it in. They had no choice but to develop it. But you will see that it will be a good, clean, honest development and nothing for anybody to be in the slightest degree ashamed of."

Warehouses, I thought. *Listen, you son of a bitch, you take your goddamn warehouses and . . .*

I didn't say anything. What was the use? I must have known even before I was conscious of it that everything was finished, my future and the future of the land writ large in whatever was printed on all those charts he was holding. I stood looking at the parvenu, hating him more than ever now that he had spoken and seemed pleasant. I stared at him for a good long moment and then back at the other.

"What goddamn warehouses?" I snarled.

The man with the charts looked at me and then at his boss. I knew what he was thinking: *This guy don't look retarded. What the hell we got ourselves into here?* He patiently explained it all again, just as before, putting a lot of emphasis on the "brand spanking new building technology" that would allow them to build a "warehouse park" in perfect harmony with the landscape.

First, though, they would need my cooperation.

"How's that?"

I would need to sign this little paper—why, he had it somewhere right here. Except he did not have it. The fat man had it. He moved for the first time, whisking the paper that awaited my signature out of his inside coat pocket and, not wanting to be too obtrusive, holding it against his chest until the other had finished his explanation.

"Yup," said the skinny devil. All they needed was for me "to sign this little paper here" so they could pay for the new water line the city would be running in front of my property. Otherwise I would be liable for the charge myself.

"What goddamn warehouses!"

The skinny chap looked at me again—really looked at me for the first time, a new light in his eyes. I guess he thought he had finally caught on. *Now ain't that just our luck. We come all the way out here and run into the family idiot. I guess every family has one. Their looks'll sure fool you sometimes. Looks as bright as the next feller, don't he? But I reckon we're just wasting our time out here talking to him.*

I watched as they began to turn away. "Guess you guys won't be happy until you've paved over every square inch of the damn county. Don't reckon it matters none. Figured I'd have to sell it anyhow one of these days, probably for a golf course, so I can send my grandson to Harvard."

The fat man who, by all accounts, was the most feared entrepreneur in the county turned and looked at me again. "We believe our work has met the very highest standards in every respect."

"I reckon we're all environmentalists."

"I can assure you that we are."

"No bloody runoffs into the bottom, no drainage ditches choked with mud—and, of course, you *are* going to run everything off into our bottom, aren't you?"

"Under state law we are allowed—required—to run all water onto the lower ground."

"My fucking bottom. That's it, isn't it? Just like the Highway Commission. Just like all those other developers over there on the other side of the ridge."

"We had hoped there wouldn't be a problem. We thought we had gone the extra mile by agreeing to pay for the entire installation of the water line without throwing this burden on the property owners."

"Anybody else sign that little paper?"

"Everyone. I believe you are the last. You are the largest property owner and, of course, would be more liable than the others. We had thought . . ."

"Gotta talk to my lawyers," I said, still glaring at him from the tiller, knowing I wouldn't get any more plowing done today.

"As you wish," said the fat man, sticking the paper into his pocket.

I knew it was all over, even before my wife started lecturing me on my despicable manners, explaining that "we might as well go ahead and sign and be done with it because we'd just make ourselves look ridiculous otherwise."

I knew as well as she that you couldn't fight them. She didn't have to tell me that.

A failed chairman of the City Redevelopment Commission, now

working for the patriarchs, came the next day. "How're you good folks today?" He sat in our parlor and ate our cookies and drank our coffee and explained that this new venture of the patriarchs was absolutely overflowing with environmental covenants and safeguards and that when I saw the results, I would kick myself for not having written editorials in support of this kind of far-seeing development.

"Yeah, a nice shiny vinyl, I'm told. Blend right in with the landscape."

We knew we would have to sign. He probably knew it as well. Not because of the entrepreneurs so much as because all the people at church and everyone else who had already signed would think ill of us if we did not. They already thought of me as the village atheist. Now, if I refused to sign, they would probably start to think of me the way they had once thought of witchy Sweet Adeline Furchess, the community "healer" who needed to be strung up for her own protection and for the good name of the community. I could imagine what they were saying. "Sho' do take after his old grandpapa, don't he? Why, they tell me he don't do nothin' 'cept sit down thar in that big house of his'n and swig corn liquor the whole day long." Some chance I'd have of ever getting *my* name in one of their stained-glass windows. As soon as we had signed the papers, the failed redevelopment chairman was out telling everybody in the community that I was a thoroughly discredited jackass with whom it was impossible to talk seriously and who would not cooperate in any way whatsoever with men who only wanted what was best for the community.

It had been no more than three months since the two men from the wax museum appeared at the end of my garden. Not even three months and, already, the first warehouse was taking shape, its steel beams casting a harsh glitter of sun all across the countryside. I first noticed it after a sleepless night of wandering from my bed to my word processor.

Each morning, now, I look out and see it looming ever more ominously on the horizon. Below me, the yard falls away dew-sprinkled toward the Big Grassy Fork, giving onto the railroad and onto the high-rising ground where Angus cattle once grazed. All of that was a very long time ago, a long time before the city came, a long time before the warehouses.

Now the city had come to stay. I felt certain that the warehouse was not there when I last turned out the lights. It seemed to have appeared like some monstrous glittering toadstool fed by the cool dews of the morning.

Ah, if only it were to fade as quickly as the sun swung on toward the zenith!

Yet you know it is there all right and you certainly know that it will not be the last. There would come a second and third, perhaps even a fourth, each larger than its predecessor, spreading across the whole crest of the hill where the county farm once stood and where, before that, some of the first settlers built their homes and barns and granaries.

Below the warehouses, the swamp I had almost reclaimed after years of work again threatened to take over the whole lower third of the bottom. The patriarchs had behaved legally and properly and responsibly, just as they promised, by dumping all the water from their gutters and outfalls onto our property. Just like the Highway Commission.

How long before we would ever have a stand of grass over that part of the bottom? Now there is only the swamp, with scrub willows and sassafras and all sorts of weed trees beginning to sprout along the ditch line. Even a good wildfire probably couldn't save us now. Perhaps the swamp would bring back the mink and the muskrats, perhaps even the trapper, whom we hadn't seen for more than three or four years. I felt certain that he left hating us for our secret plot to drive him off the land. How large and grotesque would the swamp finally get to be? Perhaps it would spread all up and down the bottom, all the way up to Rural Hall, five or six miles to the north, and become, in time, another Great Dismal. So even if the patriarchs were well on the way to destroying our bottom, I guess you have to look at it in a larger sense—one thing balanced against the other, warehouses and office parks in exchange for the return of a great wilderness area of the sort unknown since the time of the Tuscarora and Cherokee.

In the end perhaps all the wildlife would come back, not just the mink and otter, but also the black bear and the panther and cougar and wildcat, the gray foxes and finally the wolves that would come up into the yard at night and kill what was left of our cattle—and maybe even the Siamese cat.

Ah, yes. Perhaps I had been in too great a haste to condemn the New Patriarchs. One cannot in good conscience fail to salute those who bring wealth and progress to the community. I have therefore settled on a policy of nonviolent passive resistance, not with any hope of forcing the developers to the bargaining table but only in a spirit of wholesale capitulation. I have decided to light a bonfire in the bottom, like the druids of old, like Muck Olla on the eve of the great festival of Halloween, to celebrate the coming of the warehouses and the new prosperity of which they are the most conspicuous symbol.

Truth is, I am only acting in the oldest and most venerable of traditions. I now realize that I have acted meanly throughout the whole affair and have behaved with insolence toward my superiors—men who only wanted what was best for my land. My initial reaction, I'm sure, was not unlike that of the ancient Romans when Alaric and his Gothic hordes appeared before the gates of their city. "The first emotions of the nobles," Gibbon tells us, "were those of surprise and indignation, that a vile barbarian should dare to insult the capital of the world; but their arrogance was soon humbled by misfortune; and their unmanly rage, instead of being directed against an enemy in arms, was meanly exercised on a defenseless victim."

While those old Romans were trying to appease their gods by choking to death a princess and rumored adulteress, Alaric walked in and took over the city.

Men and women far less civilized than the ancient Romans have known how to deal more realistically with such tragedies. Often we find that the masses have acted far more civilly at such times. The Israelites dancing naked before the groves of Diana and Astarte and the great god Baal even as the Babylonians came to march them away into captivity. The people of Belgium dancing and singing on the eve of Waterloo. Richmonders drinking to the glory of the Confederacy even after all the liquor had run out and the Yankees were banging at the door.

In the same spirit, I have decided to light bonfires to honor the destroyers of our bucolic civilization rather than to plant dynamite beneath the foundations of their new buildings, as I originally intended. Naturally the builders have ignored my R.S.V.P. How could I have known that even as I was sending out the invitations, my own neighbors, men and women I had known and trusted all my life, had devised an even worse fate for our land?

Ah, but it was true. I, myself, had been brought in on their little game without realizing I was throwing away the last hope for a good life among the warehouses. Their idea was simply this: Since the whole countryside had been taken over by developers anyway, why not put our own land up for sale and at least gain some of the profits of our own devastation?

"Well, why not?" I said with a heavy guilt and great reluctance.

"If you say so," Mary Ellen added, with even more reluctance.

Now that the city was all around us, no one had anything to gain by continuing to fight. What good was any of it anymore? You sure couldn't fight the kind of money the barbaric patriarchs were throwing around.

"It will never be the same after they put that road through our bottom," Mary Ellen said. "I'm surprised that you, of all people, are going along with them."

"Weren't you the one who decreed that we really had no choice? Besides, they're my friends. How can I deny them access? That's all they're asking, only enough land for an access road. Anyway, you were the one who insisted that it was foolish to try and hold out against them. I suppose you were right. Nothing is the same anymore. Every time you look out the window you see a new warehouse going up. No wonder the trapper never came back. I guess he knew something we didn't."

"We can't do anything about the warehouses, but we can at least do something about our own bottom."

"Why, the city already has sewer and water easements running all over the place. They say you can't do anything with it, that it's all flood-plain. But that doesn't stop them from putting the easements in."

The neighbors finally won her over with a promise of almost half a million dollars for a mere three-hundred-foot right-of-way. I knew her real estate experience would eventually pay off for us in a big way. Our advantage wasn't that we had access; it was that we had the *only* access. Meantime, we would lose only about four or five acres. Once we had signed the pact, all sorts of fraudulent salesmen and zoning experts came in. We went before the planning board. The board threw us out, mainly, I suppose, because nobody had the kind of money it would take to buy off the members.

"Get out of here and develop a better plan," the chairman said. "There'll be a lot of opposition to this kind of development out there."

I argued that nobody protested when the patriarchs came in with their warehouses and office complexes. Why deny us the same right? The chairman banged down his gavel and nodded ominously toward the bailiffs, or whoever they had hired to keep order.

We left and spent many a night talking over a new plan. We hired more experts. Landscape architects. Lawyers. There were murmurs of dissension as the biggest and richest family in the enterprise sought to gain the ascendancy. Being president or vice president of our Bethania Station Development Association suddenly seemed more important than The Plan itself. We eventually got it all put together, after spending untold thousands in the process, despite growing feelings of ill will among members of the association.

Back we went before the planning board, which approved our proposal on condition that we agree to a public hearing.

"Lots of opposition to this kind of development out there," the chairman said.

We held the public hearing and found ourselves cursed by other men and women long thought to be our friends. The planning board, meanwhile, had called in its own zoning experts, who took one look at our property and decided that we would need three or four acres of landscape "berms" to muffle the sound of the big trucks. More land gone without any promise of more money—and it was all coming out of our bottom.

Anyway, now we were able to talk at last to developers about bringing in a new office complex. No eyesores. No unsightly warehouses. Everything properly landscaped, and very little noise. All kinds of setbacks and building restrictions. Everything would smell just like new mown grass and fresh air. We got nowhere. The would-be developers brought in by the people now running our association would take their proposals down to city hall and run into all kinds of obstacles. No explaining it, but for whatever reason something always got in the way.

Each developer would give up, in his turn, but there would soon be another to take his place. The new man was always full of confidence: just let him have a talk with those folks down at the planning department. No doubt in his mind that he could talk them into supporting our project! Eventually, back he would come, shaking his head like all the others and echoing the same old theme: "This town is never going anywhere. No imagination. No vision."

I had long known, of course, without caring much about it, that the people in the zoning office did not give a hang about "building up the town." All they really cared about were their rules and regulations. Why, I knew from my own experience that it was a regular chamber of horrors down there. You would answer one objection and then run smack into another. All they really cared about was the development of their artistic skills—drawing neat little lines on their maps and coloring them in with nice fancy colors and hanging them on the wall as a signal to visitors that they had better be prepared to deal with people "who sure as hell knew what they were talking about."

As I say, I had been down there often enough to see it all for myself. All the neatly diagramed charts and maps. All the reasons why you couldn't do this, that, or the other. Why did the rules seem never to apply to the new patriarchs? Something funny about all that. You go out and walk through the bottom and see the monstrous new clusters of office buildings looking down at you and then go hat-in-hand before the zoning board and listen as some joker explains why all the good land lying along the Grassy Fork is next to worthless.

"Well, it's some of the finest land in this whole part of the world," I said during one of our visits, "and yet you say we can't stop all the big millionaires from dumping their stump-water on us? That we can't even provide access to adjoining property owners?"

I knew the true worth of the land, because I knew that that was why the German Moravian settlers had chosen it in the first place.

This meant nothing to the zoning flack, who muttered something to the effect that after more than two hundred years maybe "we were finally getting our priorities in order."

I almost had him by the knot of his tie, ready to drag him over the counter, when my wife pulled me back. "I didn't come all the way down here to spend the night trying to get you out of jail."

The fellow gave a haughty sniff and shifted some papers around, explaining that he could not recommend a road through our bottom as "an economically sound expense for the city" and that "maybe the developers will need to understand all that before laying out good money for the land."

A last gratuitous insult to one who hadn't wanted the road there at all, who out of his unfailingly generous and winning disposition had decided to go along with this nonsense merely as a favor to his neighbors. The agent irritably tapped his pencil on one of his newly drawn charts, an invitation for me to get the hell out of there and never come back.

"The problem is this particular approach. It just lies too low."

"We offered you three or four different approaches," I told him. "You didn't like any of them."

"Look, fella, I'm telling you that what you really need is a new access."

"I don't care where they put the access. We get paid anyway, goddammit!"

We were in England and on the Continent for almost two months after that, and when we came back in late May, we found that everything had changed and that the dirty work was now far advanced. New men in charge, a new real estate agent brought into the deal without any consultation from our side. The biggest and richest family, and also the most landlocked and, therefore, the most helpless without our access, had purposely worked it all out before we had a chance to come back and complain. A *fait accompli* in the most exact sense, and I hadn't had to go all the way to France to find out how to describe what had been done to us.

We had never even heard of the new man the pact had agreed to hire—assuming, of course, that we would go along. We soon found him to be the most subtle of the lot. He had once worked for the city and knew his way around the labyrinth of rules and regulations.

"I really hate this," Mary Ellen said. "You know I've always hated it."

"Dunno. There's something about the whole thing that smells."

I didn't realize how close to the truth I was until the next meeting. It smelled all right, and not merely as a figure of speech. Still, it would be a welcome hunk of cash if he could make the sale. Taxes had got to be a real problem.

What we heard at first sounded like good news. The agent, taking a good long look around the room, informed us that he had lined up a prospective buyer. A murmur of excitement ran through the crowd. I could see from the eyes of the representatives of the biggest and richest family that they already knew who it was.

"The city," he said.

The city? What would the city want with it?

"Why, they're the very ones who have been standing in our way all these years," I said.

Even as I said it, I had guessed the worse. Of course, the city and its planners had stood in the way, wanting to make sure nobody else got their hands on it before the time came when they could take it over for their own iniquitous purposes.

"Well," the agent said, worriedly, "I know it isn't what a lot of you want to hear, but the city wants to expand the landfill."

"A landfill!" I said. "Did you say 'landfill'?"

"Just hear me out."

"The landfill is way the hell and gone out beyond everything," I said. "Now they want to bring it into the city. That's what they've had in mind all along, isn't it?"

After a prolonged pause, he went on to explain that the city had done its own appraisal and that the land wasn't worth anything like what we had anticipated.

"How much?"

"Only seventy-five hundred dollars an acre."

"My good man," I said, in the snottiest, most patronizing tone I could muster, "even you must know that we started off asking twenty, and not a soul who ever looked at that land didn't doubt that it was worth every penny."

The agent looked at me ingratiatingly, indulgently. A former employee of the city planning department turns real estate agent and suddenly whips up a deal like this? I looked around at my neighbors. They had been in on it from the start. As I said, it was all in their eyes.

The agent explained that he had not yet got around to "the really good news."

Everybody looked at him with growing scorn, everybody except all my one-time friends who had been a party to the affair. Hell, they had an estate to settle. Let them get what they could and get out. That's the way they looked at it. They would all prosper, no matter what the final figure.

"The city is willing to pay thirteen thousand an acre," the agent said. "Now think about that for a moment. They are willing to go that much above the original appraisal."

"*Their* appraisal," I said.

"Not at all. No, sir. I've checked these figures with men I've known for years—men I respect and trust implicitly."

He sat looking around the room. I guess he was waiting for applause. No applause.

I glowered at him, more than ever convinced that everything had been worked out while we were in Europe so we would not be there to protest. He smiled weakly, innocuously. Another refugee from the wax museum. Piss on him the hot piss of your despair and disgust, and watch with growing satisfaction as he slowly melts into nothingness.

"Thirteen thousand dollars," he said again. "They're willing to pay almost twice what the appraisers think the land is worth. Almost twice as much. No way anybody's ever gonna beat that price."

He nodded triumphantly and began to shuffle through his papers. I thought of jeering at the man, mocking him with ribald and devilish wit. I thought of inviting him outside, where we could settle all this on the sidewalk like real men. Instead, I only laughed. Yes, laughed! A hollow, despairing, menacing sound that set the whole party of conspirators to fidgeting and muttering among themselves.

Yep, the lunatic has done gone and done it again!

Before I knew it, I was shouting at the man in the Unknown Tongue, which only sounded like a lot of cussing to all the others.

"Won't you just please stop it?" Mary Ellen said. "Behave yourself, won't you! Must you always insist on showing yourself in front of all these people!"

In his most syrupy tone, the agent urged me not to take it so hard, insisting that we really could "trust those guys down at city hall."

"Well, you were one of them. I reckon you oughta know."

"Yessir, that's right. Sure as shooting. I know those guys, and lemme tell you something, they're always gonna do the right thing. There's never gonna be a single garbage truck on your property. Not one. Nosirreee. And you can take that right to the bank."

"They're paying all that money for an access they don't intend to use? Still wish I had me a little piece of paper to make it all legal-like."

"Oh, you'll get the paper, all right. No trucks, no smell."

"No trucks maybe. But that last part is what I'm still waiting to find out about. No kinda paper's ever gonna protect against that."

12

"Different in All Things from All People"

While waiting for the first garbage trucks, I sometimes go out late in the afternoon and take a brisk, contemplative walk along the Great Philadelphia Wagon Road. What damnable irony, I tell myself, to think that the city plans to place the world's largest garbage dump either alongside or right on top of the most historic trail in Colonial America!

Actually the road no longer has anything to do with Philadelphia or much of anything else, but it was the first pioneer trail ever to traverse the whole of eastern America and to penetrate the back parts of Carolina and Georgia—the same trail that in late 1753 led those fifteen exhausted and persevering Moravian settlers straight by the swift-flowing stream known as the Grassy Fork into a wide, lush bottom only a mile or so south of where our farm, what's left of it, now stands.

From the middle of the eighteenth century until after the American Revolution and the opening of new frontiers beyond the Appalachians, the Great Wagon Road was the way south for countless thousands of German and Scots-Irish pioneers. For another one hundred fifty years before that, it served Iroquois tribesmen as the major route along which they moved to trade, hunt, and fight wars. Though its history is still vague, seldom mentioned, if at all, in our textbooks, it was the most important road in Colonial America long before the English acquired it by treaty.

In our time not many people traveling the Great Road, the dusty side-trail of my youth, can imagine what it meant to the history of our land. Yet hardly a man or woman born in these parts before World War ll will fail to find some, if not all, of his or her forebears among the hardy breed that swamped the Carolina backcountry on the eve of the American Revolution. How different they were and how different the society they built from the Carolina and Virginia Tidewater! The Roanoke settlements and all the others, those that vanished and those that survived, were, after all, only an extension of English society. In our part of the world, it was different. The society that took shape along the Wagon Road was wholly and peculiarly American, unlike any that had ever existed on this continent or any other. Why is it, after all these years, after so many generations, I still feel vaguely a part of it all?

From my upstairs office, I can look across our bottom and the new swamp created by the patriarchs and on across the railroad and office parks toward the Great Road, all paved over now and fancied up with curb and guttering and jammed with traffic—and nothing but a single historic marker to remind travelers of its great antiquity and its crucial role in the building of Colonial America.

Before the city swooped down on us, you could follow it for miles back into the country—up the long hill beyond our land and on past the white barns and silos of the county farm, and so at last into the lower slopes of the Blue Ridge Mountains.

I think again of the land as it was before the defilers came sniffing around. I think of old August Spangenberg, the Moravian bishop who came south with a team of surveyors in the fall of 1752 to scout out the most likely spot for a new church settlement. He and his team spent more than four months in the wilds of the Carolina uplands, often without food or water, in the coldest part of the year, hacking their way through snowy forests "seldom visited since the creation of the world" and making their way by foot up and down some of the highest mountains in the southern Appalachians.

They were lost much of the time and waked each morning to the "music" of wolves—"from six corners at once, such music as I have never heard." Early in the new year they made their way south out of the lovely glens of the New River into the foothills of the Blue Ridge, where the Big Muddy Creek mingles its waters with the Yadkin River, and finally onto a tract of land that the bishop was pleased to call *der Wachau*, after the ancestral home of his Saxon patron, Count Zinzendorf.

One imagines him as he comes slowly out of the trees to the top of a hill barely visible from my window and pauses to take a long slow look all across the valley, down toward the Grassy Fork, up the long hill where the Baptist church now stands, south toward the rolling country where the communal towns of Bethabara and Salem are now mere adjuncts of the dominant industrial town of Winston, once (though no longer) the world's largest tobacco manufacturing center—and then maybe swinging round to look out across our bottom, perhaps at that time only recently burned off by the Indians "to drive the deer to a given spot," and slowly affirming with quiet conviction what his surveyors must already have been thinking: "*Das ist die land. Die Bestans. Der Wachau.*"

A thousand times and more than a thousand, I have remembered the words of the bishop—"the best land left in North Carolina"—as I sit looking up the hill toward the spot where the Wagon Road came out of the big timber.

Why, he mused, had the powers on high allowed him to spend so much time wandering the land "in ignorance" of a tract of land that seemed to have been "reserved by the Lord for the Brethren?"

How could he have known that it had actually been reserved as a site for the world's largest warehouse, a seething swampland, garbage pits, and gloomy office complexes? You think about all that and about the big-moneyed patriarchs who've taken over everything now and hate yourself all over again for falling in with your neighbors to help hasten the day of its ruin and demise. You would prefer still to be known as "that goddamn jackass that sits up there in that goddamn yaller farmhouse and won't do nothin' fer nobody."

Of all the characters to make his way into these back parts, none left quite so lively and startling an account of the rough folk that made up backcountry society as a Charleston missionary named Charles Woodmason. A strange and indomitable wayfarer, this Woodmason was. A former merchant and planter, with extensive holdings on the upper Pee Dee, he was already in his middle years when he gave up the comfortable and even luxurious life among the Charleston gentry (men and women he later ridiculed as "wearers of Scarlet and fine linen") and set out on a quixotic mission to convert thousands of wild, hard-drinking Presbyterians to the "church established."

Nobody has ever figured out what the Rev. Woodmason could have been thinking. He represented just about everything—royal government and all its institutions—that in past years had so profoundly stirred the wrath of the back settlers. Woodmason stirred it up once more, yet somehow managed to survive and leave behind a diary that contains some of the most colorful and dramatic writing in all the annals of Colonial America. Despite all his troubles, Woodmason continued to labor under the perverse delusion that he could somehow bring these formidable frontiersmen back into the Anglican Church.

Nowhere did he get much encouragement, except from the Moravians, who already agreed with him anyway and whom he once described as a society "different in all things from all people." As had so many other travelers, Woodmason flung off into an almost worshipful outpouring of praise on finding so advanced a settlement hacked out of what was still an implacable wilderness. Already the mills were humming, the forests vanishing, and the broad axes playing a merry tune on the stumps of the forests.

Everywhere else he looked as he traveled up and down the rivers and creeks and dusty wagon trails of the Carolinas, he found only degradation and savagery and poverty and despair and drunkenness. But he kept right on going, maybe because he had no consuming motive for going back. He had married once and had left his wife in England after a horse kicked him in the scrotum and rendered him impotent. So, at least he had plenty of energy for the job and, I guess, was immune from temptation in a way few of us ever are. Anyway, no other itinerant in pre-Revolutionary Carolina—not even those ever tireless, ever traveling Moravian preachers—has left so exhaustive an account of his travels or created so vivid a picture of the harshness and terrors of frontier life.

He speaks of a land where the cooking is "execrable," the dews "pernicious," and the morals vile; a land swarming with wolves, panthers, New Light Baptists, unruly gangs of Scots-Irish Presbyterians, and "all the sweepings of the jails of Hibernia"; a land where men and women as well "would do anything to come at liquor," where the Presbyterians deprived him of food and drink, stole his clothes and horses and threatened to beat him senseless or "lay him behind the fire" and once set fifty-seven dogs to fighting in a meeting house where he was trying to preach: "Behold on ev'ry one of these Rivers, What Number of Idle, profligate, audacious Vagabonds! Lewd, impudent, abandon'd Prostitutes Gamblers Gamesters of all Sorts—Horse Thieves Cattle Stealers, Hog Stealers— . . . Hunters going naked as Indians . . ."

There are times, though, when his prose is not the prose of a man rendered impotent by the kick of a horse: "The Young Women have a most uncommon Practise, which I cannot break them of. They draw their Shift as tight as possible to the Body, and pin it close, to shew the roundness of their Breasts, and slender Waists (for they are generally finely shaped) and draw their Petticoat close to their Hips to shew the fineness of their limbs—so that they might as well be in Puri Naturalibus—Indeed nakedness is not censurable or indecent here . . ."

One certainly doesn't find anything like that in the published *Records of the Moravians*. Page after page of untiring saintliness and never the first mention of *Puri Naturalibus*. Maybe that's only because Adelaide Fries, chief translator of the archival records, was herself old-family Moravian. Half the people she knew were either her kindred or took a mighty keen interest in what she was reporting about their forebears. It is a monumental work nonetheless, much the best thing we have and yet so much left to be translated and almost certainly all of the "best parts."

Not likely we'll ever know the whole truth. Even though preachers and town leaders were always busy scribbling, taking note of rebellions, wars, epidemics, political upheavals, economic developments, social change, and occasional fights at their tavern (always started by some outsider), there was never, if we are to believe Dr. Fries, the slightest outbreak of prurient interest anywhere in the town.

The Moravians have never made it easy for outsiders to get at those records. Ever since the day of Dr. Fries, which is to say, for more than half a century, the Moravian church has taken a strictly custodial view of its invaluable research materials. Church leaders have changed custodians from time to time, but whatever his or her identity, the archivist would guard those doors like a Gorgon's head or a scowling Cerberus at the gates of Hell.

The first time I ever went down there, hoping to gain stack privileges, I scarcely got inside the door. I told the lady my name, and she looked at me in stunned disbelief.

"Young man, your name again? I must tell you that I have spent all my life as a Moravian. I have studied in Bethlehem, our first home in this land. I have degrees from some of the best schools. Do I look like a fool? I can assure you we have no 'James' in here."

I explained that my ancestor had taken an Anglican name and that I was sure if she would just look under the name Jacobus, I would be able to satisfy all my curiosity. Cerberus cared nothing for that. She held her hand firmly on the drawer as though resisting rape or, what might have been worse in her eyes, the actual confiscation of those records.

Then came the American bicentennial year of 1976 and a big stroke of luck. Dr. Fries had been dead for more than two decades, and the published output from the Moravian archives had become ever more bland. That was the year, however, that the Moravian congregation in the tiny village of Friedberg, where my own people had originated, where old Jacobus had lived as a boy, where his own father had been living when he changed his name, hit upon the idea of translating the whole of their diary as a bicentennial commemoration.

For whatever reason, the fellow they hired to do the job translated everything in sight. And there they were, all of my old relatives, exposed to all the world, none more interesting than the wife of a certain Valentine Frye. The poor girl had been caught in the act of adultery, and the diarist had felt himself obliged to report every incriminating detail, though mostly in Latin. So, there I was, obligated to go out and get it translated all over again.

The diarist, old preacher Nicholas Bachhof, first minister at Friedberg, had never run into anything like that and was understandably reluctant to commit the troublesome matter to writing. Strange fellow, Bachhof. Hard as the kick of the horse that had undone Woodmason when it came to the old-time religion. Found it difficult to forgive, denying people the right to take communion for months at a time even for the most insignificant trespasses. I'm not sure Valentine Frye's wife ever even made it as far as the mourner's bench after she was found out.

The minister might well have kept the whole matter quiet if her apparent seducer, a big-mouth named Peter Volz, had not confronted her with loud, off-color remarks at a social gathering. *Adulterii causa*, Bachhof wrote, after hearing of the incident from Elizabeth herself.

She denies everything of course, complaining that she has been insulted and lied about all over the county by the "dissolute" Volz. Their liaison must have been the talk of the community for some time. Mrs. Frye had long been unwelcome at communion, and Brother Bachhof just three months earlier had kicked her lover out of the church, explaining that he was to be excluded "from all special services of the Society."

The first real dirt to come out of those archives in two hundred years, and I knew my aunts and uncles would never forgive me if I didn't let them in on the secret.

"Nothing but drunks and women of the streets," I would say.

They would show the proper amount of mock horror, sneering at me across the table as we sat at Sunday dinner and wanting to know why I seemed "to take such a delight in making trouble for everybody."

Well, there was more. In what may have been her most stinging rebuke of a fellow parishioner, Dr. Fries once described, this same Elizabeth Frye (but only as Mrs. F., not by name) as a "veritable agent of Satan," after learning that she had been pairing off boys and girls in her own home, a practice absolutely *verboten* among Moravian congregationalists.

Maybe I was making too much of it. It had been seven generations since Elizabeth was stirring up trouble among Friedberg congregationalists. Seven generations. Too long for the family to count it a real scandal. Most of the "bad blood" could have died out since then, but I guess a lot more could have come in from places we know nothing about. At least it was encouraging to realize that even Moravians sometimes got bored and wanted a little excitement in their lives.

It was an unimaginably hard life in those pre-Revolutionary days: long, hot days in the field hoeing corn or suckering tobacco, or hovering over a woodstove in a stifling kitchen. Of community recreation, there apparently was none—unless you can count as recreation the time spent at one of those boring and seemingly endless German religious services or at a "lovefeast" (which sounds like a lot more fun than it was) or at an evening *singstunde*.

So you have to wonder if people caught in that kind of life would not risk almost anything for even the briefest respite. How many were the sinners who never got caught? Must have numbered in the thousands, and, as I later learned, though not directly from the published records, some of the chief men of the town occasionally fell out of grace, among them, Dr. Jabob Bonn, supposedly the very essence of Moravian austerity and piety. But what was good old Dr. Bonn doing while on his medical rounds?

Looking for wives whose husbands were in the fields or out of town.

" . . . He liked to be among the sisters," one Moravian leader (not Dr. Fries) had written, "and annoyed them by paying them long visits when their husbands were not at home."

Annoyed?

Ha! I rather got the idea that most of his clients impatiently awaited his coming. Just don't look for anything like that in the official accounts. I found it in some material I'd had translated for my own use. One little detail out of so much that is missing. If we could only get Cerberus away from those doors, there's simply no telling what we might find: Lovely young witches in *Puri Naturalibus* practicing their rituals while the Elders in Bethabara slept? Accounts of orgiastic rites in our own Grassy Fork creek bottom? Is that why I keep finding those mystical, perfectly formed, dark circles down there—or at least was able to do so before the developers came and turned the whole place into an impenetrable swamp? Why, there was a time when they came up fresh and new with every spring rain!

Not so much anymore. I would say that the city lost a wonderful opportunity to parlay this strange phenomenon into a real tourist attraction, a hint perhaps of ancient Satanic worship on our own land, or maybe only a reminder that the UFOs have been paying us regular midnight visits without our knowing anything about it.

The city, of course, passed up the chance to promote itself as another Stonehenge and has now conspired to rob us of our own Devil's Tramping Ground, covering with garbage and swamp refuse not only the Great Wagon Road but also the sacred witching woods where not long ago we longed to dance in *Puri Naturalibus* on nights of the full moon, build fires of praise and thanksgiving to the great Muck Olla, and consecrate ourselves by means of ancient rites once practiced by the druids themselves—solemn and profound mysteries that alone would make life barely tolerable among all these state-of-the-art warehouses that seem to double in number with each new sun.

13

Birds of Omen,
Birds of Prey

Autumn, cold days now, leaves falling in great flurries as the bulldozers roar and more warehouses take shape on the hill across the Grassy Fork bottom, the stark skeletal-like framework of the girders catching the first sharp gleam of the morning sun—and not a day when we don't waken to the sound of croaking seagulls, flapping crazily about the creek bottoms and over the surrounding hills. What had brought them here, so far inland, so far from their native habitat, so far from where I had ever seen them before? Was the end of the world upon us at last?

Morning and evening I sit watching the impudent gulls soaring about the warehouses and the upper reaches of Mt. Trashmore, precursor of the city's greatly expanded landfill, which has already earned its designation as Mt. Trashmore No. 2. It now threatens to tower high above its rival and perhaps put itself forward as the greatest mountain of refuse in the world, if, indeed, it has not already done so—and on land where the water table is less than two feet below the surface, where wharf rats and deadly serpents wait to attack the unwary, where wild, snarling dogs run in menacing packs.

And those gulls, damn them! All this way for garbage?

Poontang?

Sometimes a neighbor drops in at cocktail time and we sit staring bitterly up at the warehouses and office buildings and tenements, at the great flocks of seagulls that have flown all the way into the foothills of the Sauratown Mountains to feast on the mounting pile of trash lying just north of our property, a great, high, and still-growing hill of garbage, shutting off much of the view of the Sauratown range and, on hazy days, even of the original Mt. Trashmore, itself.

"Lemme tell you something," I would say. "We're the only town in the state, in all of North Carolina, I tell you, where the city has allowed its utilities commission to create that kind of monstrous abomination within its corporate limits."

"Well, I think you're overlooking something," the neighbor says. "Winston isn't really a city anymore. Not a city, not a town, not anything. It has been dead for years, probably for half a century or more, and just hasn't found it out yet."

"Makes sense in a way. Yes, I would certainly say so. I guess a city is just like anybody else, or any other entity: it can be dead a long time without even knowing it."

My neighbor would look at me, without understanding, waiting for an explanation he knew he was not likely to get. Not from me anyway. I just hadn't read far enough into the occult as yet.

"Well, I still gotta wonder if that's why those old gulls are here," I would mutter. "All this way just to poke around an old garbage pit? Never saw anything like it. Must portend something strange and mysterious. Maybe the end of the world or something like that. Mighty unnatural. We've always associated those old birds with the life of the sea, evenings on the beach or on a fishing pier. Sunsets and high tide and the good days, when we were both a lot younger."

"Naw, they ain't nothing but trash birds. Pile up enough shit most anywhere, and you'll get 'em sooner or later."

After a third or fourth glass of bourbon, I would manage to persuade myself that there was indeed something very important and mystical in their appearance, if not the end of the world, maybe at the least the rising of the Lost Continent of Atlantis.

A serious matter that I learned all about from my New Age acquaintances and would explain in somber detail: how Atlantis would come out of the sea like a giant whale and cover the whole Carolina coastline in a mile-high surge of water, all the cities lost, the sea rising to such heights that—well, I guess I didn't hang around my New Age acquaintances long enough to find out how high it would rise—but it would sure be one more big mess, if there was any truth in what they were saying.

By now, with the contents in my bottle of George Dickel sinking faster than the sun, I would be more than ever convinced that the time had come to call the newspapers. "Perhaps the seabirds are gifted with a foresight that allows them to perceive what is lost on our scientists and oceanographers. I believe somebody wrote a book about that once. Seagulls, I'm told, are among the most gifted and instinctive and far-seeing species in all the animal kingdom. All animals have that extra sense that we humans have lost, but seagulls appear to have it in an extraordinary degree."

"Well, if that lost continent is gonna rise, I sure hope I live to see it."

"Well, who knows? Perhaps you will. The people of the New Age certainly think so. Why, I can imagine them right at this moment: practically standing around staring at their watches and then looking at each other and saying, 'Have you heard anything? Any news yet?'"

"Be a real shame to miss out on something like that."

"Why I'm sure they've got spotters out watching for it every night. Every now and then they lose somebody to the Bermuda Triangle, which is just about where we're gonna see all those old temples and monuments and pyramids begin to rise. Doesn't bother them a bit. Let one spotter disappear, and you'll have plenty of volunteers lined to take his place, all of them frantically looking at their watches and saying, 'Could be any time now. Sure you all haven't seen anything?'"

I still go out sometimes for walks along the old Wagon Road, what little is left of it, and take a good long look around and listen to the ominous sound of the birds, feeling vaguely uneasy at seeing so many of them out of their natural environment. Is it possible that they really are warning us to get out before it is too late?

Perhaps. But you know you can't do that; you have already spent too much time trying to save the old homestead and what's left of your grandfather's land. How could you ever just sell it and move out? How could you just violate the whole tradition your forebears brought to this country and walk off and leave it to somebody whose name you don't even know?

So, I wait and listen and walk about the bottom, while the seabirds soar restlessly above me, emitting a strange eerie croak that mingles with the even more haunting sound of the mourning doves.

Those old birds keep hovering and keep hovering, almost surely waiting for some great and tragic event, flapping about my front lawn as if still trying to decide where the next shoreline will be, like a bunch of loony highway workers trying to locate the edge of a right-of-way. Maybe one day not too far distant, the seething Atlantic will lie right at my doorstep after it has buried the town that has spent all these years trying to bury us. Or it may be the sea will not stop where the gulls have so fondly designated its future demarcation line. I mean, there is a possibility that those stinking birds don't know everything. Maybe the waters will roll right on over our house and bottom as well. So maybe it really is time to go on and get out.

All the prophets who know anything at all agree: The world is even now facing the End of the Age, the time of the Great Tribulation, with a promise of cataclysmic earth changes from one end of the continent to the other. The sun turning backward in its course. The skies raining blood and fiery cinders amid the bird droppings. No safe haven anywhere. Because even if you escape the floodwaters or keep a mountain from falling on you, you sure can't escape the great onrushing tide of the city itself.

All I can say is that those malodorous flocks of seagulls *must* have seen all of this coming. They swoop down everywhere, sometimes covering the whole of a nearby McDonald's parking lot, as though they had detected a *consommé* even superior to that being offered up by the chefs at the landfill.

"No trucks, no smell," the man had said. No trucks maybe, at least not so far, but everybody knew that the keepers of possibly the biggest garbage dump in modern times would never be able to keep back that smell, just as they would never be able to keep back all those filthy birds that feed there. And not just seagulls this time. Across the bottom they come, great flocks of screeching blackbirds. Birds of prey, birds of omen. Filthy scavenger birds of our doom. More of them than ever this year, swooping down to glean the last of the corn from a neighboring bottom. Off they go, screeching over the top of the warehouse, circling it as though threatening it in some vague way. Then back they come across the open land, across the railroad and the swamp and the creek bottom, blackening the sky and bringing the first smell of the garbage pit, screeching, drooping and rising, like the tatters of an old flag that somehow never quite falls apart.

Now they come on into our yard, clinging to the limbs of the trees, some perched upright, others hanging upside down, some coming in small swarms to the bird feeder below my window, ferreting out the last of the seed, their filthy bodies glistening eerily with a kind of green frost. Only six or seven at a time pecking around the bird feeder. The others remain remarkably still, not stirring at all until the leader, wherever he or she might be, whistles them into action.

Then off they go like another black cloud rolling in across the prairie, shrieking madly as a clamorous diesel appears at the crossing. They make a mad dash for the engineer, who draws back in alarm and sounds his whistle to drive them away. Off they go again, back up the bottom toward the cornfield in the adjacent bottom, with an insidious flapping of wings and another menacing screech.

It is always like that at this time of year, great flocks of black starlings swooping down over the bottom with loud shrieking cries of rebuke and damnation, grown fat on the refuse of the landfill. So it is with the seagulls, having come all this way to feast on the indescribable delicacies of the world's largest garbage pit—or at McDonald's on days when the food chain introduces a new specialty. I watch them as they flap lazily across one of the new office parks or drift down across the swamp before turning north toward the dump: the sky now black and white all at once with the foul scavenger birds of our untimely doom.

14

The Last
Agrarian

By chance, a book called *Why the South Will Survive* has come to hand.
A kind of neo-Agrarian tract written by fifteen of the South's leading
intellectuals and celebrating the fiftieth anniversary of *I'll Take My Stand*,
an even more famous Agrarian manifesto that has baffled and inspired a
certain kind of Southern intellectual for the past five decades.

By an odd coincidence, *I'll Take My Stand*, which was as much an
attack on the capitalist order as a defense of the Southern tradition, hit
the literary market just as the country was entering the Great Depression. But it is no coincidence that *Why the South Will Survive* comes out
just as the great tide of industrialism which those first Agrarians so
greatly feared is sweeping across our pristine fields and threatening to
complete the destruction of what we once fondly thought of as our
"Southern way of life."

These neo-Agrarian authors long ago gave up on the idea that "the
triumph of industry, commerce, trade, brings misfortune to those who
live on the land," as the late novelist and uncompromising Agrarian
Andrew Lytle said, and are now set to wondering, in the words of Chapel
Hill sociologist John Shelton Reed, whether the values of the Old South
can somehow "be translated into an urban and industrial context?"

Well, the Lord only knows. Maybe it will survive somewhere, if
only in the memories of the last of us who spend our time contemplating its strange and eventful history.

As I again sit looking out the window, across the creek bottoms,
where, until recently, quarter horses romped free of human restraints, I

keep wondering how those old Agrarians came by their ideas anyway. For more than half a century, a whole gaggle of Southern boomers had tried to turn the South into an industrial wonderland paid for by Yankee investment capital. They had succeeded by bringing low-paying textile mills into almost every Southern town of any size and sometimes creating towns where there were none before.

"Bring the factories to the field!"

That was the great cry of Southern uplifters during the years between Reconstruction and the boom times of the twenties. Bring in the hustlers and the "malefactors of great wealth!" And the malefactors came, by the hundreds and by the thousands, urged on by fulsome orators like Henry Grady and many others who looked at their native South as a region ripe for investment and exploitation.

Out went the carpetbaggers, in came the investment bankers, anxious to take advantage of every inducement the South could provide; and the South could provide plenty of what the investors wanted: an abundance of readily accessible raw materials and cheap water power, free building sites, liberal tax write-offs and rebates, and an unlimited supply of compliant laborers willing to work for as little as ten cents a day to manufacture raw cotton materials that would be sent for processing to Northern industrial plants, where the real money was, before being shipped to the consumer.

It is an old story: how politicians, newspaper editors, and chambers of commerce in a South desperately short of capital conspired to bring back the hated Yankee, and how, at the same time, the poor whites, drifting down from the mountains or from the marginal lands where the quality of cotton was inferior and life was hard, were grateful to be part of the new order, no matter how miserably they had to live, as long as it would allow them to escape from an even more demeaning life among the black sharecroppers in the cotton fields.

If what was best of the Old South is to survive at all, it will have to survive mostly in our common memory, to be handed down like silver plate or old artifacts through the generations: the memory, or what may be more important, the myth of the South that never was.

Perchance we can get rid of the smokestacks, the dirty air, and dirty water. But how do we get rid of the clamor and those mile-high piles of garbage or those masterfully engineered office buildings and warehouses and apartment complexes built to blend in so engagingly with the landscape that "why, mister, you'll never even know they're in the neighborhood!"

A sorry piece of change we got in return for all the inspired speechmaking of the New South people. Mostly what we got were crummy textile mills that looked more like jailhouses than centers of manufacture, degrading pay, filthy working conditions, child labor, stretch-out systems— a life appalling to all except the Yankee capitalists who put up most of the money. The irony was that the factory system failed the white man where he most hoped to succeed. It did little to improve his lot; yet, maybe even that didn't matter so much at the time. Bad as the pay and working conditions were, the factory at least gave whites a kind of social status they had never known before, shattering a developing class awareness among poor farmers of both races. No small thing to have at one's disposal a job for which no black man was eligible.

That was it then: Yankee money, Yankee hucksters, Yankee domination, with New South boosterism merely serving as a cover for it all and Southern capitalists themselves acting as nothing more than front men for the Mellons and the Du Ponts and the House of Morgan. So that by the turn of the century, the South was still the colonial outpost it had always been, its railroads a fixture of the Morgan empire, its textile plants mere feeder bins for Northern factories, its oil wells dominated by Eastern pipeline interests, its iron and steel mills deprived of natural competitive advantages by inequitable rate differentials in rail transportation—an evil never wholly corrected until midway through the twentieth century—and by tariff schedules that reflected Northern commercial imperatives rather than Southern aspirations.

Such were the forlorn circumstances on which many an old Southern market town, idle and half forgotten, built its hopes for future prosperity. The trouble was partly that the Agrarian "redeemers" had come to their work half a century too late. Industrialism of this inferior and degrading type, thanks to the boomers of the 1880s and 1890s, had already seized upon a region that had begun to look nothing at all like the South of their children.

Ah, the factory system! An "insidious spirit" to be borne, if borne at all, "with a very bad grace," said Agrarian poet and essayist John Crowe Ransom. The bloom quickly died off the faces of the young girls when they disappeared beyond the gates of the textile mill. The system bred whole generations of dispirited teenagers, anemic young wives, lethargic and dull-eyed slatterns of thirty. The light of orator Henry Grady's "Grander Day" was suddenly a dispiriting sinkhole from which escape was rare and rescue impossible.

So, maybe those old Agrarians were already twenty-five or thirty years too late. Maybe they had always been too late. Maybe that is why their little book has been more interesting as literature and social commentary than as an actual prospectus for political, social, and economic reform.

We didn't see quite as much of the new degradation in our town. There was still plenty of old Moravian money lying around in the attics, and soon Old Salem and new Winston were up and going. The town had its textile mills, like all the others. The difference was that the Moravian Brethren had embraced capitalism as a way of life even before John C. Calhoun had introduced his famous doctrine of interposition and begun to talk of war.

Another ten or fifteen years, and maybe we would have had no war. We would have become so seduced by Northern ways that there would have been no cause for war, or at least no good excuse for it—unless, as some believe, one of the great causes of the civil conflict was the Yankee fear that Southern textile men, like the Fries family in Winston-Salem, were indeed well on the way to gaining an economic advantage over Northern manufacturers, what with their monopoly of the raw product and their growing industrial know-how.

Anyway, the war came, and the Moravians dodged it as much as possible and hung on to the factories that had allowed them to enjoy the beginnings of a real prosperity long before hostilities broke out. So, we had the technology, and we didn't need their money. But mainly our prosperity was built on tobacco and banking. It's not going too far to say that we were unique to the New South of those days. Cigarettes had come in, and the pay was better than in the cotton mills, and we were the biggest town in the state, and nobody doubted but that it would always be that way.

This is not to say that booming, homegrown wealth brought relief to the godforsaken cotton mill workers and their kind. We had our slums too, mostly black slums in east Winston, and we had our mill villages. But at least they were *our* mill villages, and many is the time that I would walk through one of those places to see shabbily dressed, bare-footed women sitting on unpainted front porches drinking beer with their grizzled paramours. But there was always good pay in the tobacco factories, if you could get on there, and many a man or woman who would have died in poverty in most Southern mill villages found economic salvation as a hireling of the R.J. Reynolds empire.

There was so much work available during the boom times that even blacks often could get on as floor sweepers or for the rough work of loading freight cars and such. There had never been much of a slave economy in these parts, and we were therefore spared the iniquitous sharecropping or "furnishing" system that sprung up after the war—and was almost the first cousin of slavery itself—across so much of the lower South.

I'm not sure very many people have ever thoroughly understood the Agrarians. The least sophisticated of their critics depict them as a bunch of lean, undernourished, tobacco-chewing dirt farmers with hound dogs snoozing at their feet, Confederate flags flapping from their automobile aerials, and license tags that say "FERGIT HELL!" Even the more astute have depicted them as bookish intellectuals without a firm grip on reality.

Of *I'll Take My Stand*, the late literary critic and essayist Gerald Johnson, a Baltimore iconoclast who grew up near the raw New South town of Thomasville, North Carolina, wrote, ". . . One can only say . . . of such a philosophy . . . that it was library-born and library-bred, and will perish miserably if it is ever exposed for ten minutes to the direct rays of the sun out in the daylight of reality."

That put Johnson in direct and irreconcilable conflict with some of the great literary masters of the day: Ransom himself, Lytle, Robert Penn Warren, Donald Davidson, Allen Tate, all of whom achieved fame long after they had abandoned their Agrarianism as an exercise in youthful naiveté. The years did not change Johnson much. In the early 1970s, in a foreword to a book celebrating H.L. Mencken's contribution to the Southern literary renaissance, he wrote that the author was "kinder to the Fugitive group in Nashville than some of us would have been, but the most carping critic cannot deny their intellectual brilliance."

I have often wondered if Johnson ever went back and read those old Agrarians very carefully. Maybe he didn't realize it, but there was an awful lot of neo-Agrarianism in his own reminiscence about the South of his youth. I found that out soon after accepting a job as an editorial writer for Johnson's old employer, the Baltimore *Sunpapers*.

On my first day there I met the great man at the elitist Hamilton Street Club, a noonday retreat for all the intellectuals, socialites, bankers, big-moneyed corporation lawyers—in other words, for all the people who amounted to anything in the workaday world of downtown Baltimore. I was there only as a guest of my editor and a popular political columnist for the *Evening Sun*. And there to greet me was Johnson himself, sitting back unobtrusively in the crowd, white-haired and quite genteel, holding an enamel-tipped cane across his lap, well into his second sherry.

He was an immensely friendly man, a little deaf, yet always happy to meet a fellow Carolinian. Johnson, a brilliant stylist, with a head crammed full of classical knowledge, was exactly the sort of intellectual who in other circumstances might have embraced much of the Agrarian philosophy.

"To accept industrialism but with a very bad grace," as Ransom had said, might have been written by an older and wiser Johnson himself. But he was too caught up in what at that time passed for "liberalism." He had heard too many hound dogs barking forlornly at the moon on warm Southern nights and seen too many "darkies" contentedly working the tobacco and cotton fields, to be kept in their place and lynched if necessary, while their children were shipped off to a third-rate schooling.

In time he had thrown in with H.L. Mencken, who, like most of the gentry at the Hamilton Street Club, closely identified with the courtly Southerner of myth and lamented the shameful cultural backwardness that had afflicted the South ever since The War between the States. The truth is that Johnson and Mencken had very little in common. With a literary style even more graceful, though a mite less powerful, than that of his mentor, Johnson had made his name as a critic of Southern institutions and Southern boorishness.

Brought north for the good work he had done as an essayist and editorial writer, he soon found himself working side-by-side with the inimitable Mencken on the *Baltimore Evening Sun*. During the late twenties and early thirties, before parting company over the merits—if that is the word—of the New Deal, they were putting out the best editorial page in the country. There has been nothing like it since. But Roosevelt's big government policies gradually forced the two men apart.

Gerald Johnson embraced Roosevelt's policies with the zeal of a new religious convert and would remain a confirmed New Dealer for the rest of his life. Mencken, meanwhile, was one of the most outspoken Roosevelt-haters in the country and was even beginning to find nice things to say about Adolph Hitler and the Nazis.

More than most, he could say whatever he liked in those days.

No one knows how many times he refused to let himself be appointed editor of *The Sun*. With or without the title, his power was supreme in the paper's editorial offices, his prose sacrosanct; he was one of the few journalists in history whose work was never allowed to fall into the hands of meddling copy editors.

What a glory that must have been! To alter a word of Mencken's prose was said to have been a firing offense. When the war came, and when eventually we learned a great deal more about the real import of Nazism, his influence waned, and he never regained the prominence of his earlier years. Once, when asking after the whereabouts of an old friend, he was told that the man had died in 1948. Mencken ruefully shook his head in a lugubrious acknowledgment of his own fate, "Yes, I believe that was about the time of my own passing."

The end of Mencken's real influence in the literary life of America marked the beginning of Johnson's career as an independent journalist. He eventually wrote more than thirty books, along with countless essays attacking, among other things, the demagogic South he had known as man and boy. Harry Golden, the Charlotte author who became an overnight celebrity after his publication of *Only in America*, believed Johnson to be one of the two or three finest literary stylists in America. He had a nice turn for irony, though he lacked Mencken's withering satiric gift for comic overstatement.

He sometimes wrote in too much haste and in Baltimore gained a reputation, whether deserved or not, for being a trifle careless with facts. That is one reason I have always wondered to what extent he investigated the Agrarian philosophy before condemning it as smelling "too much of the lamp."

In learning and eloquence, as well as in their love of Southern gentility, the Agrarians were, almost without exception, Johnson's intellectual equals. They were schooled in the best European conservative tradition. Behind every passage they wrote seemed to lurk the suave, eloquent, and formidable presence of the great Edmund Burke himself.

Johnson was as gracious and accommodating to strangers as to old friends. When he learned that I had grown up (though with nothing like his early stock of classical learning) only thirty miles or so from his own home, he brightened as if a kinsman long thought lost to the world had just come back into his life. As we talked, I became even more convinced that he had far more sympathy for those old Agrarians than he would ever allow himself to admit. Johnson seemed to understand that the South of his boyhood had not come off well in its encounter with industrialism, as Ransom had said and as Johnson himself had implied in one of his novels.

Although he had seen too much of a depraved and racist South ever to look beyond its faults, as the Agrarians had, to see the higher, more abstract philosophy that governed their thought, he had written enough, as one Johnson specialist writes, to convince his detractors "that he could be as severe a critic of industrialism as they themselves."

The Agrarian Fugitives, as they were also known, had never for a moment concerned themselves with the whys and wherefores of growing a crop of corn or with the worn-out South of Erskine Caldwell's novels, but only with a style of life that could not co-exist with the industrial order and was rapidly being destroyed by the patriarchs of "progress," whose cause failed to take into account what one of our latter-day Agrarians has called "a gradual attrition of spirit in us."

Almost the first words out of Johnson's mouth that day at the Hamilton Street Club seemed to evoke all of the Old South nostalgia he had once attacked. "It is truly disheartening to see what is happening to so much of our country down in Carolina. Some of us here will be very sorry about that one of these days. Not me. My time is about up."

It was not so far up that he had failed to see the disaster facing Southern cities, just as the Agrarians had, and had addressed the problem in some of his most lucid prose. In one of his last books, *The Man Who Feels Left Behind*, he actually took out after the developers and urban development pioneers in the best Agrarian fashion: "No big city is physically fit for human habitation. The noise, the crowding, the atmospheric pollution, and the inconvenience are such as sentient beings should not be called on to endure save for compelling reasons. Only as the city offers psychic benefits to counterbalance its physical hardships does it become tolerable and even attractive as a place of residence; and American cities are steadily losing the capacity to offer such benefits . . . Gregariousness and privacy must be supplemented if the American city is to survive as a city and not as a sort of concentration *camp de luxe.* . . ."

He went on, in his best Menckenesque style, to suggest that there was a very "real danger that the people who have been in control of American cities from the end of the Second World War may go down in history as the most worthless generation since the foundation of the Republic."

Did Johnson know his own mind? Not for me to bring up so touchy a subject. It was only my first day in Baltimore, and I was not about to remind the great man that much of what he had written in recent years might have come from the pen of Ransom or Lytle himself. That would have looked bad on my first visit to the Hamilton Street Club. Besides, it was just then that I realized I was the only person in the whole place drinking bourbon.

A certain coldness grabbed my loins as I looked around the room. I feared that I had committed some monstrous *faux pas* by ordering hard liquor rather than sherry. But I had never been able to find much redemption in sherry. I was needing another shot pretty badly, what with my nervousness in the presence of a man I had long known and admired from afar. Not that I would ever have dared hold out my bourbon glass and ask the white-jacketed waiter to "freshen 'er up." So I sipped it much more slowly than was my wont and mostly kept my mouth shut lest the other members look up in astonishment to find a loud, vulgar Southerner in their midst. I would merely have enhanced the crude notion of an Agrarian as anti-intellectual and as an exceedingly uncouth character.

"Yeah," they would say, whispering behind their hands, "just some more of that white trash *The Sun* brought up here 'cause they know they'll work for nothing."

These Baltimoreans, I later learned, regarded themselves—and so had Mencken—as much the better part of the old patriarchal South. They would always remind you that the Mason-Dixon line ran north of their city and state. But Baltimore had become an industrial powerhouse on the Yankee mode, once richer than New York, and the city could never entirely throw off its split personality.

Now well into his seventies, Johnson had recently returned from a book-signing tour of his native state and had come back in despair over the madcap manner in which developers were gobbling up great chunks of the rolling Piedmont farmland he had known as a youth.

"I was surprised at how much lovely country we still have down there," he said. "On the other hand, I was shocked and put under the weather for the remainder of my stay when I saw how fast so much of it is disappearing."

North Carolina could boast no monster cities, a condition that present-day Charlotte and Raleigh, and even the "Triad" cities of Winston-Salem, Greensboro, and High Point, are trying valiantly to correct; yet at the time of Johnson's last visit, the state already had the tenth largest urban population in America. This, oddly enough, was news to the old editorialist, and on learning of it, he smote the floor rather sharply with the enameled tip of his cane, whether to emphasize a point or call for more sherry, I was not sure. At any rate a black man in a white jacket was quickly at his side, filling his glass. He held it out with all the graciousness of a white-suited Agrarian ready to make his round of the Negro quarters and pick out the best-looking little "darkie" he could find for a night of fun and rambunctiousness.

On his recent trip South, Johnson had talked at great length with Governor Terry Sanford, a liberal and Kennedyite whose support for civil rights in the early part of the decade had just about made a hash of his political career and ruined any chance he might have had for naming a successor to his office. Sanford's cry for a check on the kind of unfettered economic growth that was turning much of Piedmont North Carolina into an industrial wasteland had impressed Johnson greatly. Out of office now, he would have preserved vast amounts of green space as a way of preventing the Piedmont from turning into another Silicone Valley. His plan had won great applause from the editorial writers back home, and Johnson himself had been impressed by Sanford's neo-Agrarian concept.

"Can the industrial piedmont be saved?" he asked, with another sharp rapid-fire tap of his walking cane. "Was Sanford ever able to get any support for his ideas?"

("Not much, I'm afraid."

"Not too surprising, I suppose. He appeared to be a man of real vision. He has been very good on civil rights—I would say much better than Kennedy himself."

I had never cared a great deal for Sanford; his vision of North Carolina's future never quite seemed to match the vision of his own self-importance. But I cared even less for his successor, "Mountain Man" Dan Moore, whose sympathies were all on the side of the land-grabbers. I had written countless editorials about the need to set aside some of our good land and place it off-limits to developers. Nobody paid the slightest bit of attention.

"Yes," Johnson said. "You had a mighty good man in Sanford. A pity that he couldn't get more of those bankers and big-money men behind him."

He was silent for a moment, holding up his glass for a fourth sherry. "I suspect that the last real chance for preserving very much of our land in its natural state has passed us by. Our politics are changing now, and I doubt that anything like the mood that prevailed briefly during the Kennedy years will come round again anytime soon."

I was still a little nervous in the jacket and trousers I had bought especially for the occasion. I looked around the room and wondered if anyone had noticed. I feigned a lofty urbanity I did not entirely feel. But mostly I just kept thinking about the old man, marveling again at the unconscious transformation that had taken place in his thinking—if indeed he had ever seriously read the old Agrarians in the first place.

Here he was, half a century too late, echoing the same ideas he had denounced as "library-born" and "library-bred" in a 1920 essay. Perhaps a nice subject for an essay himself, I thought, as I fondled my second bourbon, offered without my having to signal for it: *Gerald Johnson, the Last Agrarian*. It would sure surprise a lot of those old Vanderbilt Fugitives who had once whooped it up for a South that would refuse to model itself after the Northern industrial pattern.

"Sanford was certainly the most far-sighted governor North Carolina has elected in my time, perhaps in its entire history. Is there no one at all left to carry on where he left off? Or do they lay all the blame for this civil rights furor at his door?"

"More that than anything else, I think."

"Yes, I find that a great shame. Very much to be regretted. I'm afraid that is a political commitment he will have a very hard time overcoming."

Another tap of his cane, a last long sip of sherry. "Why is it so everlasting hard for us to learn from the mistakes of the past? I tell you, they will have to act quickly if they hope to save much of that country down there."

"They are already trying to pull many of our towns together as one," I said. "Instead of Greensboro and Winston-Salem and High Point and your own Thomasville, they now have something they call the Piedmont Triad, with everybody supposedly working together for the greater glory of the real estate developers and investment bankers."

"Yes," Johnson said. "Tell me more about this Triad. I must say I don't care much for the name. I have to tell you, this 'Triad' of yours sounds more like a consortium of Chinese gangsters—a front of some kind—than a proper name for a new urban conglomeration. Do you think it is only that—a name—or does it truly signal another victory for the real estate interests? It does sound to me like they are begging for the same kind of growth that has already ruined so much of the country. I fear we are in for a very difficult time down there."

A real man of the land, I thought, maybe born out of his time. Definitely the subject for a future essay. I was thinking of all that when the dinner bell rang, a mere tinkle rather than the thunderous gong from afar that I had known while working in the tobacco fields as a child—and the black men in white again coming around in true Old South fashion, nodding and smiling as they beckoned us to table. Here, indeed, a true Agrarian would be quite at home, and I never saw anyone more at home there, in all my later visits, than Gerald Johnson himself.

Once he looked at me across the table to continue the conversation, boasting again of Terry Sanford and all his good works.

"North Carolina, I'm afraid, is doomed to repeat the mistakes that have made so many of our Northeastern cities unfit for human habitation. Maybe you can't blame people for not listening. They are hungry for all the benefits that urbanization brings. I suppose we can hardly blame them. They have been poor for so long—though much richer than they think in many of the things that truly matter. And they are scared. Yes. They have no idea where this new freedom of the young is taking us, and they're quite frightened by it all. So they're very likely to give us Nixon back for awhile. And after Nixon, what? The apocalypse? I don't know. I rather think not. I think our new desire for stability will win out over our more radical forms of politics for many years to come."

I could say little in response. I knew he was almost deaf and that I would have to shout across all the other diners, all the way down to the end of the table, and that he would only stare at me, trying to make out what I was saying, and then my fellow elitists would again start whispering behind their hands to remind each other that they had another one of those loud Southern rednecks in their midst.

I was anxious to confirm the existence of an upper-class graciousness for which the South had once been famous—Mencken's South, the feeling of community, of family, of the right to invade the slave quarters at your leisure and to select the best-looking of the mulattos for your pleasure, as no less an eminent character than Thomas Jefferson had often done. I was not sure how much of that South had ever existed. All I really knew was that I had never been a part of it. Still, I felt that I owed it to myself and the Hamilton Street Club to keep up appearances.

"Preservation is its own *raison d'etre*," I said at last, with a faint look of hauteur. "But I doubt that it's going to mean very much in the long run."

I sneaked my empty bourbon glass under the table and at once kicked it over, with a faint clattering of ice. Everyone turned to stare at my part of the table, while I delicately shoveled a slab of roast beef into my mouth.

I looked around with another fancied look of superciliousness. "Hope to be seeing you boys again first chance I get."

All I got were empty stares and a bunch of unanswered questions about my accent.

15

The Last Days
of Big Grassy Fork

Johnson is dead now, and my Baltimore days are long behind me. But I often think of our conversation at the Hamilton Street Club as I look out at the great dust clouds rolling across my bottom or as I lie in bed at night and listen to the clang of tractor trailers being unloaded and the loud, raucous shouts of the stevedores way up on the hillside among all the warehouses, always remembering the day in my summer garden when the patriarch and his flunky had assured me that I was a lucky man.

"Why you'll never in this world know those warehouses are there. You ever heard a warehouse make any noise? Think of what we might have put up there. A low-rent housing district, say. Think about all those cars. The gunshots. Sirens. Hell, why, we're gonna build them warehouses so they'll blend right in with the countryside, and, so help me, I guarantee that you'll thank us when all this is over. As pretty a bunch of warehouses as you'll ever lay your eyes on. A whole lot better than a big batch of kudzu taking over the whole countryside."

Why the South Will Survive. The book of that name still lies on my desk, along with the yellowing review I finally wrote for my old editors at *The Sun.* Was I to regard this new exercise in agrarianism as Johnson regarded the first, a bookish philosophy smelling of old wicks and lamps? I'm not sure. I do know there are plainly too many of us who refuse to acknowledge the dreadful malaise closing in on us from every side. Some of the essays penned by these new agrarians are very fine indeed, one written by an old and dear friend. So I finally turned out a review in which, like the intellectuals, I tried to hide the truth from myself. The incessant clamor of the Grassy Fork building boom had grown too great really to hide it for long, so that it took a great exercise of will and imagination to support these latter-day "Old South" apologists in the hope or belief that their philosophy could still find a place in the Sun Belt South of our undoing.

The South of our youth? Not only will it not survive; it most definitely has ceased to exist. I did not tell the truth, of course. That would have been disastrous for old friendships. Yet the clangor I once celebrated with an immense bonfire after the fashion of the ancient festival-kings is now bigger than any of us.

Night comes on apace, and now the old textile mill I have always hated has taken on an even more ominous and macabre aspect. With smokestacks shooting up huge fiery blasts into the black sky and weird floodlights beaming and the roar of all the fabricating machines going at once and the clang of the great diesels, it looks and sounds like the nucleus of a vast new industrial complex, as though some unearthly force had contrived to transfer every blast furnace in the whole Ruhr Valley to our once-tranquil Piedmont countryside, all in the space of a single night. You go to sleep thinking you are still living in the days before the great highways had come, and waken with the sun shining through enormous beams of skeletal latticework.

Perhaps I should not write the truth about that either. I must contrive to hold on to old friendships for as long as I can. That at least is one attribute for which we Southerners are famous, true or not, so I will at least fool myself yet awhile longer with the cunning chimeras of the day.

At this hour, before the sun is quite up, I can sit at my word processor and imagine the bottom as it was in my grandfather's day, when nothing disturbed our insular world except the big friendly four o'clock train that we managed to accept as something different from what it was: the promise of a new industrial age of which the railroad tracks were only a forerunner.

Now morning is on the wing again, infusing the creek bottom with a shifting mist that shuts out the warehouses, railroad, and factories all from view. At such a moment one might indeed imagine that something of the Old South still lives and will again assert itself. But, alas . . . the sun rides clear of the warehouses now, a relentless winter sun that soon banishes the mist and with it all the frail hopes of the morning hours.

Perhaps we may still hold on awhile to the old dream, but we may also know that whatever it is that has made us Southerners a breed apart—the shared infamy and glory of our history, our isolation, our religious primitivism—is still giving way before Yankee dollars and Yankee TV culture the way the Reconstruction generation gave way before Yankee bayonets. In the same way the South that many of our sanguine writers would restore is rapidly dying, if not already quite dead. Yes, I am more certain of it than ever, for the last threads of mist have finally lifted, and now one might hear the far-off haunting wail of a cumbersome diesel, and again as though magically transported from afar, the towers of the Ruhr Valley seem to be glowering down at me. In another six or eight weeks, the creek bottom, where even now one might occasionally discover a half-buried Cherokee arrowhead or hatchet or some other pre-Revolutionary artifact, will be loud with mowing machines and tractors, awakening us to a reality sometimes hidden from the authors of *Why the South Will Survive* and consigning our dreams as well as theirs to the library shelves.

Well, I still have my fancies, though seldom do I go out for a walk anymore without finding that something new has come along to alter my old perception of the land. I often look back and think about all the damage and when it began and whether there was ever a time when we could have stopped it—or at least stopped the utter annihilation of old landmarks. Perhaps there was never a time when you could have said with complete conviction that "this is the end of civilization as we have known it."

All I can say for certain is that the end had begun a long time before I came home from Baltimore, hoping to pass my last years nostalgically roaming the fields and woodlands of my youth. Many a man spends half a lifetime rummaging through the musty hay-bin of his past. Then at last there comes a day, perchance a rare summer weekend, when he can shake loose from his confining life in the city and go wandering again down country lanes or across broomsedge fields alive with aster and goldenrod.

If, by chance, fresh rains have left the canebrakes that line the creek and river bottoms all but impassable, he clings to the ridges, leaving behind both the mystery and peril of the swamp. Here there are only the dry, rock-strewn footpaths, the crisp dry grass, the clumps of honeysuckle and wild hedge. Here, too, are scattered patches of butterfly weed, brilliant oranges and near reds, the aristocratic Queen Anne's lace, the lobelias and bull nettles and wood sorrels, and the insidious nightshade; the tall, blue-flowered stalks of wild chicory; the spiked pink of the pigweed.

For it is the high noon of summer, a time of lushness amid decay, a time when the ripening fruits and vegetables remind us, somewhat wistfully, that the great earth itself is rapidly turning to seed. Now, in the high noon of his own life, a man's early ambitions lie buried in the realm of half-consciousness, like the trumpet vine amid the jimsonweed—lost amid the responsibilities of raising a family or paying off a mortgage.

Perhaps there is also a moment, as he wanders the old familiar fields again, when he can put behind him, however briefly, thoughts of the cutthroat culture that has come to dominate much of American life: gang slayings, wholesale perversions, drive-by shootings, devil cults, vacant-eyed teenagers wandering the streets, ready to strike, ready even to murder for the money that will purchase a shot of heroin, a vial of crack.

Abortionists and anti-abortionists manning their barricades verge almost daily on open warfare. After raping his wife (a husbandly duty), a man in Virginia wakes in the night to find that she has brazenly cut off the instrument of her undoing and maybe thrown it to the hogs or something and left him bleeding all over the bedsheets. Other men sit anxiously awaiting the day when their daughters will be old enough for them to seduce or rape.

Don't tell Mommy, goddammit, I'll kill us both.

A whole new way of boosting one's "self-esteem."

Meantime the deadly specter of AIDS stalks the land, like an Old Testament plague ordained by an angry Yahweh. Date rape, child abuse, patricide—the stuff of everyday headlines, transforming Rockwell's America into a bubbling cauldron of greed and deceit and frenzy; all the dark springs of the American spirit flowing madly to the surface of our lives, even as the masses of the poor huddle grimly in their crowded, sweltering tenements.

One swears that he will allow himself no excess of emotion; he will lose himself instead in the woods and thickets of summer, lulled by the jarflies and night insects, carried away on the streams of Lethe, unable to stir or act decisively even as the last curtain of tragedy drops over the land. He reads that this great country is losing her grip, not to mention her sanity, and will never again stand for anything worthwhile in the world—that we are in the last age of our imperial decline.

He wonders vaguely what has happened to the old promise of America. Have we lost forever the good feeling about our land? Is it all theft and lies and violence and political chicanery? Perhaps. Yet it is difficult for one to convince himself that those visions of his youth are now quite dead. Like the goldenrod that brightens the waste places, our hopes bloom again along the weed-choked roads of memory. For in the noon of life, there is still time to plan and dream—to give way to those moments of reverie that obsessed us so long ago, when every waking hour brought a fresh challenge and when even the most remote object of our ambition seemed easily within our grasp.

Autumn brings other voices, other memories. Often now one wakens on those first cool mornings in September or October to find the past hanging over him like a haze over autumnal fields—to find himself thinking of another quite different time in his own life, another quite different America. The America of small towns and slow, easy twilights filled with squeals of laughter, echoes, faint voices, or the far-off thud of an ax cutting into oak timber. The call of the hunt on clean windless nights; boys seining the Yadkin or the Pee Dee or the Big Grassy Fork; a lone hound dog barking at three A.M., a rooster crowing at four; fields of ripening corn being gathered into shocks; the smell of tobacco turning yellow and bronze in a log curing barn; men combining hay in the low level meadows that run down to the river's edge; crowds flocking to the Saturday matinee, the drugstores and sidewalks alive with laughing, high-spirited teenagers; a haunted and unchangeable land filled with plenty, with hope, with glorious promise.

Alas, in the true autumn of his life, he often wakens again to find that the land from which he has drawn so many fond memories and so much comfort has been rudely stolen from him and, like youth itself, is now forever irrecoverable. So it was with my return to the land of my forebears. Even the old railroad depot where Mr. Will and Aunt Effie often met for a Sunday afternoon rendezvous has been gone for many years. Not only the depot, but the house in which old Jacobus and his German wife spent all their adult years. I do not remember visiting their house; both were dead before I was born. After that it became just another rental property.

I never knew any of the renters either, except for one scroungy little low-life who lived there for awhile and rode my school bus and sat beside me in class and was always trying to pick a fight. So I thought very little about it and did not realize until it was gone (it vanished with the depot) that it was truly a very important historic house. The family eventually sold the timbers to Old Salem, which had run short of authentic eighteenth-century building materials during one of its restoration projects.

Maybe it was then, when I saw both the house and the depot gone, that I first realized the city really meant business. I just looked up one day, and there it was, its giant earth-moving machines and concrete mixers reared up against us in a truly threatening manner, like a bunch of mangy guests that hadn't had the common decency to announce themselves.

Until the two men had come with their charts and maps, the city had more or less kept its distance, and for awhile, I had forgotten about the big concrete mixer and the new subdivision that had taken the place of the wild fields where old Jacobus once grew his crops and eventually died from an overdose of laudanum. But we always knew it was there, that old concrete mixer, bellowing down its yellow smoke and glowering at us as though daring us so much as to open our mouths in protest.

For a long time after the city set up shop and before the environmentalists started making a fuss, the Big Grassy ran black with dye and waste. I remembered forlornly the days when it was a clear stream brimming with catfish and perch. Maybe the environmentalists would get rid of the dye and waste, but I doubted that it would ever be quite the same. At least no one would think of seining it again; and certainly no one would ever think of going out, as we once had, and picking blackberries along the railroad—unless he liked them sweetened with dioxin.

On the whole I guess the railroad has accommodated itself to city ways better than the rest of us. But the foxes and raccoons no longer come out to say howdy, and the trains no longer make the slightest effort to ingratiate themselves. They come at all hours of the day and night, banging and scraping, mingling the sound of their great iron wheels with the shouts of truckmen constantly unloading their wares.

I guess the real problem is that someone forgot to remind the railroad people that the tracks were put there for the benefit of the common man—for long afternoons of walking and relaxation—as well as for the convenience of trains. Or, I guess I should say, for the financial betterment of all those faceless moneychangers who, without ever being invited to do so, have brought the unremitting clangor of the city into our lives.

One other thing: I don't think that trapper ever did get a mink or otter out of our bottom. I knew the place well all during my childhood and since have investigated the bottom with new vigor and purpose. No mink. No otter. Maybe in the old days, in my father's youth, maybe even in my own, when the stream still swarmed with perch and catfish—but now that the water had turned green and black and gray with pollution? Not a chance. Surprising, indeed, if in these troublesome days, even the catfish would consent to come back.

DATE DUE

DEC 0 9 2019			
DEC 0 9 2019			
DEC 0 9 2019			